NEEDLEPOINT
Stitch by Stitch

Anna Pearson

NEEDLEPOINT
Stitch by Stitch

BALLANTINE BOOKS · NEW YORK

AUTHOR'S ACKNOWLEDGMENTS

A great many people have helped in the preparation of this book. The needlepoint projects
would have been quite impossible to produce without a helpful, patient band of stitchers, all
of whom helped me sew the projects and some of whom also lent me back things to be
photographed in the Inspirational sections at the end of each chapter. In particular, I should like
to thank Angela Kahan, Annette Southward, Brian Synge, Connie Levy, Liz Salmon, Joan Downes,
Joanne Rebholz, Ruth Levy, Sara Low and Val Darby.
Thanks are also due to DeDe Ogden who, beside lending the Russian doll, was a great
inspiration during the writing of the A – Z of Hints and Tips between pages 134 and 141, sharing
her special tips with me; Sue Strause, DeDe and I designed the Butterfly panel together and it
was kind of them to let me use it in the Inspirational Stitchery section.
Heartfelt thanks to all the very special people who introduced me to needlepoint and
helped me grow more confident in my ability to design, teach and write. Finally, thanks are
particularly due to Fiona Holman, my editor at Rainbird and my husband, Patrick.

Library of Congress Cataloging-in-Publication Data
Pearson, Anna
Needlepoint stitch by stitch
Includes index.
1. Canvas embroidery.   I. Title
TT778.C3P424 1987   746.44′2   86–48010

ISBN 0–345–34055–8

This book was designed and produced by
The Rainbird Publishing Group Ltd
27 Wrights Lane,
London W8 5TZ

Text set by Wyvern Typesetting Ltd, Bristol, England
Color origination by Hong Kong Graphic Arts Ltd
Printed by CAYFOSA, Barcelona, Spain

Editor: Fiona Holman
Designers: William and Ingrid Mason
Line artwork: Lindsay Blow, Karen Daws, Jane Cradock-Watson,
Ray Burroughs and Richard Phipps
Photographers: Charlie Stebbings and Terry Trott

Manufactured in Spain
First Edition: August 1987

10 9 8 7 6 5 4 3 2 1

Illustration Acknowledgments
Bridgeman Art Library Ltd Pages 115 and 119
The Burrell Collection, Glasgow Museums and Art Galleries Pages 27 and 112
The Victoria and Albert Museum Pages 66 and 67
The Henry Francis du Pont Winterthur Museum Pages 113 and 117

CONTENTS

Introduction

Needlepoint Stitch by Stitch is a fresh, up-to-the-minute guide to all aspects of embroidery on canvas. Packed with information on yarns, types of canvas, stitches, design and color, the book will appeal to needleworkers of all levels of expertise.

The uniqueness of the book lies in the scope of the projects covered, some traditionally associated with canvas, some less so. The five main stitch categories covered are: Tent stitch, historically the stitch most usually associated with canvas work; Florentine, which probably has been more responsible than any other stitch for the present popularity of needlepoint; Cross stitch and its variations, so useful for its hard-wearing qualities and its use on commemorative samplers; Stitchery, which with its decorative textures and stitches is excellent for geometric designs; and Pulled thread, traditionally associated with fine linen work and especially attractive when applied to canvas.

Within each main stitch category there is a progressive learning concept. Each of the five stitch chapters starts with a Simple project or learning piece which teaches the basic techniques of that stitch, for those who have done little or none of that type of stitchery. From this Simple project the stitcher progresses to a second piece, the Advanced project and, finally, to an Inspirational section which illustrates a range of further ideas based on the techniques covered in the Simple and Advanced projects. Not all the ideas in these Inspirational sections are particularly complicated; many of them suggest ideas that are different in scale or are spectacular but simple to stitch. I also show you how to mix stitches from different chapters to obtain beautiful results.

Before embarking on any projects, the first chapter, 'Materials and Techniques' outlines good working methods to follow when stitching as well as describing the materials needed before you can start.

Following on from the project chapters, 'A Look at History' brings alive the stories of the individuals who stitched and looks at their domestic surroundings which affected the designs worked. For the purposes of this book I have started with Elizabethan needlework, with a look also at the early years of the United States, a period rich in needlepoint. The chapter 'Finishing and Aftercare' is designed not just to help you finish off your pieces but to give you a better understanding of how they are made so that you can better plan your project from the outset. Custom-finishing your piece can work wonders and make it look really professional. The 'A–Z of Hints and Tips' is meant for dipping into; it is a personal collection of ideas to help you achieve better stitching. This is followed by a large and comprehensive Stitch Glossary where all the stitches used in the book, except the Florentine ones, are explained in detail and accompanied by a clear diagram and photograph of a stitched area.

The book closes with a list of museums, collections and educational guilds that you may find useful, as well as some helpful suppliers. On page 174 you can find out how to order kits of some of the projects in the book.

So, Happy Stitching!

Anna Pearson

CHAPTER ONE

MATERIALS AND TECHNIQUES

Both the Simple and Advanced projects in each chapter of this book clearly list the required materials and order of work. Follow these instructions carefully, otherwise the finished size of the work will differ and the ply recommended will have to be adjusted.

This first chapter aims to guide you through the mass of materials that is currently available; also, to help you buy the best ones if you are inspired by any of the designs in the Inspirational sections of the project chapters. The pieces shown in the Inspirational sections take motifs, ideas or stitches from the Simple and Advanced projects which are fully documented.

This chapter covers four distinct areas:

1. Materials such as canvas, threads and needles that are essential for your needlepoint.
2. Frames, lights, magnifiers and all the extra tools that make stitching better and more fun.
3. Techniques such as transferring designs, marking canvas and starting and finishing threads – these instructions are general to all the projects in this book.
4. Color and how to achieve harmony in different color combinations with the use of the color wheel.

Finishing and aftercare of needlework are dealt with in the chapter beginning on page 122 and 'A-Z of Hints and Tips' on page 134 gives an alphabetical list of ideas that I hope you will find helpful, in addition to the basic facts given in this chapter.

◇

MATERIALS

CANVAS

Most good-quality canvas is 100 per cent cotton but pure linen and plastic canvases are also available and are suitable for certain needlepoint projects.

There are two main types of canvas, Penelope or double-thread canvas and mono or single-thread canvas. The mono canvas is available both with an evenweave (sometimes called regular) or interlocked thread. Zweigart's mono evenweave cotton canvas has been used for most of the projects in this book (in each instance the mesh has been specified), but it is as well to understand the potential of other canvases. When talking about the number of canvas meshes a stitch covers I have used the expression 'canvas threads'.

EVENWEAVE OR REGULAR MONO CANVAS: This is used in all the projects in the book except for the Apple Box on page 21 as its woven construction makes it easiest to block into shape after working and it also 'gives' in use. This is very important for pillows and upholstered pieces. This canvas needs binding on the cut edges before starting work.

INTERLOCK MONO CANVAS: Interlock mono canvas looks similar to evenweave canvas but, on close inspection, you can see that at each intersection the threads are bonded together rather than weaving over and under each

TYPES OF CANVAS: *1. Interlock mono canvas. 2. Double-thread canvas. 3. Congress cloth. 4. Plastic canvas. 5. Linen. 6. Evenweave canvas.*

other as with evenweave canvas. Thus, the canvas does not unravel and can be trimmed extremely close to the worked area; it is an excellent choice for small items such as napkin rings and spectacle cases. This canvas is not suitable for pillows, upholstered pieces or anything else that requires a certain amount of 'give' – if you sat on a chair cover worked on interlock canvas a thread could snap easily, leaving a hole in the canvas.

PENELOPE OR DOUBLE-THREAD CANVAS: Penelope, with its double thread, is the only choice of canvas for a pictorial scene where a wealth of detail is required in certain areas and a larger stitch is required as background. If you look at nineteenth-century canvas work, frequently a bunch of flowers or the human figures are worked in little stitches (petit point) and the background is worked in the same stitch but double the size (gros point) – the stitcher has split the double threads and stitched over each one for the fine areas and worked over the pairs of thread for the larger background stitches.

PLASTIC CANVAS: Plastic canvas is used in the Simple Tent project on page 21. It comes in sheets approximately 27 × 34 cm (10½ × 13½ in) in both 7- and 10-mesh. It is available also in circles, hexagons and diamonds in varying sizes. Its rigid construction makes it simple to finish into boxes, tissue-box covers, luggage labels and key tags. Children also enjoy using plastic canvas.

LINEN: Elsa William's linen canvas is particularly suitable for all Pulled-thread stitches and so I have used it in that section. It was also used for the Hydrangea Rug (see page 28) as I wished to make the design in one piece and the linen canvas is 137 cm (54 in) wide, slightly wider than most canvases. Further notes on the advantages and disadvantages of designing a rug on a single piece of canvas are discussed in Finishing and Aftercare on page 130.

CONGRESS CLOTH: This is fine cotton canvas made by OOE in Denmark and is available in white, pastels and bold colors. It is a good choice for samplers and was also used for the Evening Purse on page 47 where the Diagonal Florentine pattern needed to be the same as the Vest but scaled down.

Canvas is generally available in white and shades of ecru. The color is a personal choice. However, if you wish to paint a design, have a pale background or leave some of the canvas exposed, white is the most satisfactory color; if the background is dark, the wool will appear to cover the canvas better if ecru is chosen.

Before making a decision on the color also check the widths available in the mesh you need. Some canvas is only available in 68 cm (27 in) widths, which is suitable for chair seats but less satisfactory than the 1-m (40-in) width canvas which will give two good pillows across the width.

The canvas mesh (the number of threads to the inch) is indicated for each project. If you want your work to be the same size as shown in the project use the same canvas mesh as indicated. When planning your own designs remember that the more detail you require in the space, the finer the canvas mesh will have to be. For example, if you adapted the ideas in the Country Cottage (Advanced Stitchery page 83), which uses 18-mesh canvas, to work a large house but only wanted a small picture at the end, the canvas you used would have to be fine, for example, 24-mesh. If, on the other hand, you wanted to make a wallhanging with the same house, the canvas could be considerably coarser such as 12-, 10- or 7-mesh if you wanted it to be really large.

If you enjoy working some of the designs in this book it is great fun to work them again on finer canvas with a different thread such as floss, silk or other interesting threads.

Note: If 17-mesh or 13-mesh canvas is unobtainable, 18-mesh and 14-mesh should be used instead.

◇

THREADS

Wool gives the longest wear so is recommended for all upholstery pieces. The following list gives details of all the threads used in the book, together with a few extra ones that you may enjoy experimenting with on projects such as the Vest on page 40 or the Country Cottage on page 83 when the question of wear is not of primary importance.

To avoid confusion with the different thicknesses in which the various threads are available, I have used the word ply when talking about the units or correct amount of yarn (whether wool, cotton, or silk etc.) to use for any one stitch. When using this word I mean the thinnest strand of the yarn you can take apart easily.

For example, the Appleton's Crewel and Medici wools come in single ply, Paterna Persian

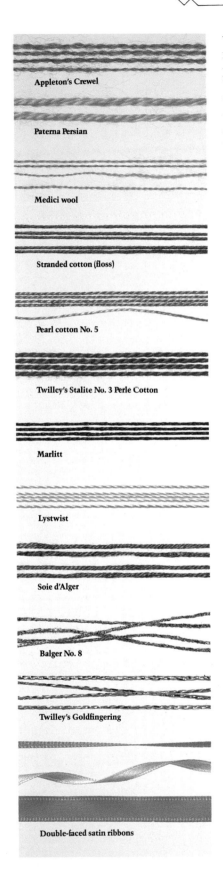

Appleton's Crewel

Paterna Persian

Medici wool

Stranded cotton (floss)

Pearl cotton No. 5

Twilley's Stalite No. 3 Perle Cotton

Marlitt

Lystwist

Soie d'Alger

Balger No. 8

Twilley's Goldfingering

Double-faced satin ribbons

wool hangs together in threes but is very easy to pull apart, and pearl cotton is twisted so it would be extremely difficult to separate. The only one that might confuse you is Marlitt. This has four plies which hang together closely, but because of the static in the thread it will work much more satisfactorily if the instructions for damping and 'stripping' it before use are followed (see page 12). If in doubt, consult the following list where each of the threads used in this book is explained in detail.

WOOL: Three different kinds of wool have been used in the book – Appleton's Crewel, Paterna Persian and Medici. Each one is particularly appropriate for its project. Paterna Persian is the thickest of the three wools, followed by Appleton's Crewel and Medici is the finest.

Appleton's Crewel and Paterna Persian both have color range names and numbers that are universal and Medici has just shade numbers, but these are standard worldwide.

All three are divisible wools, that is one or more plies can be pulled easily from the cut hank and used in a multiple that will suit your canvas. The correct number of plies for each stitch is given in the instructions for each project. If you substitute one brand of wool for another or move to a finer or coarser canvas, experiment until you find the number of plies that gives good coverage of the canvas.

When working with very dark colors an extra ply might also be necessary to cover a light-colored canvas completely. Refer to the list of stockists on page 174 if you have difficulty in obtaining any of the threads which are mentioned.

Appleton's Crewel: This is an English wool that has a very fine range of shades in each color hue; it is, therefore, very good for detailed shading and also for Florentine work. Individual plies come ready separated.

It is available in two quantities, a 25-g (1-oz) hank or a very small skein, which is useful if only a few stitches of a shade are needed.

These wools are known by both their color name and reference number.

When working on 14-mesh or coarser canvas cut new hanks into two equal lengths to get a good working length. When working on a finer canvas, cut the wool into three equal lengths – the reason for this is that there will be more friction on the wool as it passes through the holes of the fine canvas and a long length would wear thin before it was finished.

Paterna Persian: This is an English wool of fine quality. It is 3 ply but these are easily separated. It is generally available in 15-g (½-oz), 25-g (1-oz) and 100-g (4-oz) hanks although some shops will sell it by the strand.

These wools are known by both their color name and reference number.

Persian wool has a 'right' and 'wrong' or rough and smooth direction; always use the thread in the smooth direction. To find the right direction, run the thread lightly against your upper lip, you will feel the difference. It also helps the wool to remain flat during stitching if you run your fingers down the length between the plies before threading the needle.

Medici: This is a fine French wool, originally produced for the

manufacture of Aubusson carpets. It has a smaller color range
than the previous two wools.
However, both the natural earth
and deep shades are particularly
good and forty new colors have
been added to the range recently.
The names given to the shades in
this book are my own and purely
for your guidance. The shop will
go by the reference number. It
works up beautifully smooth.
Individual plies come ready
separated.

It is available in 50-g (2-oz)
hanks (that are further divisible
into five hanks) and small skeins
which are useful for the odd
stitch or if you wish to experiment with color before paying
out money for a big project.

FLOSS: In this book the DMC
range has been used and the
reference numbers given are
theirs. If you substitute another
brand for DMC note that they are
all 6-ply divisible and come in
8-m (9-yd) skeins.

There is no easy way to cut the
skein into working lengths ahead
of time but I find it worthwhile to
wrap the thread around a suit-
able-sized object, such as my
frame, and then cut it into equal
lengths before threading it onto a
palette. This avoids the floss
getting snarled up during stitching and also helps if only a few of
the plies out of the strand are
needed to work the stitch.

The floss needs 'stripping'
before use; cut a length about
50 cm (20 in) and pull the 6
individual plies apart. Lay them
flat, side by side. Follow the
project instructions for the correct number of plies to use for a
particular stitch and then thread
the needle. 'Stripping' makes the
floss lie smoothly on the canvas
and gives better coverage.

PEARL COTTON: The shade numbers in this book refer to the
DMC range. It is a softly twisted,
single-ply thread that comes in
three thicknesses. No. 3 is fairly
thick and good on 12-mesh canvas. No. 5 (used in this book) is
good on 14-, 16- and 18-mesh
canvas and No. 8 on 22- and
24-mesh canvas. No. 5 is available both in 25-m (27.3-yd) skeins
and 48-m (53-yd) balls.

The thread is used just as it is.
To prepare a new skein for use,
take off the two wrappers, un-
twist the skein and cut through it
twice, once at the knot holding it
together and once at the opposite
end; this will give two lengths of
thread approximately 48 cm (19
in) long. Thread the wrapper with
the color number back on one
length and keep this for reference.
This is an easy way of checking
the quantity – when you finish
the first half of the cotton have
you done half the work?

**TWILLEY'S STALITE NO. 3 PERLE
COTTON:** This is a matt pearl
cotton made in Britain. It is
available in a small color range in
50-g (2-oz) balls. The thread is
used as it is.

RAYONS: These are not the
easiest fibers to use, but they give
a sheen to things that will receive
only light wear, such as the Vest
on page 40.

Marlitt: This is a 4-ply, divisible,
high-lustre floss available in 10-
m (11-yd) skeins. I recommend
that you cut it into working
lengths, 38–46 cm (15–18 in)
ahead of time, using the same
method as for cotton floss – the
tangle that it can get into is
indescribable! It frays easily so
use the short lengths recommended. Damp each length with

a small sponge and 'strip' it, using
the same method as for cotton
floss, before threading the needle.

Lystwist: This is 100 per cent
viscose available in 20-g (¾-oz)
balls. It is used as it is but
damping before threading the
needle helps to prevent fraying.
As it frays easily, use short
lengths, 38–46 cm (15–18 in).

SILKS: These are expensive but
not that difficult to use. They
have a long-lasting sheen.

Soie d'Alger (Au Ver à Soie): This
is a 7-ply, slightly twisted silk. It
has a wonderful low sheen and an
extensive color range. It is available in both small (2-g) and large
(12-g) skeins.

It is used in short lengths,
38–46 cm (15–18 in). Prepare the
skein in the same way as a skein
of pearl cotton. The lengths then
need 'stripping' before use.

METALLICS: As far back as
Elizabethan embroidery, spang-
les and mica were used to catch
the light. Metallics used in short
lengths add glamour to needlepoint, especially to fashion
pieces.

Balger: The easiest metallics to
use are the Balger range, a synthetic metallic made in France.
Gold, silver and many basic and
blended colors are available in
four thicknesses.
1. Blending Filament – this is
wonderful for mixing with other
thread such as floss. It is available
in 50-m (54-yd) and 100-m (108-
yd) reels.
2. No. 8 – this is suitable for 22-
or 24-mesh canvas. It is available
in 10-m (11-yd) reels.
3. No. 16 – this is suitable for
14-, 16- and 18-mesh canvas.

It is available in 10-m (11-yd) reels.

4. No. 32 – this is suitable for couching on the surface of worked areas. It is available in 25-m (27-yd) reels.

Twilley's Goldfingering: This has been used in some of the projects in this book. It comes in a good range of colors, including gold and silver, and is washable. It is prone to unravelling, so use short lengths, 38–46 cm (15–18 in), and take care not to disturb the cut end of the thread when threading the needle. I find a needle threader a great help.

RIBBON: In the book I have used double-faced satin ribbon by Offray. There is a good range of colors that come in different widths. The 1.5-mm (1/20-in) width is good for stitching with on 14- and 18-mesh canvas. The 3-mm (1/10-in) and 6-mm (1/5-in) width is used for couching on the surface of the canvas. Use a normal Tapestry needle.

NEEDLES

Always use a blunt-tipped Tapestry needle. The size of the needle depends on the mesh of the canvas and the thread used. They range in size from 14, the heaviest, to 26, the finest. Too large a needle will distort the canvas and too small a needle will fray the yarn.

Use the following sizes: size 18 for 7- and 10-mesh canvas; size 20 for 14-mesh canvas; size 22 for 16- and 18-mesh canvas; size 24 for 22- and 24-mesh canvas.

Generally, Tapestry needles are available either in packets of mixed size or all one size. I find the packets of one size more convenient.

SCISSORS

Two pairs are essential – a small embroidery pair with sharp points and a larger pair for cutting hanks of wool and canvas.

A stitch-ripper is useful for cutting stitches out (this is usually easier from the back of the work) and tweezers for plucking the cut thread out.

ADDITIONAL EQUIPMENT

It is more a decision of what not to buy as, particularly in the United States, the extras can be expensive. However, if you get better results by using a particular tool or are more comfortable stitching if you have a good stand or lamp, I suggest you try and buy it. The single most expensive thing you invest in your needlework is your time and you should have fun while doing it.

The following are just a few pieces of equipment that I enjoy using and which have proved their worth.

FRAMES

In doing canvas work these are not an extra but essential. Any frame will make one's work better in all cases except when working on plastic canvas. Stitch tension is smoother, the canvas is

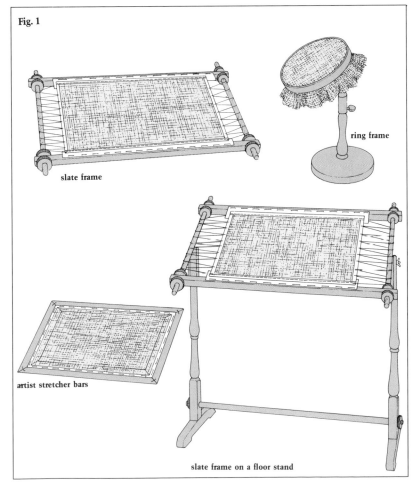

Fig. 1

slate frame

ring frame

artist stretcher bars

slate frame on a floor stand

easier to see and there is no distortion; it is impossible to work Pulled-thread stitches or to do any couching without a frame.

There are various types of frame (see Figure 1 on page 13) but the simplest and most adaptable one is assembled from artist stretcher bars available from art or craft shops. These are bought in pairs of varying lengths which slot together simply. For most of the projects in this book two pairs of 40- or 46-cm (16- or 18-in) bars would be suitable. For different shapes such as a long stool, a further longer pair can be purchased and fitted with one of the shorter pairs to give a suitable rectangle. Fit the canvas on to the assembled frame as tautly as possible, using flat-headed push pins.

There are a number of stands available that hold the frame, leaving both hands free for stitching. There are both floor-standing models and ones that fit under your knees or clamp to a table. Some stands can be angled easily to allow you to sit on either a high or low chair or even in bed – I find that useful, but would you?

The other important points I watch for are ease in turning the work over to finish threads off on the back and also ease of changing frames over – I like to switch from project to project and I want to be able to do this quickly.

◇
LIGHTING

Good light for stitching is essential. A small lamp that can be angled on to the work is vital. However, there are some lamps with built-in magnification that are wonderful. Again, choice is personal and depends on space and funds available. There are two questions to ask yourself when considering the various types:

Many of these newer magnifying lamps rest in heavily weighted floor stands, so will you wish to travel with it?

Other lamps clamp on to a surface such as a table or desk edge, so do you like sitting upright at a table or is there something close at hand to which the clamp could be fitted?

◇
THREAD ORGANIZERS

Looking at current equipment catalogues issued at American needlepoint seminars the stitcher is totally spoilt for choice; in other countries it would appear that organization does not rate so highly!

Look at the thread organizers available and which you think will work best for you. The following are examples: a simple wooden palette for wool and a smaller plastic one for silks and flosses, a folder with a series of cards for each project or a roll-up bag that will take both your frame and yarns.

Even if you are stitching for pure pleasure it is far more relaxing to have the threads together, to know what the reference numbers are and to be able to run a quantity check from time to time. But do be organized, it will make stitching more fun.

◇
GENERAL TECHNIQUES

ESTIMATING YARN QUANTITIES

It is very important to buy sufficient yarn from the same dye lot to complete the project. The most satisfactory way to determine the right quantities is to test stitch a 3-cm (1-in) square in the yarn, using the stitch you plan to use for the project. Approximate the number of squares in the canvas design to be worked in each color and multiply the number of squares by the length of yarn used for the test area. You will then have a fairly accurate figure for the amount of yarn you need to purchase. Add on 10 per cent just to be on the safe side!

One simple example of the importance of this quantity check is when working a set of dining chairs – it is obviously most important to purchase all the wool you think you will need from the same dye lot. Then, simply divide the wool into what you think is sufficient for one individual seat cover. When this first seat is completed you will then be able to assess whether or not more wool is needed to finish the set.

However, if when working the piece you see there will not be enough, do not despair – there is a way to minimize any variation between dye lots. Buy the extra yarn at once as matching unworked wool is easier than matching new wool to worked canvas.

You will be able to introduce the new yarn in stages; keeping to the number of plies already used, first of all use one ply from the new wool and the remainder from the old. After a few needlefuls of this combination, move on to two new plies and the remainder from the old stock and continue in this way until all the plies are new wool.

◇
PREPARATION OF THE CANVAS

Always allow at least 5 cm (2 in) of unworked canvas on all sides of the design. This will be needed for making up the finished work and will be trimmed as necessary by the upholsterer.

Always bind with masking tape or machine stitch all cut edges of the canvas before starting to stitch. Plastic canvas is the exception and needs no such preparation.

◇
MARKING THE CANVAS

This can be done in three ways. Each suits a specific type of design.

1. A sharp pencil is best when copying one of the project charts given in this book or when each space has a known thread count. The pencil point stays in the channel between 2 canvas threads and marks the straight or diagonal lines easily. However, lead pencils are apt to smudge and can make the wool dirty, so when the drawing is complete, give the canvas a very good rub with paper towels.

2. When designing your own geometric piece or when you do not know exactly which thread count will suit the stitches best, it is wise to stitch the lines in with a contrast wool thread as these can easily be moved if necessary. I used this method when originally planning both the Simple Stitchery and Simple Florentine projects. Once you know the stitches fit, you can then use a pencil to draw in the lines.

3. When marking a picture or curved design, such as the Pigs in Clover rug on page 61, use either oil paint thinned with Turpentine or choose a mid-colored indelible marker pen. Nepo or SC-UF are good. Be sure to check the color fastness of any marker pen on a piece of the same canvas you

plan to use it on – the layer of sizing on some canvas can affect the fastness of even those pens that claim to be indelible.

◇
ENLARGING DESIGNS

The pictures diagrammed in this book (the Rooster on page 27 and the Pig and the Flower pot on page 63) will need to be enlarged before drawing them on to the canvas. The outlines have been drawn on a grid, each square of which represents a stated size (see Figure 2); you simply draw a larger grid, following the instructions for the size of each square, and draw the outline square by square (see Figure 3). In some areas there are copy or photostat shops that are able to enlarge (or reduce) any drawing – if you are fortunate

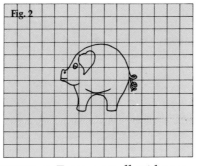

FIGURE 2. *Trace a small grid over the design you wish to enlarge.*

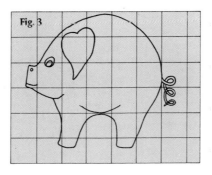

FIGURE 3. *Next draw a larger grid with the same number of squares and copy the design square by square.*

enough to have one close at hand all you need to do is to make a tracing from the book and say what enlargement you require.

◇
COPYING DESIGNS

When the design is the correct size make sure that the outline on the paper is easily visible through the canvas – it may help to ink it in; with simple pictures, such as those diagrammed in this book, position the canvas over the

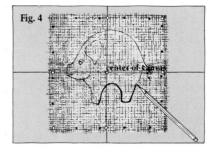

drawing, centrally or wherever it is needed and mark the design on to the canvas with either the brush or pen as described.

If the design is more complicated further preparation is needed (see Figure 4). Mark the center of the design on the paper and also the center of the canvas by folding it; draw straight horizontal and vertical lines through the centers, both on the paper and the canvas. Place the canvas on top of the drawing and push pin the two centers together on a board. Pin on the vertical and horizontal lines. Then, fill in the spaces with push pins about 5 cm (2 in) apart around the edge, pulling the canvas taut. Trace the design as already explained above.

◇
STITCHES

In this book all the stitches used in the project chapters, except the

Florentine ones, are explained in detail, diagrammed and photographed in the Stitch Glossary beginning on page 142. The Florentine stitches are explained and charted in detail within their own chapter beginning on page 32.

◇

STARTING A NEW THREAD

There are three different ways of doing this, and each one is suitable for a specific occasion.

A WASTE KNOT: Make a small knot at the end of the thread and place it on the right side of the work in the direction and about 5 cm (2 in) away from where the first stitch will be made. When you have worked up to the knot, snip it off carefully with sharp scissors – it will be firmly caught by the back of the stitches just worked.

AN 'AWAY' KNOT: This is used for working any isolated motif (see the Samplers on pages 66–67) or when the stitch will be surrounded by exposed canvas or Pulled-thread work. Make a small knot and place it anywhere about 10 cm (4 in) away from the work. When the stitches are worked this long thread can be picked up in a sharp sewing needle and securely woven into the back of its own stitches.

WEAVING INTO EXISTING STITCHES: This is useful when working a second stage to a stitch, possibly in a contrasting color. Simply weave the tail of the thread (no knot is necessary) backwards and forwards into the back of previous stitches; the amount of weaving depends largely on the density of the existing stitches.

Remember, with all three methods, to be generous with the distance between the knot and the starting-point as nothing is more tiresome than a thread that works undone.

◇

COLOR

Color is such a personal means of expression that its application frightens many people; however, it gives such individuality to needlepoint projects that I always encourage my students, even on their first sample pillow, to work in their color preference.

Color is frequently the part of an object that first attracts attention – a dress in a shop window, an eyecatching fabric or an abstract picture that is difficult to understand until the color combinations, having caught one's attention, begin to become clear.

A color must always be considered, both in regard to the other colors that are used with it in the project and also to the location planned for the finished work. The way to achieve harmony in color compositions is explained in the section on the color wheel.

It is necessary to take into account where a chair seat or pillow will be put when finished; vibrant, eyecatching combinations should be used to 'furnish' a small entrance hall, dark, dramatic schemes would look good in a dining-room used mainly in the evening and soft pastels will add airiness to a traditional sitting-room.

Let the professionals help you in your color selection; if you have a fabric or wallpaper that you love take a sample with you when choosing yarn for a project. Match colors to a favourite painting but do it either in the proportions of the original or completely reversed; for example, a green fabric with a coral dot would set off a coral pillow with small amounts of green.

My inspiration for fashion items frequently appears in wrapping paper or packaging of scent or cosmetics. Keep a scrap book for reference and tear out color photographs of anything that appeals to you to refer to later on.

◇

LIGHT REFRACTION

One final point to consider is that the texture of both stitches and yarns affect the shade of a color. Tent stitch always makes a color appear darker; a raised stitch, such as Rhodes, catches any light and so appears lighter; and silk or rayon threads will look brighter than wool.

◇

COLOR WHEEL

On the facing page is a 12-hue color wheel to refer to.

PRIMARY COLORS: There are only three of these – red, yellow and blue. Mixed together, these primary colors make all the other hues. They are equidistant on the wheel. (Black and white are not colors, they provide shades of each hue.)

SECONDARY COLORS: These are green, orange and violet and are formed by mixing two of the three primaries in equal amounts. For example, red plus yellow equals orange, or blue plus yellow equals green. These secondary colors are positioned mid-way between the primaries.

TERTIARY COLORS: These are a mix of a primary and a secondary color; there are six altogether –

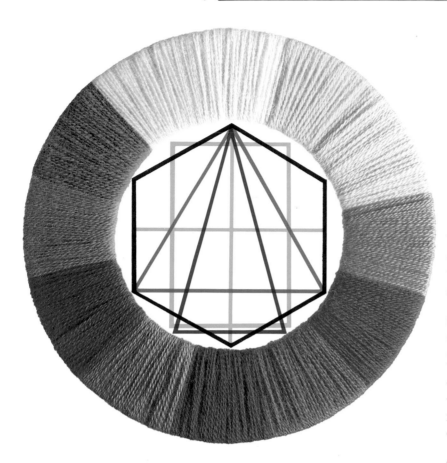

green, violet and yellow. They are shown by the two straight green lines on the chart. These usually work best if used in unequal amounts, for example tints and shades of violet used in flower petals and just the center of the flowers in yellow.

If you use the shade of one hue (color plus black), you must team it with the tint (color plus white) of the hue directly opposite; therefore, if you take a tint of blue-green then the shade of red-orange must be shaded (darkened) to the same degree as the blue-green is lightened.

SPLIT COMPLEMENTARIES: These are formed if one color of the complementary dyad is replaced by its two neighbors, for example, yellow with blue-violet and red-violet. The geometric figure is an isosceles triangle, marked in red on the chart.

TRIADS: These harmonies are formed by the use of any three colors formed by an equilateral triangle, marked in blue on the chart.

TETRADS OR PAIRED COMPLE-MENTS: These are two pairs of complementaries whose connecting diameters intersect each other at right angles, marked in green on the chart.

Other tetrads are formed with a rectangle connecting two complementary pairs, also shown in green on the chart; for example, yellow-green, yellow-orange, blue-violet and red-violet.

HEXADS: A hexagon can be rotated around the color wheel, marked in black on the chart, giving six harmonious colors for a scheme.

yellow-orange, red-orange, red-violet, blue-violet, blue-green and yellow-green.

All these hues can have black added and form a shade, have white added and form a tint, or have grey added and form a tone.

The hues on the right-hand side of the wheel, yellow clockwise through red to violet are termed 'warm' and those on the left-hand side are termed 'cool' colors.

However, with this color wheel there are a great many schemes that work well.

MONOCHROMATIC HARMONIES: This involves the use of only one color with its tints and shades. This is probably the most restful of the color schemes and is a good choice if many different textures are being planned.

ANALOGOUS HARMONIES: These are formed when colors adjoining each other on the wheel and related through one primary color are used.

FURTHER USE OF THE COLOR WHEEL: Diagrammed on the color wheel are various triangles, squares, rectangles and lines. If you make a circular disc out of card or construction paper the same size as the inside dimension of the color wheel circle and draw on the same shapes, using the same colors, you can then dial a color scheme, giving you many successful and contrasting color combinations.

DYADS OR DIRECT COMPLE-MENTS: These are hues directly opposite one another on the wheel, for example, red and

CHAPTER TWO
TENT STITCH

I have decided to make Tent stitch the first project chapter in the book for various reasons.

First, it was the introduction of Tent stitch in the sixteenth-century, when this hard-wearing stitch was used to copy the expensive, imported carpets to cover the plain furniture and to make pillows for the simple, hard benches, that has made so many more needlepoint pieces of the period survive to this day.

Second, Tent stitch is used in most of the other projects in this book, either as a background to set off a textured or patterned area or simply as a few stitches that are part of a more complicated composite stitch.

Finally, there is much confusion about how best to work the stitch, so, please, even if you think you have 'done' Tent stitch before, check through the basic techniques on the following pages.

I have divided the Tent stitch chapter into four parts. First comes the techniques of the stitch itself. There are two ways to work Tent stitch; both are explained and when to use them. Then comes the Simple project which shows you how to shade an object. Even though the object here is just an apple, the project shows you how to look at the subject matter properly before stitching, how to prepare the yarn mixes and stitch the piece. The same rules apply when stitching a more complicated object or arrangement.

The Advanced project, the Rooster, is adapted from a Roman mosaic, so that the principles explained in this section will not only enable you to copy this handsome bird for yourself, but will help you also to look at many other paintings, stained glass as

well as other mosaics, and plan and stitch them for yourself. Finally, there is the Inspirational section which covers antique textile and rug design, miniature needlework and Tent stitch used for backgrounds.

◇

THE TWO BASIC TENT STITCHES

CONTINENTAL TENT STITCH

Only use this version of Tent stitch when there is a single line of stitches to be worked either horizontally across, vertically up

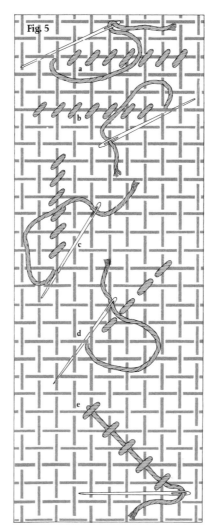

or down or diagonally from the upper right to the lower left.

Work the stitch as shown in Figure 5a with a long stitch behind your work. It will wear well and not distort the canvas. When turning a corner make sure that you still have a long stitch behind the work and have not started Half-cross stitch with very little wool behind the work. This does not wear as well and looks thinner from the front.

If a diagonal row from the lower right to the upper left is needed the stitches do not touch each other and it may be necessary to run a thread under the row of stitches on the surface of the canvas afterwards – this will visually connect the stitches. This is particularly useful when working some initials such as the first stroke of 'W' (see Figure 5e).

Figure 5a shows the direction of the stitch when working from right to left, 5b shows from left to right, 5c shows a vertical row down and 5d shows from the upper right to the lower left. Figure 5e shows the other diagonal with the thread running under all the stitches.

◇

BASKETWEAVE OR DIAGONAL TENT STITCH

This is the method of Tent stitch to use in all other places. On the front of the work it looks the same as Continental tent stitch but on the back of the canvas it forms a basketweave texture that wears well and does not distort the canvas. It uses about the same amount of yarn as the Continental tent stitch.

If you have never tried it before, take a scrap of canvas and work a diagonal line up as in Figure 6a, holding the needle horizontally and passing under 2 threads of

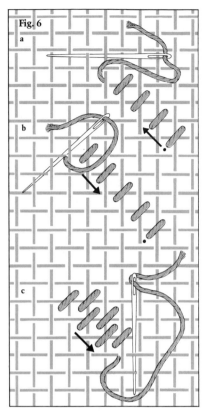

Fig. 6

When you understand the technique fully you can work even very small areas with this stitch.

READING THE GRAIN OF CANVAS: On evenweave or regular canvas there is a way of achieving even better results with the Basketweave tent stitch. This is to make use of the weave of the canvas threads.

Look closely at a piece of canvas and you will see that the threads weave over and under each other. At one intersection or

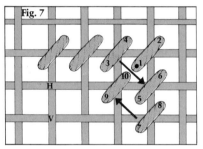

Fig. 7

canvas. After about 5 cm (2 in) change direction by coming up through the hole at the side of the last stitch (Figure 6b) and then with a vertical needle work down the row (Figure 6c).

If you have not worked the stitch before, do not start in a corner, otherwise you will have to change direction constantly to go up and down; it is the turning-point that confuses people and where they miss a stitch.

When you are confident with the technique draw yourself a corner on the canvas scrap and practise, following Figure 6c.

When you reach the top of a row and cannot go further, think of rotating the needle one hole towards the center of the design; likewise, when you reach the bottom of the row and the next stitch would be over the marked line, rotate the needle one hole towards the center of the design.

mesh the vertical thread is on top and at the adjoining one the horizontal thread is on top. Look at a diagonal line of intersections and they will either be vertical or horizontal – they alternate on each diagonal.

Look at Figure 7. Always work the row down (with the needle in the vertical position) over vertical threads; and work the row up over horizontal threads with a horizontal needle.

There are many advantages of this method. Besides a really smooth result, you can work different areas of the pattern; for example, flowers in different places on the canvas and when you come to do the background there will be no diagonal ridges where two lines that may have been worked in the same direction are side by side.

There is no need to leave the wool unfinished in the middle of

a row so that you can tell where you were up to. You simply look and if you see vertical threads to be worked over on the next diagonal you start at the top and go down, and if they are horizontal, you must go up.

While these are the most important tips for good-looking Basketweave tent stitch, there are a few extra points worth remembering. If there is a large motif already worked in the middle of the canvas and you do not wish to take the yarn across the back of it, choose the shortest distance for the point where the two halves will join up (see Figure 8). Stitch down one side to your chosen point and then return to the top and stitch down the other side. The join will be least noticeable at this point.

If there is a smaller motif which you can work across, anchor the yarn in the back of the motif stitches and pick up the correct diagonal (the grain of the canvas helps a great deal) on the other side.

Finally, finish off the thread by running through the back of stitches on the vertical or horizontal (never up the last diagonal row). When starting a new thread take the waste knot out to the side of the last stitch (not diagonally in front).

Everywhere else in this book I have stressed the importance of placing the waste knot in the direct path of your stitches. This is the one exception.

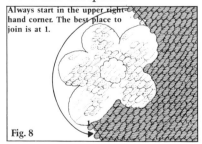

Always start in the upper right-hand corner. The best place to join is at 1.

Fig. 8

Simple Project

Right from the very first project in this book you will have something pretty and useful when finished. The apple worked on the top of this little box helps you master all the rules of shading. It is worked on plastic canvas which is easy to finish off yourself and all instructions on doing this are given.

There are also many adaptions of this basic idea that you might like to try; a box, either square or rectangular, would be attractive in the simple check pattern that is used on the sides. The apple panel by itself could be the start of a set of coasters (you could even design other coasters with a different fruit on each one!); or the apple could be worked on regular evenweave canvas and mounted on a pillow front or be made into a pincushion for a keen stitcher.

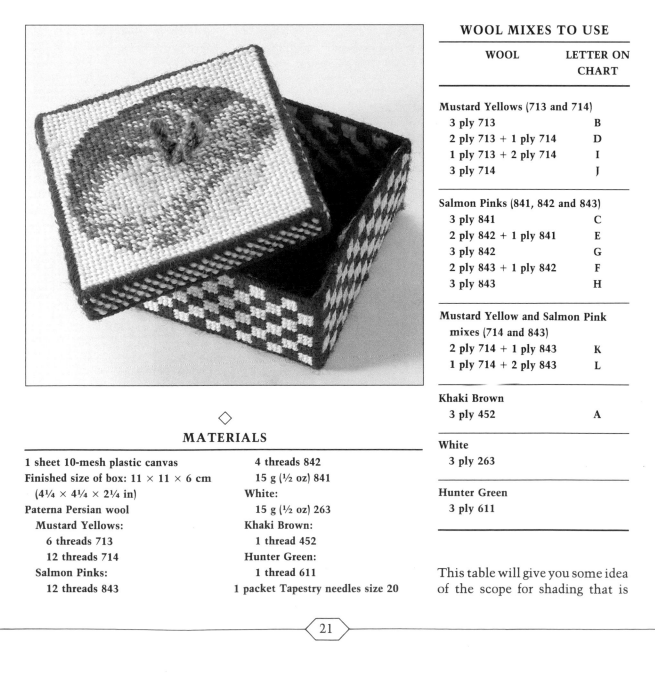

WOOL MIXES TO USE

WOOL	LETTER ON CHART
Mustard Yellows (713 and 714)	
3 ply 713	B
2 ply 713 + 1 ply 714	D
1 ply 713 + 2 ply 714	I
3 ply 714	J
Salmon Pinks (841, 842 and 843)	
3 ply 841	C
2 ply 842 + 1 ply 841	E
3 ply 842	G
2 ply 843 + 1 ply 842	F
3 ply 843	H
Mustard Yellow and Salmon Pink mixes (714 and 843)	
2 ply 714 + 1 ply 843	K
1 ply 714 + 2 ply 843	L
Khaki Brown	
3 ply 452	A
White	
3 ply 263	
Hunter Green	
3 ply 611	

This table will give you some idea of the scope for shading that is

◇

MATERIALS

1 sheet 10-mesh plastic canvas
Finished size of box: 11 × 11 × 6 cm
  (4¼ × 4¼ × 2¼ in)
Paterna Persian wool
  Mustard Yellows:
    6 threads 713
    12 threads 714
  Salmon Pinks:
    12 threads 843

4 threads 842
15 g (½ oz) 841
White:
15 g (½ oz) 263
Khaki Brown:
  1 thread 452
Hunter Green:
  1 thread 611
1 packet Tapestry needles size 20

possible with a thread such as a floss that has 6 plies or silk that has 7 plies. Even one range of an Appleton's Crewel color (these normally have eight or nine shades ready-made) would give you, if you used 3 ply and mixed them as explained above, twenty-five blends, ranging from light to dark.

◇

SHADING

Realistic representation of flowers, fruit or people are most frequently worked in Tent stitch. It is the smallest canvas-work stitch and therefore, can give the greatest detail and opportunity for portraying light, shade and depth. However, the method explained here of blending various plies of different shades of thread can be applied satisfactorily to any stitch if you so wish. One particular example to look at is the brick and plasterwork on the Country Cottage (see page 83).

As explained on page 10, a 'ply' is the thinnest unit of wool that is easily divisible. In this chapter when I refer to a 'strand' of wool I mean the mix of ply that is listed against the code letters in the table on page 21.

The aim with all but the most basic shading is to achieve a gradual transition from one color to another. To obtain this, a mixture of any divisible thread gives multiple steps between light and dark shades as one more ply of the darker color can be introduced to the needleful at regular intervals. Blends of two contrasting colors produce a speckled effect.

Take, for example, the Paterna Persian wool used for the apple; on 10-mesh canvas 3-ply wool is necessary for good coverage.

There are eight colors used – Khaki Brown and Hunter Green, which were only used full strength for the stalk and stalk base, White for the background and five others, two Mustard Yellows and three Salmon Pinks. By mixing the two yellows in different proportions, the three pinks in the same way and then the light pink with the lighter mustard yellow I achieved eleven color shades. If I had mixed the pinks and yellows in every combination of ply I would have obtained more different shades.

◇

PREPARATION FOR SHADING

From experience I cannot stress enough the importance of organization of the threads. By setting the threads out before starting work the actual stitching is much more fun and you are not

tempted to stitch too large an area before changing shades (this is only too easy if the threads are not ready).

While the apple is completely charted for you to copy on page 24, I should like to go through the various stages of preparation so that, for future projects, you can experiment and shade for yourself.

First, I found a ripe apple, one with quite a lot of color variation. I took a number of photographs of it, as although I referred to it while it was still fresh, fairly soon it seemed to change color and fade. Besides making a record, looking through the view finder of the camera helped me find the most interesting angle for stitching it.

Next, I made a stitching card (see Figure 9). I used a strong piece of foolscap paper and folded it in half across the middle. On the

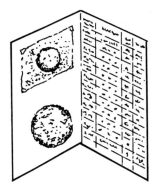

Colour mixes and number of plies	Parking lot	Code letter	Quantity
Mustard Yellows 3 x 713	···	B	
2 x 713 + 1 x 714	···	D	
1 x 713 + 2 x 714	···	I	
3 x 714	···	J	
Salmon Pinks 3 x 841	···	C	
2 x 842 + 1 x 841	···	E	
3 x 842	···	G	
2 x 843 + 1 x 842	···	F	
3 x 843	···	H	
Mixes 2 x 714 + 1 x 843	······	K	
1 x 714 + 2 x 843	······ ···	L	

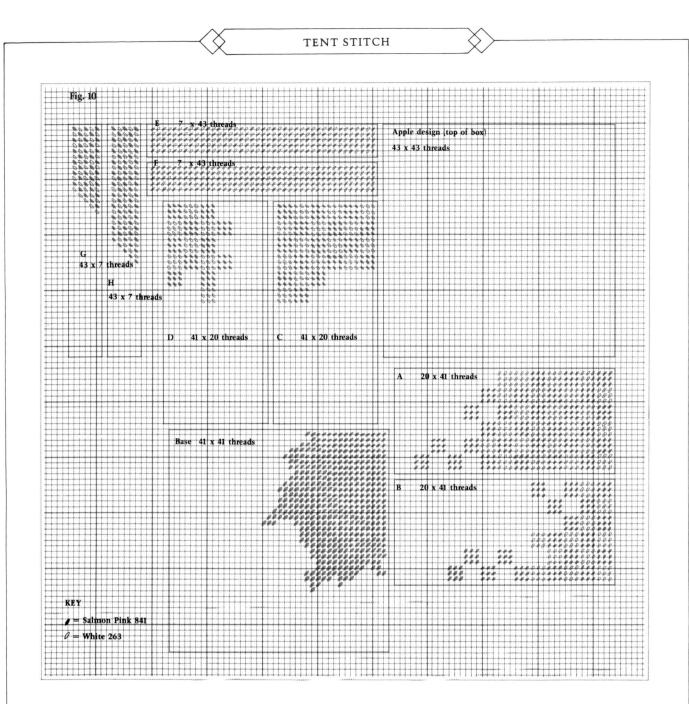

Fig. 10

E   7 x 43 threads

F   7 x 43 threads

Apple design (top of box)
43 x 43 threads

G
43 x 7 threads

H
43 x 7 threads

D   41 x 20 threads   C   41 x 20 threads

A   20 x 41 threads

Base 41 x 41 threads

B   20 x 41 threads

KEY
∕ = Salmon Pink 841
θ = White 263

inside left-hand lower page I did a drawing of the apple – this really made me look at the fruit.

Was it round? Was it red and green or was it more yellow? Were there patches of each color or did they mingle in some places? Were the blends more yellow or more red?

Next, I colored the drawing with three red crayons and two yellow (the same number as the shades of wool I planned to use)

and checked where the colors had to be dark, light or blended.

I left the upper half of this left-hand page for the photograph.

On the right-hand side of the page I made four columns, two narrow and two wide. I wrote out each mix in the first column and the relevant code letter in the third column. In the second column I 'parked' the strands themselves. The easiest way to do this is to ply the wool in the right

proportion, knot it at the end and take it through the card, leaving the knot on the right side to hold it. For this project I made up three working lengths of each mixture to start with. The 'Khaki Brown, Hunter Green and White were used straight.

I tied the three strands of the same color mix loosely together, only untying them when I was stitching with that blend. By only having one combination untied it is easy to know which one you are using.

Finally, in the fourth column I put three dashes to indicate the three strands that I had started with. If I had to make up any more strands, I added extra dashes so that I knew how much I had used at the end of stitching; or the remaining wool could be counted at the end if you should wish to make another identical canvas.

Now, ready to go I could enjoy the actual stitching!

◇

SPECIAL TIPS FOR PLASTIC CANVAS

Plastic canvas does not have an identical mesh count, either horizontally or vertically; therefore, it is important that all the pieces for one project are worked and cut in the same direction so that they can be joined together easily.

Plastic canvas needs no blocking; however, do not stitch it too tightly as the canvas can curl.

No seam allowances are needed for plastic canvas as it does not unravel. All the pieces in Figure 10 are diagrammed allowing 1 extra thread on each side. This is used for binding the pieces together when the design is complete.

Wherever possible use the natural edges of the plastic sheet as there are no nubs sticking out on these edges. Other edges must be trimmed carefully with sharp scissors before working the Binding stitch otherwise the nubs will poke through the stitching.

◇

WORKING THE BOX

See Figure 10 for the layout of the pieces on the sheet of canvas. These pieces are charted in a

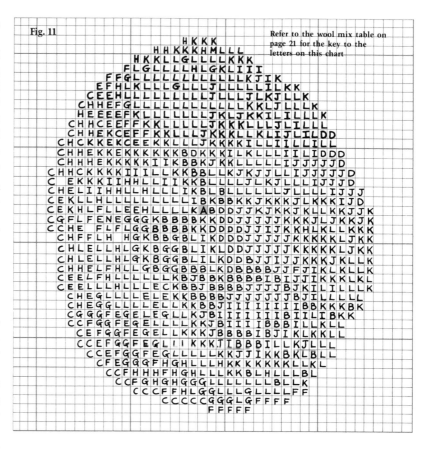

Fig. 11

Refer to the wool mix table on page 21 for the key to the letters on this chart

different way to the apple design (see Figure 11). Each stitch here in Figure 10 is drawn over a graph line indicating the actual stitch on the canvas thread. This will make leaving the outer thread clearer.

The outer solid line on all the pieces shows the final canvas thread on all sides which is used for joining the pieces later on. Mark out the pieces on the canvas but do not cut them out at this stage. It is far easier to stitch the small pieces when they are still part of the main sheet of canvas. Use the upper right-hand corner of the canvas so as to get a professional edge with no nubs to as many sides as possible.

Use 3-ply wool throughout and Basketweave tent stitch wherever possible. Stitch the apple design on the top of the box first,

following Figure 11. Start with the one stitch in the Khaki Brown, 'A' on the chart, and continue to work the 'B's, then the 'C's and so on.

When stitching like this it is more convenient to place the waste knot right out to the side or use the back of existing stitchery for beginning and finishing threads.

When the apple is complete, work the background with 3-ply White 263 in Basketweave tent stitch. Remember to leave 1 thread of canvas on all four sides of the panel which will be used later for binding the pieces of the box together.

Work the four sides of the top (E, F, G, H) with the pattern shown in Figure 10, using Salmon Pink 841 and White 263. Repeat the pattern shown all over.

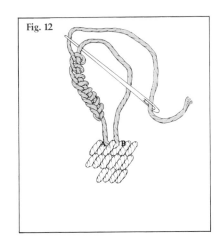

Fig. 12

Work the four sides to the base (A, B, C, D), using the same color wools but following the different pattern (see Figure 10). Repeat the pattern shown all over.

Work the base with just the Salmon Pink 841 in Basketweave tent stitch.

To make the loop to help remove the top of the box, thread a needle with 3-ply Hunter Green wool and bring it up through the canvas on the same stitch as the stalk at A (see Figure 12).

Leave a loose loop, about 3 cm (1 in) long, and return through the canvas over one thread at B. Come up again at A and buttonhole stitch along the length of the loop (see Figure 12). Make a second loop in the same way.

◇
ASSEMBLING THE BOX

The Binding stitch used here (see also Stitch Glossary page 143) can be used again in any home‘ finishing, either in a decorative contrasting color or in a matching thread.

When working Binding stitch start the stitching in the center of a side. It will then be easier to round a corner and will make the corners stronger.

◇
THE BASE

Using the Binding stitch, stitch over the unworked threads with 3-ply Salmon Pink 841 to join the four sides together along the short edges (see Figure 13,1).

When complete, join the four sides to the base (2). Using the same color wool and Binding stitch, stitch along the top edges of the base (3).

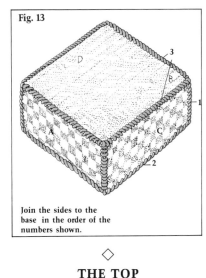

Fig. 13

Join the sides to the base in the order of the numbers shown.

◇
THE TOP

In the same way stitch the four top sides together along the short edges (see Figure 14,1) and then join the sides to the top. Stitch along the lower edges, using the same color and stitch.

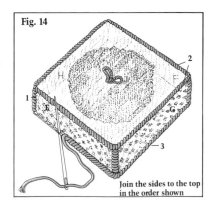

Fig. 14

Join the sides to the top in the order shown

◇
PLANNING YOUR OWN SHADING

The stitching card suggested is always extremely helpful, even on the smallest project. After years of stitching I am now totally converted to the idea of a few minutes of organization working out the color mixes before stitching.

When working out your own shading, make up as many 'mixes' as you can and mount a few of each in the 'parking spaces'.

Start by working the 'skeleton' of the object. With the apple this was the stalk, followed by the sharp yellow markings radiating out from the stalk, and then the deep pink outline.

If, for any reason, you might wish to repeat the design again, in particular if it is a prototype for a church kneeler, chart the stitches in pencil, as you go along. You always think it will be easy to remember afterwards, but it is not!

Instead of the usual symbols I used letters of the alphabet to represent the colors, this acts as an easy-to-follow order-of-work.

The tip for tying the strands of the same color mix together works particularly well on a more complicated project such as the Advanced Tent stitch project, the Rooster. When you wish to use a particular combination simply untie the knot, use the strand(s) needed, repark any usable length that is left and retie the bundle. This way you always know which combination is being worked with. Again, you think it will be easy to remember afterwards, but interruptions occur and it is only too easy to forget!

Advanced Project

T his handsome rooster is adapted from a Roman mosaic of the first century BC in the Burrell Collection, Glasgow, Scotland.

Early pictorial mosaics were always made from natural materials; indeed, those of the fourth and third century BC were made of pebbles with the outlines emphasized in lead. However, by the period of this rooster, small pieces of colored marbles were chiefly used. These small pieces are called tesserae. Frequently they were cut to a rough cube shape but sometimes the shape of each tessera was cut to enhance the area of the animal or other subject it was going to embellish. This is very evident with the rooster; on the tail feathers there are long curved tesserae, on his plumage they are long and narrow and on his body they are roughly square in shape.

Understanding the piece being copied helps to determine the shades of wool to use. Marble is a natural material and so the tesserae have small variations on their surface. However, to take an example, in one feather of the rooster's plumage the craftsman would have set marble fragments as closely matching as possible. So, while the rooster is not shaded in the true sense of the word, by blending shades of the fine Medici wool subtle variations can be achieved.

Evenweave, mono 18-mesh canvas was used to obtain the fine detail and the background can be completed in either creamy Basketweave tent stitch or by continuing the tesserae in pale shades.

MATERIALS

18-mesh evenweave, mono canvas
The rooster is 27 × 20 cm
(10½ × 8 in). A good size for a
pillow would be 40 cm (16 in)
square. If you wish to make
something else such as a firescreen
or stool top, measure your piece,
add 5 cm (2 in) on all sides for
making-up and center the rooster
in the area.

The quantities given are sufficient for
the rooster and the ground
underneath.

Medici wool
  Browns:
    3 small skeins each 500 and 306
  Golden yellows:
    2 small skeins each 321, 322
    and 327
  Greens:
    2 small skeins each 411, 413
    and 414
  Coral:
    1 small skein 104A

Floss
    1 skein each DMC 920 and 921
1 packet Tapestry needles size 22

WORKING THE ROOSTER

The drawing in Figure 15 needs to be enlarged, either at the copy or photostat shop or by the method explained on page 15. Draw the design on to the canvas with a marker pen.

It is only necessary to draw the outline of the rooster; the individual outlines to the marble tesserae can be stitched in freehand.

Make a stitching card as described on page 22. Add in letters as you make up the card.

WOOL MIXES TO USE FOR FILLING IN SPACES

WOOL/FLOSS	NUMBER OF STRANDS
For the plumage and legs	
2 ply 321 + 1 ply 322	8
1 ply 321 + 2 ply 322	8
3 ply 322	8
2 ply 322 + 1 ply 327	8
2 ply 327 + 1 ply 322	8
3 ply 327	8
For the cockade and head	
1 ply 104A + 4 ply 920 floss	3
1 ply 104A + 4 ply 921 floss	3
1 ply 104A + 2 ply each 920 and 921 floss	3
For the tail	
2 ply 413 + 1 ply 411	5
1 ply 413 + 2 ply 411	5
2 ply 414 + 1 ply 411	5
1 ply 414 + 2 ply 411	5
2 ply 414 + 1 ply 413	5

I recommend that you work the tesserae outlines in one area at a time and then fill in, using the wool mixes in the table. Use 2-ply wool for all the tesserae outlines. Use the dark brown (500) for outlining the chest area of the body and use 1-ply 500 and 1-ply 306 mixed for all the other outlines (the darker color is necessary to show up on the chest).

Start by stitching the plumage on his neck first. Outline a feather, work free-hand Tent stitches to represent the gaps in the marble and then fill in with the chosen blend of wool, using Basketweave tent stitch. Each feather should be the same blend down its length but the feather that lies next to it should be a good contrast.

After the plumage is complete, work the head and cockade, introducing the floss to give a slight sheen. Then work the body and finally the tail.

The ground under the rooster's feet is a blend of Medici wool 321 and 322. If you decide to work a

Fig. 15

1 square = 16 mm

mosaic background around the completed bird you may like to experiment with 2-ply Medici wool 306 for the outlines as it will be less harsh against the creamy shades of the background tesserae. The shades I suggest for the background are 502, 329 and 509. Depending on the final size of the piece you may like to buy 50-g (2-oz) hanks of these last three shades. One hank will cover approximately 52 sq cm (8 sq in).

Inspirational Projects

I have chosen several very different items to give an idea of the many interesting ways in which Tent stitch can be used.

The floor pillow (see page 30) is copied from a Turkish rug. It is particularly interesting as in sixteenth-century England carpets and rugs from the Near East were so prized that needleworkers copied them in Tent stitch for table carpets, pillows and bed-hangings to make their homes more comfortable. The large rug (below) has hydrangeas tumbling all over it. It has a Florentine border and Basketweave tent stitch as a background to set off the texture of the flowers.

Inspiration for the three-dimensional doll (see facing page) came from a Ukrainian peasant figure and was stitched by DeDe Ogden of San Francisco. It is stitched on 18-mesh canvas with appliqués of congress cloth for her needlecase and chatelaine, and footstool behind her. It is stitched in three pieces – the doll even has a base that is stitched with lacy bottoms to its bloomers and very lady-like sized feet!

Doll's-house miniatures (see page 31) are a delight to make if you have good eyesight and patience. Tent stitch is by far the best stitch to use; it allows the detail needed for the scale and also allows the furniture to stand firmly. Larger stitches would tend to make the pieces topple over.

Read on for more details of these beautiful pieces, together with other inspirational ideas for projects using Tent stitch.

FACING PAGE: *The Hydrangea rug.*
LEFT: *The Russian doll.*

The pieces I have selected use Tent stitch in very different ways. Each one set off a train of thought down interesting avenues, some of which I have enjoyed exploring, others which I hope to have the time to do one day.

The floor pillow is a good example of what Tent stitch is suited to. First, it is a very useful project to make and more examples of pouffes and stool tops are discussed in Finishing and After-care on page 128. The pillow also opens up a whole area of design that lends itself particularly well to needlepoint. Carpets and rugs were never made specifically to go on floors until the nineteenth century – they were also hung on walls and balconies, used to cover tombs and tables and even in some regions, draped over chairs.

Looking at Oriental carpets and rugs you have to be able to judge whether or not a particular design will translate well on to canvas at a reduced size. Obviously, any design can be copied but a 6-m (6½-yd) square carpet with a Savonnerie or Aubusson-type floral design all over will not scale down to a pillow at all satisfactorily. The design on the floor pillow is a particularly good example; there are six squares with a similar star design in each and then a series of borders round each square and a multiple border round the whole design. The design is quite time-consuming to work out initially on graph paper but Brian Synge, who planned and worked it, enjoys the mathematical challenge of such designs. I have charted a small area for you (see Figure 16).

When looking at rugs or antique textiles as a form of inspiration remember that straight lines and angles at 45 degrees are simple to work on canvas. Other angles and arabesques are much more difficult.

Two of my most successful class projects are taken from rugs; one I saw in a shop window on Madison Avenue, New York and I unashamedly stood there and did a quick sketch. Using very different scales this design has been made into a wallhanging, a pillow front incorporating ribbons and Pulled-thread stitches and an evening purse. The purse is photographed in Inspirational Stitchery on page 93. The other one is a Hajji Babi rug design that I have adapted with silk, ribbons and metallics into a purse front.

You will find many beautifully illustrated books on rugs in your local library: look through them and see if any of the designs inspire you. In an attempt to itemize areas of inspiration, I realized that most of the tribes that made carpets were nomads and the great centers of carpet production were situated along the famous Silk Route in Asia, the busy trading route used by merchants of many lands for over a thousand years.

Try and look also at the Persian Garden carpet designs; neatly compartmented like formal gardens, the designs usually include flowerbeds, paths, and fishponds with borders running between each section.

Geometric kilims are also a wonderful source of inspiration for modern pieces. The Bergama region of Turkey has designs with large geometric ornaments and bold unshaded colors. Even when the main design is difficult for you to see translated into stitches examine the borders carefully as I

ABOVE: *The Turkish floor pillow.*

am sure you will find a wealth of ideas to incorporate into future projects.

Adapting carpets for projects leads me on to antique textiles; even fragments can have wonderful repeating designs that would be easy to stitch. Traditional patchwork quilt patterns, in general, make attractive designs and if you wish to mix and match, say a set of dining chairs, it is frequently 'safe' to take different designs from the same source as they will go together. Here are two examples of this; a student of mine wished to work some pillows for a set of country pine chairs and found very compatible patchwork star designs, each one slightly different but, scaled to approximately the same size, they made an interesting set. If you wished to do a pair of chairs with high backs, two animals executed in mosaic, so long as they were drawn relatively the same size, would make a far more interesting project to work than repeating the same design twice. I have already discussed mosaics

when working the Rooster on page 26, but there are useful geometric designs which, even when copied from postcards, can be translated with a stitch for each tessera. Colored tiles, set in a geometric pattern, are common for garden paths in Victorian homes and make good patterns.

While it is not my favorite thing, many people enjoy copying paintings. I am not referring to Old Masters and trying to 'needlepaint' a Rembrandt oil painting, but artists such as Vasarely, Mondrian and Ben Nicholson use abstract form from which you can gain inspiration. Any painting is worth looking at for pleasing color combinations.

The Hydrangea rug (see page 28) is a very English piece and shows our love of gardens with hydrangeas tumbling in a riot all over it and spilling on to the border. At the design stage I made

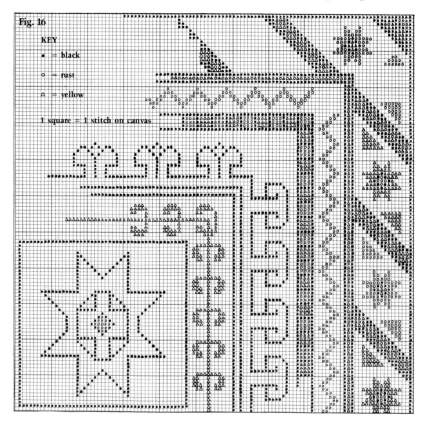

Fig. 16

KEY

• = black

○ = rust

△ = yellow

1 square = 1 stitch on canvas

many studies of the flowers in the garden, drawing some that were still not completely out and others that were fully blown. When I had about six flowerheads in appropriate sizes that pleased me, I made a few photocopies of each one. Then I cut them out and placed them (overlapped in some cases) on a strong piece of paper that corresponded to the final size of the rug.

Next I traced the flowers on to the linen canvas I had prepared. I used 13-mesh linen canvas for two reasons: first, its extra fine quality, and second, it is a little wider than most canvas – 150 cm (60 in). This meant that the rug could be stitched in one piece. Rugs stitched in one or more pieces are discussed in Finishing and Aftercare on page 130.

Basketweave tent stitch has been used purely as a background to the free stitching of the petals and the Florentine border. The French knots have been worked on top of the Tent stitch. The smooth stitching makes an excellent foil for the texture everywhere else and also means that the rug will wear well. This piece of needlepoint was planned for a low-traffic area, in front of a fireplace in a formal drawing-room. With its long stitches it would not be suitable for somewhere walked on a great deal.

The Russian doll (see page 29) is worked in fine detail on 18-mesh canvas with appliqués of congress cloth. It gives an excellent idea of how unusual fibers can be used to great effect. If you are looking for hard wear for a chair seat or rug there is really no substitute for the finest quality wool available. If, however, you are planning something purely decorative such as this doll or the Country Cottage (see page 83) any

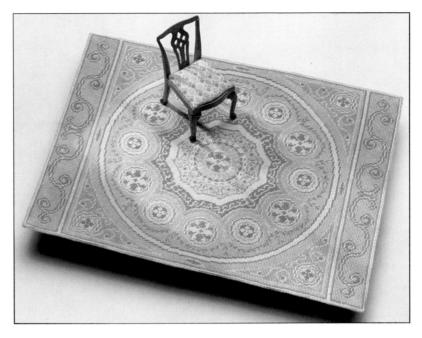

fiber that works on the canvas, i.e. that will go through the canvas mesh if you wish to stitch with it or can be couched on to the canvas surface and looks good, is fine. This particular piece was planned as a workshop project and so the chance to try many different fibers was one of its important features.

The other range of projects that fine canvas and Tent stitch are particularly suitable for are doll's-house miniatures. Many years ago I found a Victorian doll's house in need of restoration and I fear most of the work still has to be done. However, my husband, Patrick has needlepointed some beautiful rugs and furniture for it. It seems that men, when they enjoy stitching, are challenged by the mathematics of rescaling designs and plotting them on graph paper.

Generally speaking, doll's houses are built to the scale of 1 inch to the foot and we have found that stitches other than Tent are too 'bumpy', especially for floor coverings. They also

ABOVE: *Doll's-house miniatures.*

tend to make the delicate furniture wobble and rock alarmingly. The coarsest canvas we have used is 24-mesh congress cloth, and the finest 48-mesh silk gauze. Anything you would consider making for your house can be made, with patience, in miniature – screens, wallhangings, pillows, footstools and we have even made a backgammon board! The canvas count depends, as with all canvas work, on how much detail you require in a given area.

Two final tips – you may not have a frame small enough for miniature pieces; simply mount the piece of canvas (allowing the normal margins) on to a large piece of strong cotton fabric or calico that will fit your frame. Mount the fabric on the frame as normal, then carefully snip away the backing fabric from behind the area of canvas you wish to work. Work in a good light and invest in magnification of some sort if it makes you more comfortable.

CHAPTER THREE

FLORENTINE STITCH

Simple Project

I t is probably Florentine work that initiated the current interest in needlepoint. Many patterns are easy and quick to work and the overall look can be altered dramatically by the use of color.

Avid stitchers find having two pieces of needlepoint on hand a good idea; one that needs concentration and good light and another one that can be done when traveling or when without special equipment. Many Florentine patterns fall happily into the second category.

The Simple Florentine pillow incorporates eight Florentine patterns, plus a dramatic border. Any one of these patterns can be worked singly for an attractive project.

Each of the patterns is charted fully here next to the relevant instructions rather than in the Stitch Glossary, and I have given suggestions for other uses of the patterns too.

◇

MATERIALS

14-mesh, white evenweave, mono canvas
Cut size: 56 cm (22 in) square
Finished size: 48 cm (19 in) square
Frame: 56 cm (22 in) square
Appleton's Crewel wool
  Sky Blue:
    25 g (1 oz) each 561 and 563
    50 g (2 oz) 564
  Early English Green:
    25 g (1 oz) 541
  Pastel Shade:
    25 g (1 oz) 874
  White:
    75 g (3 oz) 991
1 packet Tapestry needles size 20

◇

MARKING THE CANVAS

Tape or machine the edges of the canvas. Mark the canvas with either a pencil or basting thread in a contrasting color. Marking diagonals with a sharp pencil and ruler can be done by lining up the diagonal threads of the canvas. If basting thread is used remove it from the work just ahead of the stitching.

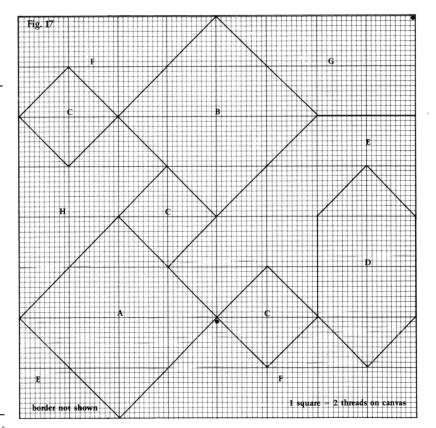

Fig. 17
border not shown
1 square = 2 threads on canvas

Mount the canvas on to the frame as tautly as possible.

◇

WORKING THE PIECE

Use 4-ply wool for all the Florentine stitches and 3-ply for the Tent stitch.

◇

A HORIZONTAL MOTIF

(see Figure 18)
Work this pattern in the lower left-hand corner. Find the central hole by running the point of a needle across the canvas from both the side and top points.

The Simple Florentine pillow.

Work the central stitch from 2 threads above the central point to 2 threads below. Work two stitches either side, making five in all.

Next, work a ring of 16 white stitches still over 4 threads. The spots either side of the green stitches on the diagram show how two white stitches fit one above another and share a hole.

In the diagram all the white stitches have been left void but when there are two rows of them sharing the same canvas holes I have put a spot to show the correct length of the stitches – no stitch is longer than 4 threads.

When all the Florentine pattern is complete, three horizontal running stitches in Early English Green 541 can be worked between the pairs of white stitches in the second white ring – in the diagram I have shown these only on the right-hand side.

Complete the background to this area with stitches over 4 threads of canvas in white wool. Figure 18 shows the edge of the design area with a dotted line and the length of the white stitches with spots. Do stitches over 1

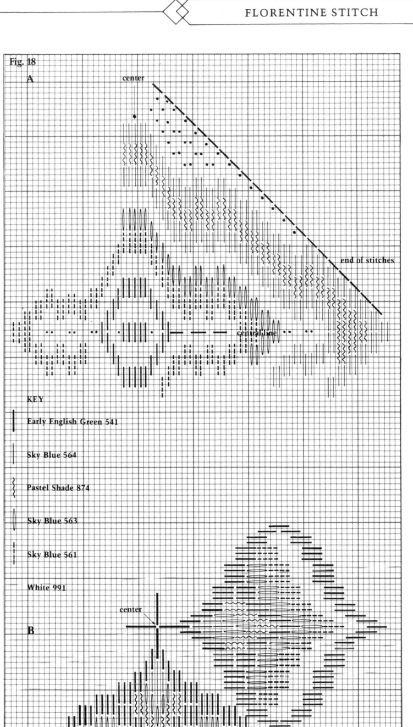

Fig. 18

A

center

end of stitches

central line

KEY

Early English Green 541

Sky Blue 564

Pastel Shade 874

Sky Blue 563

Sky Blue 561

White 991

center

B

thread of canvas only where necessary to get a smooth diagonal edge to the area.

FURTHER PROJECTS: Either a purse front in bold Aztec colors for daytime use or in metallics for the evening. Or use finer canvas (so that the pattern is smaller) for a checkbook cover, make-up purse or eyeglass case.

◇

B 4-WAY POMEGRANATE

(see Figure 18)
Work this pattern in the top center. Find the central hole of the area by running the point of the needle across the canvas from both the side and top points of the large diamond. Start here with the four stitches over 6 threads that join the four pomegranate shapes together.

All other stitches in this area are over 4 threads. Continue to work first one outline and then another, turning the frame or not depending on which is most comfortable. After the outlines and 'flame-like' peak (which is in the same Early English Green 541) are worked fill in with the rest of the colors.

Complete the background between and around the pomegranate shapes in Basketweave tent stitch with 3-ply White 991.

FURTHER PROJECTS: As the central motif with an interesting border for a pillow or pillow front. The design looks particularly good set in a circle so it would be perfect for a round pillow or foot stool.

This motif can also be worked with all the motifs on the vertical as an all-over design. Work one pomegranate and you will see that the single stitch in the middle of each outward curve becomes the top stitch of the next one. This is called a 'half-drop' pattern repeat (see also Figure 30 on page 53).

◇

C BARGELLO FLOWER PATTERN

(see Figure 19)
This is worked in the three small diamonds placed diagonally across the canvas from the upper left to the lower right.

Start by working the Flower outline. Each of the four long stitches over 6 threads starts 2 threads in from the corner points. Start with one of these long stitches and work round the flower doing four stitches over 2 threads and then another long stitch over 6 threads before changing direction. Repeat the pattern until the outline is worked.

Work a circuit of long inner stitches over 6 threads in White 991, and then continuing in the same color, work the short stitches over 2 threads, each quarter radiating out from the center.

Finally, work eight stitches down into the center (only three of these stitches are shown so that the stitches underneath can be seen clearly).

Leave the Basketweave tent stitch background to these three areas until later on.

FURTHER PROJECTS: Worked as an all-over design for pillows or small bedroom chairs. The design is very pretty with the colors reversed; for example, colored flowers on a white background instead of white flowers on a dark background.

The pattern looks very pretty, if a little delicate, with all the long stitches worked with the narrow satin ribbons used in the

Advanced Pulled-thread project. (The 1.5-mm (⅛-in) ribbon stitches well on 14-mesh canvas).

Both the short central stitches and the background can be worked in either a pearl cotton or a rayon thread.

◇

D ARROW HEAD

(see Figure 19)
This is worked down the right-hand side of the canvas. Work the outline around the area and the two dividing lines. Most of these stitches are over 3 threads of canvas but follow the diagram at the lower and upper points and where a vertical line branches off from a diagonal line.

Next, work the central area stitching inwards. Both the straight and hollow stitches are all over 2 threads of canvas. The wavy stitches form a diamond over 2, 4, 6, 8, 6, 4, 2 threads at the central point.

Fill in the two outer areas, again working inwards and following the colors given in the diagram.

FURTHER PROJECTS: Either elongated or repeated down the length, the pattern would make a lovely bell-pull.

With a pointed base and a straight top it would make an unusual eyeglass case. Recently, I saw an attractive one hung on a cord round a lady's neck – her glasses never went missing! The design here would be fun with a small tassel at the bottom.

◇

E WAVE PATTERN

(see Figure 19)
This is worked in the area immediately above the Arrow Head. Start above the point of the Arrow Head pattern which is shown in

the diagram. Work up into the horizontal line drawn on the canvas which marks the edge of the border between areas E and G. All the stitches are over 4 threads of canvas. The stitches are worked in groups of 5, 4, 3, 2, 2, and 1. Follow the diagram for the reverse of the pattern. All subsequent rows follow the first one exactly.

The pattern is continued into the lower left-hand corner, seeming to reappear from behind the horizontal motif already worked. I counted mine carefully across but if you are a thread or two out no one will know so long as you stitch the rows of color in the same order.

The colors are stitched in rows in the following order: Early English Green 541, White 991, Pastel Shade 874 and Sky Blue 563.

FURTHER PROJECTS: This pattern is lovely for large pillows but asymmetrical designs (ones that do not balance either side of a central point) are not good for upholstered pieces such as chair cushions – it makes the chair look as if it is going to fall over!

If the piece was big enough, for example a bedhead, where the pattern would work down and then back up again, it could look very dramatic.

If you have perfectly proportioned tall windows and are dextrous and patient when making something up, a curved window valance would look stunning.

◇

F TRELLIS

(see Figure 19)
Work this in the top left- and lower right-hand corners of the design. In the lower right-hand area there is a spot in the point

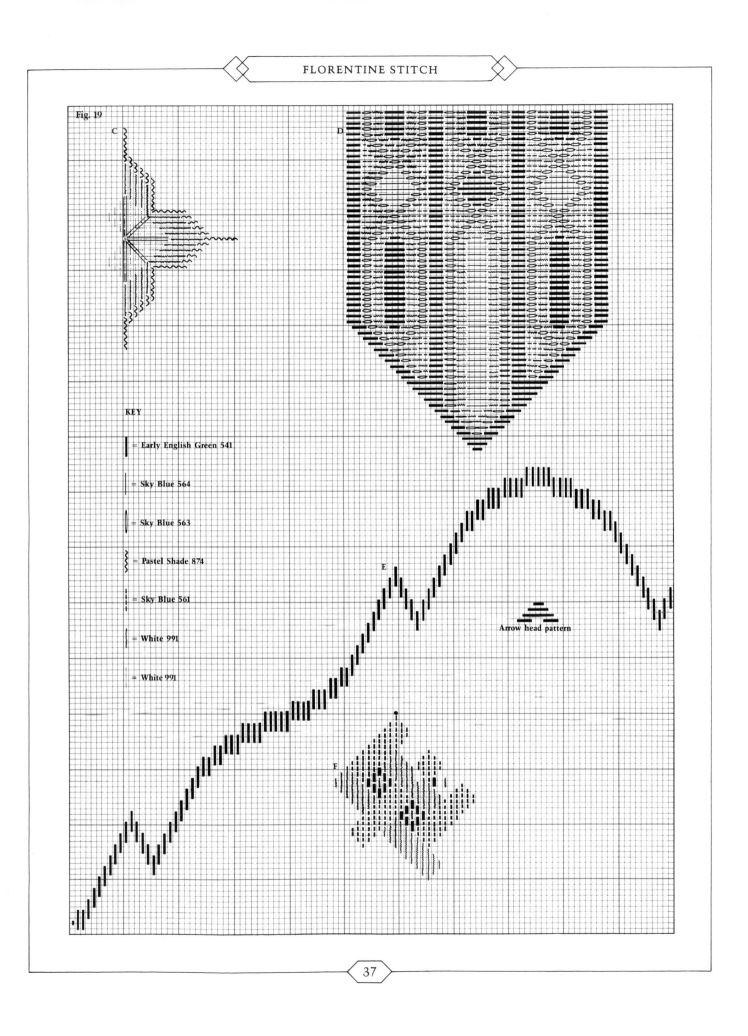

Fig. 19

C

D

E

F

KEY

⌡ = Early English Green 541

⌡ = Sky Blue 564

⌡ = Sky Blue 563

⌡ = Pastel Shade 874

⌡ = Sky Blue 561

⌡ = White 991

⌡ = White 991

Arrow head pattern

between areas A and C. Start at this spot, matching it to the one on the diagram and the pattern will then fit the area.

Each full Trellis band has one stitch over 2 threads, one over 4, seven over 6, one over 4 and finally one over 2. The shorter bands shown on the diagram are the compensation bands needed for the area being stitched.

Two needles, one for each color of the Trellis, are particularly helpful as it is easier to work the different colors in turn rather than fit one in later on. The short filler stitches can be worked at the end.

FURTHER PROJECTS: Pillows, stool tops, dining chairs and eyeglass cases. This is such a small repeating pattern that it is extremely versatile.

◇

G   SCALLOPS

(see Figure 20)
Work this in the upper right-hand corner. Start in the upper right-hand corner, matching the spot on the diagram to your corner. Work all the outlines over 4 threads in Sky Blue 564.

When these are complete fill in each area starting at the top. Note that on the third and fourth rows down there are side stitches over 6 threads of canvas and on the last (sixth) row there are two stitches over 2 threads on each side.

FURTHER PROJECTS: This pattern is slightly larger in scale than the Trellis one but would be suitable for all the same things except for the eyeglass case (unless, of course, it was worked on very fine canvas).

◇

H   6, 2, 2 FLORENTINE

(see Figure 21)
Work this midway down the left-hand side. Match the spot on the diagram to the top left-hand point. Follow the Sky Blue 564 outline on the diagram and the upper right-hand stitch will fit perfectly into the upper right-hand corner of the design area.

FURTHER PROJECTS: Pillows, stool tops and dining chairs. The pattern has been used also as a border for the Rug on page 48.

◇

BACKGROUND TO BARGELLO FLOWERS

This can now be worked with 3-ply White 991 in Basketweave

tent. Follow the instructions in the Stitch Glossary on page 168 and you will find it necessary to tuck certain stitches under the long outline stitches of the flower to cover the canvas satisfactorily.

◇

BORDER

(see Figure 21)
This is not yet marked on the canvas. The complete border is worked over 40 threads and now is the time to mark it in, together with a miter line on each corner.

Miter lines: Any time a design needs to be turned around a corner, such as in the case of a photograph frame, the design has to change direction along a diagonal line known as a miter. When working the stitches into

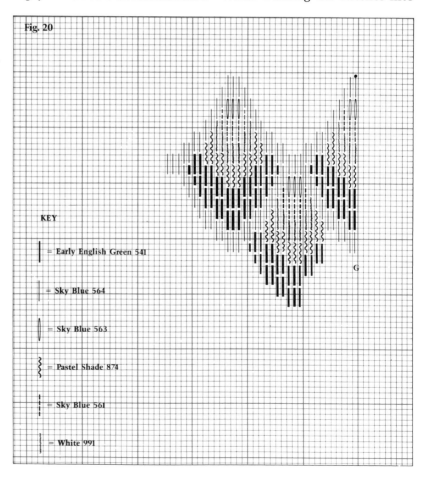

Fig. 20

KEY

| = Early English Green 541

| = Sky Blue 564

| = Sky Blue 563

} = Pastel Shade 874

| = Sky Blue 561

| = White 991

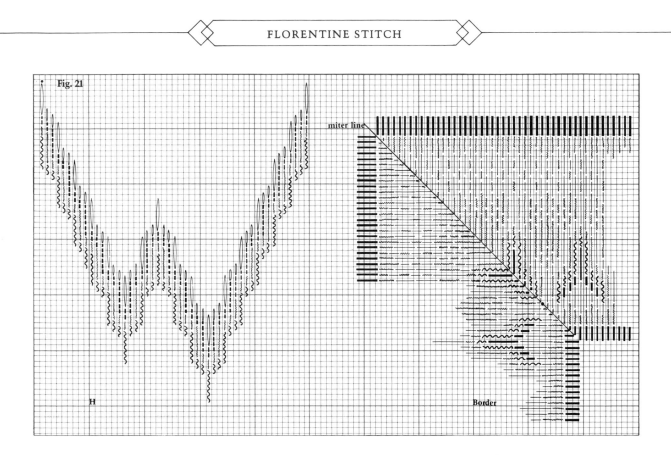

Fig. 21

the holes along the diagonal line, continue the pattern as closely as possible and shortening stitches only where necessary. When working away from the miter line your stitches on both sides of the miter line must be the same color and length.

To make the miter on the upper left-hand corner start at the top stitch of the Trellis pattern and mark out a diagonal line, using either a pencil or a basting thread, and moving up a canvas thread at each intersection. Each miter is done in this way, radiating out from the main design.

These lines will help when working the corners as all the stitches go down into this diagonal line at the corner and compensation stitches may be necessary.

Work the border outwards, starting with the line of Straight Gobelin over 3 threads of canvas in Early English Green 541. This stitch will share on all four sides with the patterns you have already stitched.

Next, work the Straight Gobelin stitch over 2, 3 and 4 threads in White 991. Next work the 2, 2, 6, 2, 2 spire shapes in Sky Blue 564, starting in one corner and matching the spot on the diagram to your miter line.

Fill in the spaces inside each spire. It would be easier to fill in some complete spires along one side before attempting a mitered one on a corner when you will need to work compensation stitches.

Work the 2, 4, 2, 2 border beyond the spires in Sky Blue 564.

Fill in with stitches over 2 threads in White 991.

Fill in the area between the spires and this last border with a continuation of the 2, 2, 6 pattern but worked in White 991 only. Note that some of these stitches are over 3 threads on the miterd corners.

Work a border of Straight Gobelin over 2, 3 and 4 threads in White 991 and finally work one of Gobelin over 4 threads in Early English Green 541.

This pillow is larger than many and would make an excellent stool top or floor pillow. In the Finishing and Aftercare photograph on page 122 you can see it made up with tassels made from matching Appleton's Crewel wool.

Advanced Project

Vests are a wonderful stitching 'investment'. Depending on the fibers and stitches used they can be either extremely glamorous and tailored-looking for city wear or ethnic-colored to wear with tweed skirts or trousers at the weekend. Stitching a vest brings flair to a simple outfit, as well as giving you a little added warmth and, above all, it is a great conversation piece!

My design here is very versatile. It uses a commercial paper pattern as a base and the Florentine stitching is designed so that it will repeat if you wish to make a longer-style vest or have a more generous fit.

The matching evening purse on page 47 is just as adaptable, as the needlepoint panel can be slipped out and replaced by another one with a different color scheme or pattern.

Colors that fit into a wardrobe are so personal (and seasonal as well) that I have given an alternative color scheme. This variation would make an evening version of the same design in black and gold. This vest design is an advanced piece, so please either use the design as it is here or just some motifs from it to create your own beautiful outfit.

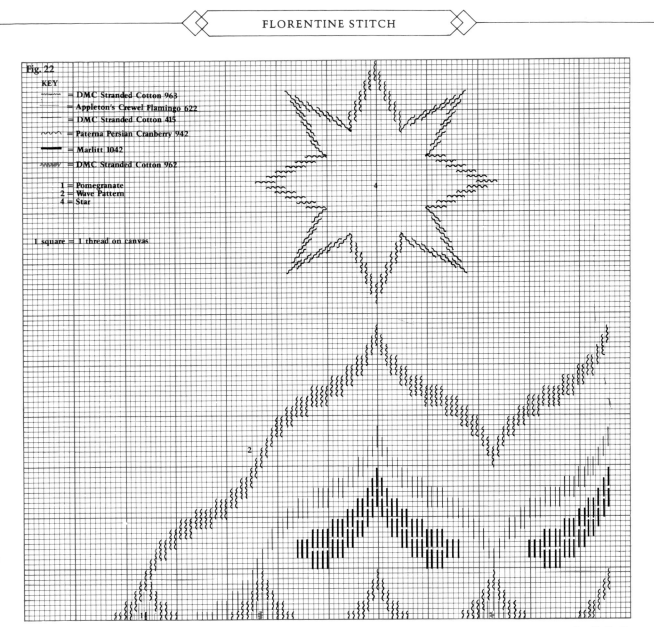

Fig. 22

KEY

⩔⩔⩔ =	DMC Stranded Cotton 963
=	Appleton's Crewel Flamingo 622
=	DMC Stranded Cotton 415
∿∿∿ =	Paterna Persian Cranberry 942
▬ =	Marlitt 1042
∿∿∿ =	DMC Stranded Cotton 962

1 = Pomegranate
2 = Wave Pattern
4 = Star

1 square = 1 thread on canvas

continued in Fig. 23

STITCH SUMMARY

Number	Stitch	Thread	Number of plies
1	Pomegranate	*For the outline:* PP Cranberry 942. *For infilling:* Appleton's Crewel Flamingo 621 and 622 and Bright Rose 943, and DMC Stranded Cotton 415 and 963	Use 3 for Paterna Persian (PP) wool
2	Wave pattern	Same as above plus Marlitt 881	Use 4 for Appleton's Crewel wool
3	Diagonal Florence	PP Strawberry 954 and 955, Appleton's Crewel Flamingo 622, DMC Stranded Cotton 415 and 963, Marlitt 881 and 1042, and Balger Silver No. 16.	Use 2 for DMC Pearl Cotton; Use 8 for DMC Stranded Cotton except for the initial which uses 6; Use 1 for Balger No. 16
4	Stars	*Main star:* PP Cranberry 942. *Initial:* DMC Stranded Cotton 962. *Basketweave tent stitch:* Marlitt 1042. *Other stars:* DMC Stranded Cotton 415, 962 and 963, Marlitt 1042 and Balger Silver No. 16.	Use 4 for Marlitt
5	Wave pattern	PP Cranberry 942, Appleton's Crewel Flamingo 621 and 622, DMC Pearl Cotton 893 and 894, DMC Stranded Cotton 353, 415 and 962, and Marlitt 881 and 1042	
6	Vertical stripes	*For the outlines:* PP Pearl Grey 212 and 213, and Bright Rose 943. *For infilling:* DMC Pearl Cotton 893 and 894, DMC Stranded Cotton 415 and 963, and Marlitt 881	

◇
MATERIALS

A commercial paper pattern for a vest. The Florentine design will adapt well to any style of vest. I made mine in a medium size but the design can easily be adapted.

Sufficient fabric for the back only and piping the edges. I used raspberry-colored ultra-suede.

Fabric for lining. I used finely striped gentleman's sleeve lining.

17-mesh Elsa Williams linen canvas. Cut size: 65 × 80 cm (26 × 32 in). This allowed the two fronts to be worked side by side on the same piece of canvas, with approximately 8 cm (3 in) between the two front edges. It is much easier to match the design working side by side in this way, so even if your vest pattern is slightly different from mine, lay the pattern front out twice to allow for this, and add on 5 cm (2 in) on all sides and 8 cm (3 in) between the pieces. Measure your layout and buy the canvas accordingly.

If the linen canvas is unobtainable, 18-mesh Zweigart is a suitable alternative.

Wools:
Paterna Persian
Pearl Gray:
   15 g (½ oz) 212
   10 threads 213
Cranberry:
   40 g (1½ oz) 942
Strawberry:
15 g (½ oz) 954
25 g (1 oz) 955

Appleton's Crewel
Flamingo:
   15 g (½ oz) 621
   15 g (½ oz) 622
Bright Rose:
   40 g (1½ oz) 943
Cottons:
DMC Pearl Cotton
4 skeins 893
3 skeins 894
DMC Floss
2 skeins each 353, 962 and 963
4 skeins 415
Metallics:
2 skeins Balger Silver No. 16
Rayons:
Marlitt
   2 skeins each 1042 and 881
1 packet Tapestry needles size 22

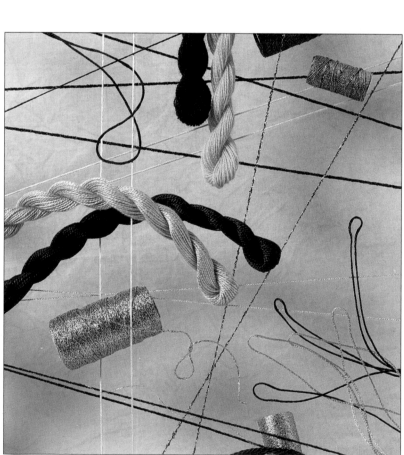

◇
THREADS

The colors listed above are only a suggestion: you may wish to substitute some or all the colors. However, if you wish to achieve the same dressy appearance try and substitute wool for wool, floss for floss, metallic thread for metallic thread and so on.

In the instructions the tone of the color has been indicated where it is important; for example, the outline of the Pomegranate should be quite bold. This will help you to get the same balance if you change the color scheme.

If you wish to make this vest in another color scheme, substitute

My suggestions for an evening version of the vest in blacks and shades of copper and gold metallics.

continued in Fig. 22

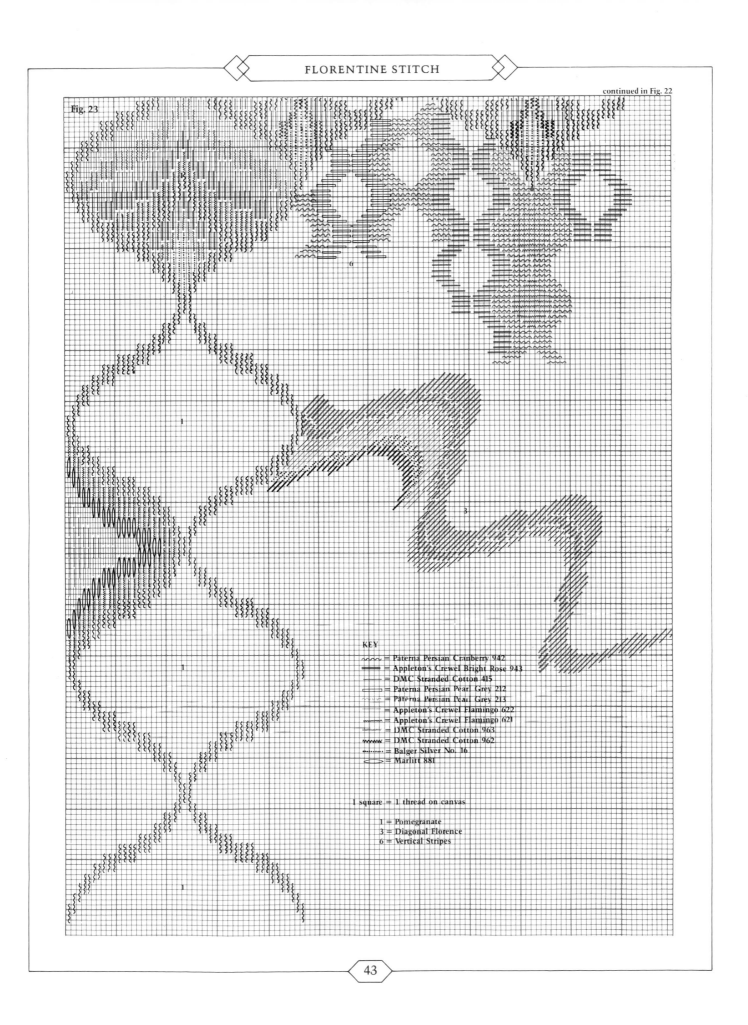

Fig. 23

KEY

≈≈≈ = Paterna Persian Cranberry 942
━━━ = Appleton's Crewel Bright Rose 943
━━ = DMC Stranded Cotton 415
━━ = Paterna Persian Pearl Grey 212
━━ = Paterna Persian Pearl Grey 213
━ = Appleton's Crewel Flamingo 622
≈≈≈ = Appleton's Crewel Flamingo 621
≈≈≈ = DMC Stranded Cotton 963
≈≈≈ = DMC Stranded Cotton 962
∙∙∙∙∙ = Balger Silver No. 16
⬭ = Marlitt 881

1 square = 1 thread on canvas

1 = Pomegranate
3 = Diagonal Florence
6 = Vertical Stripes

two other colors for the pinks and grays and choose silver or gold highlights. For example, if you want jade greens and deep blues, find four shades of green wool (to substitute for the pinks) and two of blue (to substitute for the grays); take a selection of floss and pearl cotton and any rayons that fit in with the color scheme.

Here are my suggestions for an evening version of the vest in blacks and golds. As I wanted shades of copper and gold metallics rather than golden yellow wools, the substitution was slightly different. Instead of four rose- and apricot-pink wools I selected five different textures of black wool, two rayons, floss and pearl cotton. I chose dull mustard shades which I planned to use only in small quantities and various shades of copper and jet metallics. I felt that bright gold looked too 'new' and I thought that the copper shades would be far more flattering.

Shown here are the threads I selected for this version:

BLACK: (Wools) Paterna Persian 220 and Medici black; (Rayon) Lystwist black – shade 1 and Marlitt 801; and (Cottons) Floss and Pearl Cotton DMC 310.

MUSTARD SHADES: (Wool) Medici 8325; (Cottons) Pearl Cotton DMC 729 and Floss DMC 676; and (Rayon) Marlitt 898.

COPPER/GOLD/JET METALLICS: Twilleys Gold Dust; Pingouin 'Place Vendôme'; Balger blending filament single ply, in copper 021 and Jet/copper 022; Balger No. 8 2122; and Balger Jet/copper 0522 and Jet 005.

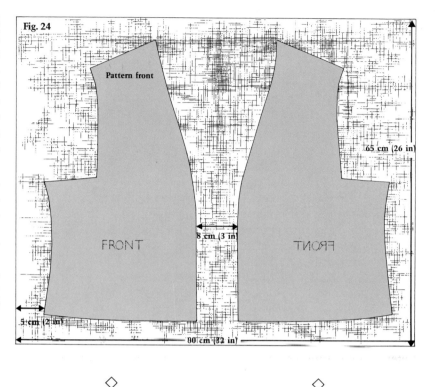

Fig. 24

Pattern front

FRONT

FRONT

65 cm (26 in)

8 cm (3 in)

5 cm (2 in)

80 cm (32 in)

PREPARING THE CANVAS

The pattern piece for the vest front is used twice (see Figure 24). Match the line printed on the pattern piece to indicate the grain of the fabric to a line of canvas thread. This will ensure that the design will be stitched straight on the weave of the canvas.

Mark the outer cutting line. Mark any seamline printed on the pattern too. When stitching the piece you will take stitches over this inner seamline but not quite as far as the outer cutting one. The reason for this is that canvas work is fairly stiff when finished and therefore, you do not want extra bulk in the seams.

Mark out the second front on the canvas, this time with the printed side down. Line up the uppermost point of the shoulders on both fronts by following the canvas thread across so that they are side by side.

ADJUSTING THE DESIGN FOR FIT

This is not a difficult job as each of the stitch designs can be continued downwards, sideways or upwards until the outlines on your canvas are reached.

However, the top Pomegranate design (there are three and a half repeats up the front edge of the vest on both sides) looks best at bust height. Therefore, if you wish to make your vest longer, work the top Pomegranate first at your bust height and then work down, with as many pattern repeats as necessary until you reach the bottom edge.

WORKING THE PIECE

However tempting it is to cut the piece of canvas in half and work each side of the vest separately, do not. Work at least the Pomegranate design up the two leading edges, a little of the Wave pattern and the first row of both Diagonal Florentines above it while the canvas is in one piece. You will find it much easier to match across from one piece to the other and as the two edges sit together in wear, it is important that the design is level!

The right-hand side of the vest only (as you look at the photograph) is charted (see Figures 22 and 23). The other side is a mirror image except that the stars on the shoulder have been left off and the Wave pattern continued across the whole area.

◇

1 POMEGRANATE

(See Figures 22 and 23)
Refer to 'Adjusting the design for fit' on page 44 for details on where to place the top Pomegranate, unless you are following the pattern exactly as the one diagrammed here.

Work the Pomegranate pattern on the leading edge of the right-hand panel. The outline (including the 'flame-like' peak) for each one is Cranberry 942. This is quite a deep tone but not the darkest. There are three and a half pattern repeats down the edge.

All the Pomegranates are filled in with different combinations of wool, metallic and floss. However, for each Pomegranate the true pink as well as the peachy tones are used, together with both the gray floss and gray metallic thread.

◇

2 POMEGRANATE/WAVE PATTERN

(See Figure 22)
When these complete Pomegranates are finished, the same groups of stitches are worked but sloping diagonally upwards. Follow Figure 22, starting with the outline color you have already used and work across from the top of the highest Pomegranate to the armhole. If your canvas is a little wider, just continue with the pattern repeat as necessary. Do not take the Wave pattern any higher at this stage.

Fill in with a combination that pleases you. The inverted hearts shown on the diagram should be in a strong color, possibly the darkest one used. I used the deeper Marlitt here.

Now is the time to copy the mirror image on the second front panel – it is much easier to do it now while there is no additional stitching. The filling in of each Pomegranate matches across with one on the same level: match or contrast as you wish.

Now work half Pomegranates (shown in Figure 23) to give you a straight leading edge. All my fillings in were the same, using wool and floss alternately, with gray floss in the center.

◇

3 DIAGONAL FLORENCE

(See Figure 23)
Next work the Diagonal Florence on the right-hand panel. Start it, sharing with the second Pomegranate down from the top, even if your design is longer than the one photographed. There will simply be more curves before you reach the bottom edge.

Immediately after working the first line work the mirror image on the other front. Again this is much easier now than later on.

The sequence is as follows: Row One is over 4 diagonal threads of canvas and is worked in wool, and Rows Two and Three are both over 2 diagonal threads of canvas and are both worked in something other than wool such as cottons or metallics. The pattern continues down the area with a wool row and then two shiny rows.

◇

4 STARS ON RIGHT SHOULDER

(See Figure 22)
If you want an initial in one of the stars like mine, position this one first (see also Alphabets on pages 72–75). Plot it on graph paper so that your letter fits the space.

The Star is the same as the one worked on the Simple Stitchery pillow (see page 79) except that the first five circuits are left out. Work the initial, using a bold color. Work the Star outline in the darkest shade and fill in with a soft shade, using Basketweave tent stitch.

Now position other Stars at random, working each one to a different number of circuits. Mine are three, four, five and six. Each was worked in a different color order but using only three colors: pink, gray and metallic.

◇

5 WAVE PATTERN ON LEFT SHOULDER

(See Figure 22)
Next work the left-hand shoulder, continuing the Wave pattern from the top of the Pomegranates all the way up. All the stitches are over 4 threads and a color order was worked out and then repeated as necessary to fill the area. (Once you have decided on your shades, it helps to mount the order of shades on a palette or piece of card.)

Now work the mirror image of these curves behind the Stars on the right shoulder, balancing the rows of color as you go. The reason for doing the left shoulder before the right will become apparent when you have to count 'across' the Stars – having the correct pattern to refer to helps a great deal!

◇

6 VERTICAL STRIPE PATTERN

(See Figure 23)

Finally, work the vertical stripe pattern between the Diagonal Florence and the base of the diamond area between the two hearts, starting at the spot on the diagram. In this way the pattern repeat matches up well with other existing stitchery.

The stripes are worked in pairs of the same color wool, four stitches sharing, then stepping away from each other and then back together, leaving an oval space to be filled in with a contrasting thread. The oval shape is made up of stitches over 2, 4, 6 threads, four stitches of 8 threads, 6, 4 and 2 threads.

The sequence of rows I used was pale gray (Pearl Gray 213), mid-gray (Pearl Gray 212), pale gray (Pearl Gray 213), mid-pink (Bright Rose 945), pale gray (Pearl Gray 213), mid-gray (Pearl Gray 212), pale gray (Pearl Gray 213) etc. The satin stitch fill ins were done at random but quite a strong color was always selected to fill in the mid-gray stripe.

Occasionally, a Ribbed spider

Fig. 25

wrong side

was worked in these ovals in the same shade as the rest of that row. The Ripped spiders are stitched over a base of Basketweave tent instead of the Satin stitch used in the rest of the ovals.

◇

MAKING-UP

Refer back to the commercial paper pattern and cut the back and two fronts in the lining fabric and the back in your chosen fabric. I used ultra-suede for the back of my vest and binding around the edges. This fabric is a good choice as it can be trimmed close and can be cut on the straight rather than the bias for making the binding.

Alternative backing fabrics are fine cord, closely woven silk or velvet. If using these fabrics it might be easier to use a decorative braid to finish the edges rather than making the necessary length of bias binding.

Place the lining fronts and back right sides together. Baste and stitch the shoulder and side seams. Press the seams open (see Figure 25).

Make two rows of machine stitching, one on top of the other, on both canvas fronts around the curved neckline of the needlework and close up to the work itself. Trim the excess canvas to about 6 threads around the work. Place the canvas fronts and the fabric back right sides together. Baste and stitch the shoulder and side seams. Press the seams open.

Working on a flat surface, arrange the lining garment with the canvas and fabric garment on top, wrong sides together. Smooth out both layers and baste together, allowing the usual seam allowance. If this goes over some of the canvas work do not worry.

Allow the vest to hang up, overnight if possible, and then check that neither fabric is pulling the other and making one 'blouse out'. Adjust the basting if necessary. Now, immediately before binding the cut edge of the canvas, check all the edges for knots that will cause unnecessary lumps under the binding; trim any away carefully.

Cut a piece of ultra-suede 4 cm (1½ in) wide by the total length. To obtain this measure carefully all the way round the edges to the center back again, plus a further 10 cm (4 in). Cut the binding as one piece or join two pieces to obtain the right length. Measure and cut similar binding of the same width for both armholes, again allowing about 10 cm (4 in) extra for starting and finishing.

Baste the long piece of binding to the right side of the vest, starting somewhere along the back hem (where it will hardly be noticed). Stitch on top of the existing basting stitches. Continue until you return to the starting-point, overlap for a short distance and trim any excess. Machine stitch. Turn the binding to the inside. Turning in the 1-cm (½-in) seam allowance, neatly slip stitch to the lining.

This is by far the easiest way to complete the vest. However, if you prefer, follow the method suggested in your paper pattern. If you decide to use a decorative braid applied just to the right side of the piece you will have to make up the lined vest first with all the hems turned in.

Advanced Project

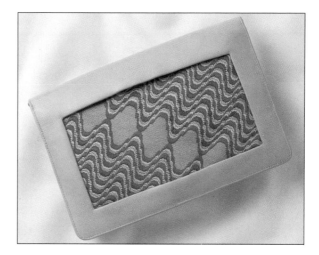

A ny of the patterns on the vest would look good on a purse front, particularly the random stars on a Basketweave background or the Vertical stripe pattern. I stitched the Diagonal Florence, possibly the most difficult of the vest patterns, but it does form an interesting diagonal across the panel and reverses well to form plain areas where you could stitch initials, or a motif of Ribbed spiders or small stars.

Use exactly the same pattern for the purse as one of the ones on the vest but stitch on a finer canvas in order to have a smaller piece at the end.

The purse itself is available to order (see List of Suppliers on page 174).

MATERIALS

24-mesh congress cloth
Cut size: 20 × 30 cm (8 × 12 in)
DMC Floss
   2 skeins each 962 and 963
   4 skeins 415
Rayons:
   Marlitt
     3 skeins 881
Metallics
   2 skeins Balger Silver No. 16

WORKING THE PIECE

Baste a diagonal line across the canvas, starting about one third in from where you want the top left-hand corner of the design to be.

Work a row of Diagonal Florence over 4 threads across the canvas (see Figure 26). The diagonal line you have marked will be a quick check on every curve to prove that you are not off-line. Use the Marlitt or your darkest shade for this first row.

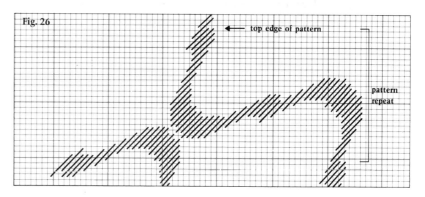

Fig. 26   ← top edge of pattern   pattern repeat

Turn the chart upside-down and work a partner row to your first row. At the bottom of each curve the rows will touch before swooping away again.

Then fill in behind these two rows. The order of colors I used was Marlitt, always over 4 threads, the two pinks DMC 962 and 963, over 2 threads, Marlitt, two grays (the metallic Balger No. 16 and the DMC Floss 415) and so on.

The areas between the two curves are filled with Basketweave tent stitch. Initials or Ribbed spiders could have been worked on top.

STITCH SUMMARY

Thread	Number of plies
Diagonal Florence	
DMC Stranded Cottons 415,	
962 and 963	6
Marlitt Rayon 881	4
Metallic Balger Silver No. 16	1
Basketweave tent stitch	
DMC Stranded Cotton 415	4

MAKING-UP THE PURSE

Trim the canvas to 8 threads around the worked area. Finger press the spare canvas to the back and slip stitch to the back of the stitchery. The piece is now ready to insert into the leather purse.

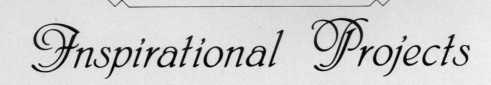

Inspirational Projects

Florentine designs are suitable for a wide variety of projects as can be seen from the additional ideas given under each pattern in the Simple Florentine project.

Increasingly, ready-made fabrics are available either woven or printed with traditional Florentine patterns so that it is important to tailor a design for stitching in such a way as to make it really special. No one would want their hand-worked piece mistaken for a length of fabric, however beautiful!

The photograph here shows a few pieces that I have made for my own drawing-room; they all demonstrate a particular way of creating a design or adapting an existing design to make it completely personal.

The two small pillows are worked in the color scheme of the room, with a border pattern from the curtains adapted into a Florentine wave pattern for one and the Diagonal Florentine pattern used in the Vest for the other. A third pillow has a Florentine border worked around my name with a background worked in floss, using a Cross-stitch variation that leaves some of the canvas exposed. The final pillow is a very small panel worked with a four-way design in ribbons. It is surrounded with lace and mounted on an existing circular pillow.

The Florentine chair was a flea-market find; it is still possible to buy single chairs inexpensively if you watch out for a good shape and are prepared to paint or distress the wood. The back of the chair is worked in an unusual Gothic spire pattern and I had great fun – and needed a large piece of graph paper – working a four-way version of the pattern to fit on the rounded cushion.

The Yellow rug has an all-over design of flower-heads in two different sizes and both worked in four-way Florentine. A wide border is stitched in the 2, 2, 6 pattern already used in the Simple Florentine project.

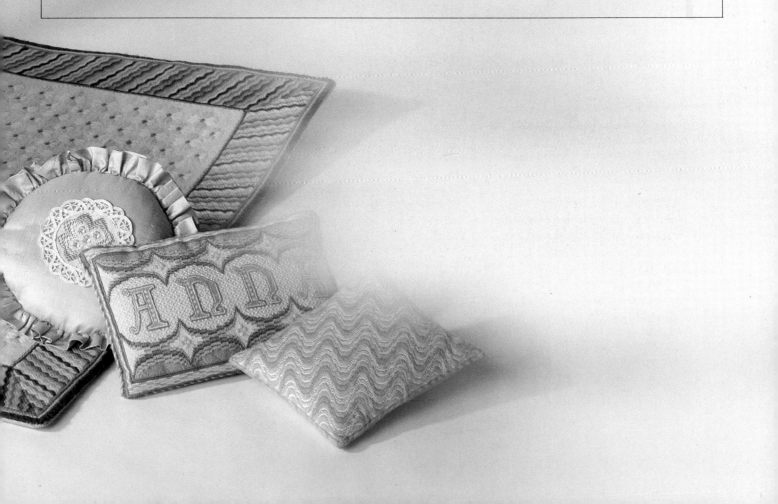

There are almost as many romantic stories about the origins of Florentine as there are names connected with it: Florentine work, Bargello, Hungarian point, Irish stitch, Flame stitch and there are even some references in Victorian craft books to Railroad stitch (no doubt because the stitching grows so quickly).

There are stories of an altruistic lady who encouraged all the female inmates of the Bargello prison in Florence, Italy, to stitch these patterns, hence the name that is most commonly used for these designs in the United States. Other sources say that it was the fifteenth-century marriage between a king of Hungary and an Italian princess that fused the traditional motifs of Hungary with the appearance of silks from the princess's native land.

◇

CHOOSING A DESIGN

Within the wide range of Florentine designs there are many simple ones, suitable either for a first-time project or for a piece to be worked on while travelling or chatting. There are small designs that are particularly versatile for a multitude of projects and there are large-scale designs that need space to be appreciated to the full.

Some Florentine designs have short, neat stitches that make them suitable for hard-wearing rugs and chair cushions and others have very long stitches that would not wear so well.

I have charted the flowers and border from the Yellow Rug (see Figure 27) and the four-way Candleflame design on the chair seat (see Figure 29) that are in the photograph on pages 48 and 49.

◇

YELLOW RUG

The rug was worked on 12-mesh canvas and has two sizes of flowers worked alternately, so it is easy to see how either to rescale them or to work them on finer canvas for a small piece. The rug is worked in Appleton's Crewel wool. The flowers are all one color, Bright Yellow 551, and the background is Off-White 992. Therefore, the wide border could afford to be worked in a number of colors — I used the Sky Blue, Grass Green, Wine Red, Flamingo and Heraldic Gold families, three shades of each with a single line of Chocolate 181 in between each color change. If you wished to copy the border on to something else with more color used in the central pattern, you may prefer to work only in one or two families with a neutral shade such as Off-White, Chocolate 181 or Iron Gray 961 in between each family.

The flowers are worked in two different scales, the smaller over 2, 4, 6, 4, 6, 4 and 2 threads, the larger over 4, 6, 8, 6, 8, 6, and 4 threads. The final location for this rug is in a place where it does not get a tremendous amount of wear. If you were planning it for an area with more traffic, consider working all the flowers in the smaller scale stitch.

The rug was worked in five pieces, the central area and four lengths of border all carefully thread counted so that they could be joined satisfactorily after stitching. Remember to stitch the long borders to run the same way as the long sides (down the canvas) and the short ends to match the short sides (across the

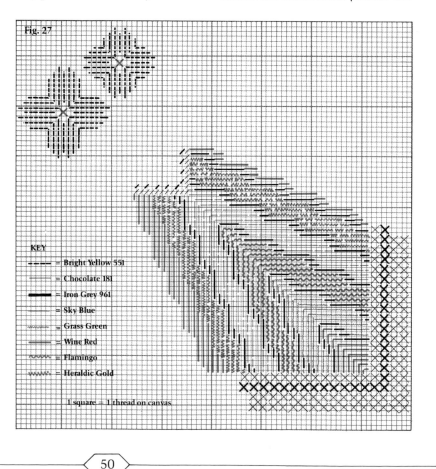

Fig. 27

KEY

- - - - - = Bright Yellow 551
━━━━━ = Chocolate 181
━━━━━ = Iron Grey 961
──── = Sky Blue
wwww = Grass Green
──── = Wine Red
wwww = Flamingo
wwww = Heraldic Gold

1 square = 1 thread on canvas

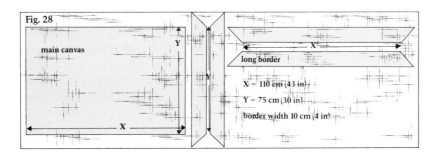

Fig. 28

main canvas

Y

X

long border

X

X = 110 cm (43 in)

Y = 75 cm (30 in)

border width 10 cm (4 in)

canvas) so that the canvas mesh will match exactly (see Figure 28).

The Florentine 2, 2, 6 pattern is a pattern you are already familiar with if you worked the Simple Florentine pillow where it was used straight in one of the areas. Here, it is mitered at each corner to give a raying-out effect to the completed piece. The mitered corner is charted here (see Figure 27) and, if you were working on one piece of canvas it would be simple to copy. Continue the color sequence as started. When the center of one side is reached simply reverse the pattern. With a rectangular piece the four corners will be identical and the centers of the two opposite sides also. With a square piece, the corners and all the centers will be identical.

The border for this rug was stitched in four pieces. First work one long border, starting from the center out in both directions, first in one and then in the other. When the same number of threads is stitched on the inner edge (the edge to be joined to the main canvas) mark the miter and then stitch it. Next, work one of the short sides, starting with the same miter reversed, working to its center (not necessarily the same color as on the long side) and then out to the next miter corner. Then work the other long side and finally the second short side.

◇

FLORENTINE CHAIR

On the chair the unusual Candle-flame pattern is worked upright on the back of the chair and four-way on the seat. It is charted here in the more complicated four-way version (see Figure 29). If you prefer to work it straight simply use the pattern charted (with the candles upright). Use the pattern repeats shown and ignore the miter line.

When copying either design start in the center of the canvas. Start the four-way pattern with the four stitches over 3 threads of canvas going down into the central hole (shown with the arrows) and set up the stitches in the Rose Pink first. If you are stitching the straight version again it would be best to work the Rose Pink outline first.

Figure 29 shows an outer motif as well – it is the same stitch repeat but using a slightly different color combination from the four central motifs.

Count all the stitches carefully as while most are over 6 threads there are some over 2, 4 and 8 threads of canvas.

◇

FLORENTINE PATTERNS

Generally speaking, Florentine patterns fall into two main categories; those that repeat across the width with a series of wavy patterns (these can have flame-like points, gentle curves or sharp, stepped inclines), and those that have some motif that repeats itself diagonally as well as vertically (for example, patterns such as Scallop and Trellis on the Simple Florentine pillow on page 34). Pomegranates and Bargello flowers can be worked as all-over designs as explained in the Simple Florentine project on pages 35 and 36 and then fall in to this second category too.

Patterns can be altered dramatically with the use of color; designs can be worked in soft muted shades for traditional interiors and worked again in bold fresh colors for a modern setting. Even the simplest wave pattern can be altered dramatically; imagine a simple flame design worked in three primary colors and then think of the same pattern in a range of shades worked from dark to light and back again – the pattern is hardly recognizable as the same one.

The wave on the small pillow photographed on page 49 was stitched to copy a similar pattern on the curtain fabric. Making a pattern such as this one is not difficult if you remember a few tips and are prepared to unpick if necessary!

The finished size of the project will dictate the scale of the repeat; for example, a large duet piano stool could take a large-scale flame pattern as there would be sufficient space for the pattern to 'read'; the scale on the front of an eyeglass case would have to be much smaller. Start any wave pattern, whether it is with a peak or a valley, in the center of the canvas – in this way the pattern will automatically balance at the sides. Odd num-

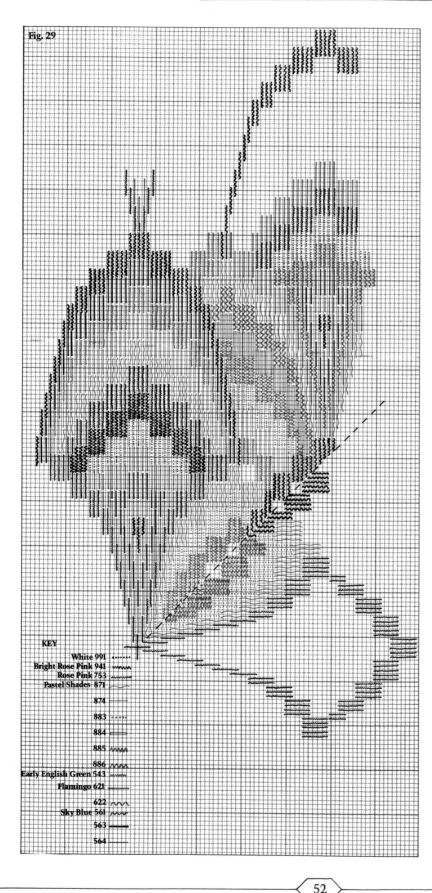

Fig. 29

KEY

White 991	....
Bright Rose Pink 941	~~~~
Rose Pink 753	~~~~
Pastel Shades 871	_____
874	_____
883	....
884	=======
885	ΛΛΛΛΛ
886	~~~~
Early English Green 543	~~~~~
Flamingo 621	_____
622	∿∿∿∿
Sky Blue 561	∿∿∿
563	_____
564	_____

bers of peaks, valleys or any other motif tend to look more sophisticated than even numbers.

In order to achieve a curved wave it is necessary to work groups of stitches, the more stitches in each group the softer the curve. This is demonstrated well in the pattern on the Simple Florentine project that is worked immediately below Scallops; it curves gently at the top of the area with groups of 5, 4, 3 stitches and then as it descends it becomes much more acute worked with only one stitch at a time.

In order to achieve an attractive curve work the largest group of stitches at the top (and bottom if required) and then gradually decrease the stitches in each group as the pattern line descends. Graphed here are some examples (see Figure 30); it is obvious that a number of groups with a lot of stitches in will give a softer curve than one with only a few stitches.

It is very satisfying creating your own Florentine patterns. When you have done some standard pieces and experimented with a few wave patterns try creating your own four-way Florentine design. These four-way designs look particularly good on circular pieces such as footstools or on rounded cushions such as the Florentine chair on page 48. Again a few tips will help you get started.

Mark the canvas diagonally from corner to corner through the center – this will give you the same miter lines that you marked on the Simple Florentine project when working the border.

Any stitch that is worked down into the miter line shares with a stitch of the same color and length worked at right angles to it. By following the chart for the Simple Florentine project border

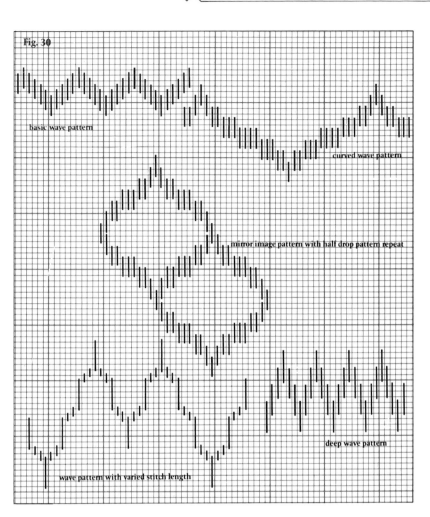

Fig. 30

basic wave pattern

curved wave pattern

mirror image pattern with half drop pattern repeat

deep wave pattern

wave pattern with varied stitch length

on page 39 you will have automatically done this. Another example using a mitered corner to refer to is the Florentine border on the Yellow Rug (see page 50).

Any design with a single-stitch point at the bottom (such as the Pomegranate) can be worked four-ways simply by sharing the four 'bottom' stitches at right angles to each other in the central hole of the canvas. The Gothic spire pattern on the back of the chair looks infinitely more complicated but, in fact, there is a single stitch at the base of the pattern and it was this stitch, worked four times radiating out from the center of the canvas that started off the four-way design for the chair cushion.

◇
DINING-CHAIR CUSHIONS

Possibly the most popular use of Florentine is for dining-chair cushions. The two main advantages of Florentine over other needlepoint techniques for chairs are speed and adaptability. No needlepoint is fast but of all the stitches Florentine covers the canvas the quickest. Many Florentine patterns simply repeat the first line stitched. Others have an outline that has to be counted carefully but can then be filled in quite painlessly. Florentine pieces make a nice starting project for children or

convalescents looking for something new to try.

Florentine is also adaptable. You can mix and match similar patterns when working a large set of chair cushions. Patterns of the same scale in co-ordinated colors look interesting, especially if pairs of chairs are worked in each pattern. An example of this would be to take different wave patterns all with approximately the same sized pattern repeat and work them with the same number of colors.

Another idea for a dramatic set of chairs in a room with not much other pattern is to work an outline pattern, for example, either of those adapted from the pocketbooks in the Winterthur Museum (see page 117) and then fill in each area with a set of colors used at random, very much like the Pomegranates worked up the leading edges of the Vest on page 40.

Finally, adaptability would pay off well if any friends offered to help you stitch a set of chairs. The stitch tension of different Florentine pieces is far less noticeable than that of a Basketweave tent design done by different stitchers!

Choose a Florentine pattern that does not have very long stitches, these could easily snag and so the piece would not wear well. The length of the stitch obviously depends on the canvas chosen. For example, a stitch over 8 threads on 18-mesh canvas will be much shorter (and more hardwearing) than a stitch over 8 threads on 10-mesh canvas. As a general rule I would not consider any pattern with a stitch over more than 6 threads on 14-mesh canvas or 4 threads on 10-mesh.

CHAPTER FOUR

Cross Stitch

AND ITS
VARIATIONS

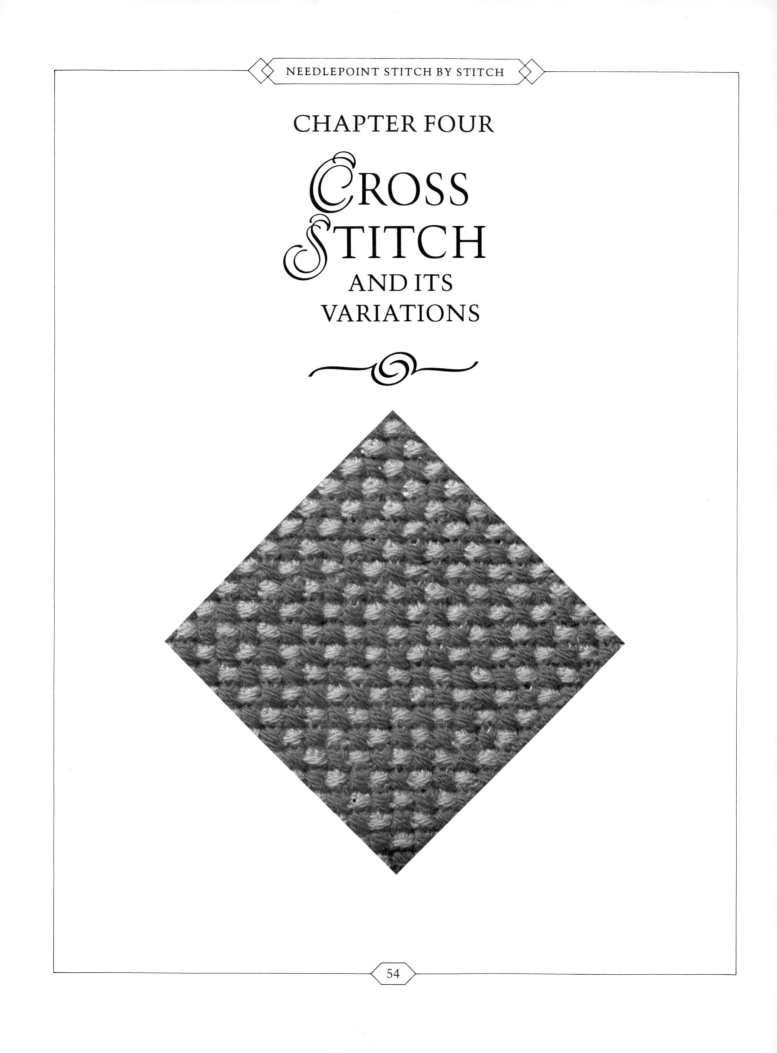

Simple Project

C ross stitch is probably the oldest decorative stitch and has been used by needlewomen all over the world for many centuries.

Basic or Diagonal cross stitch is two bisecting diagonals which form a square but there are many variations. The stitches can be either upright or oblique as shown in this chapter. All Cross stitches are counted-thread stitches which makes them ideal for canvas work.

All the variations of Cross stitch are very regular in shape and therefore, they are very suitable for geometric designs. This pillow front uses the Basic cross stitch for outlining each pattern area and a further seven variations within the pattern areas.

As Cross stitch is hardwearing this design can be adapted also as a church kneeler or door stop. Methods of making these two items is explained on page 58.

◇

MATERIALS

14-mesh evenweave canvas
Cut size: 46 cm (18 in) square
Finished size: 29 × 28 cm (11⅜ × 11⅛ in)
Paterna Persian wool
  Pearl Gray:
    12 threads 211
    30 threads 212
  American Beauty Pink:
    30 threads 901
    20 threads 903
    32 threads 904
    24 threads 905
  There are approximately 45 threads in a 25-g (1-oz) hank. If wool is only available in half or full hanks then purchase 15 g (½ oz) of 211 and 25 g (1 oz) of the rest.
2 Tapestry needles size 20

◇

MARKING THE CANVAS

Mark the design shown in Figure 31 on to the canvas. Each square on the chart represents 2 canvas threads. It is easiest to start in the middle of the chart, matching it to the approximate center of the canvas.

◇

WORKING THE PILLOW

The numbers on the chart and in the Stitch Summary refer to the stitches to be used in each area. Work in the order suggested.

◇

1 BASIC CROSS STITCH

(See Stitch Glossary page 147)

Work all the narrow channels marked over 2 threads of canvas with Basic cross stitch. Start at the top left-hand corner of the

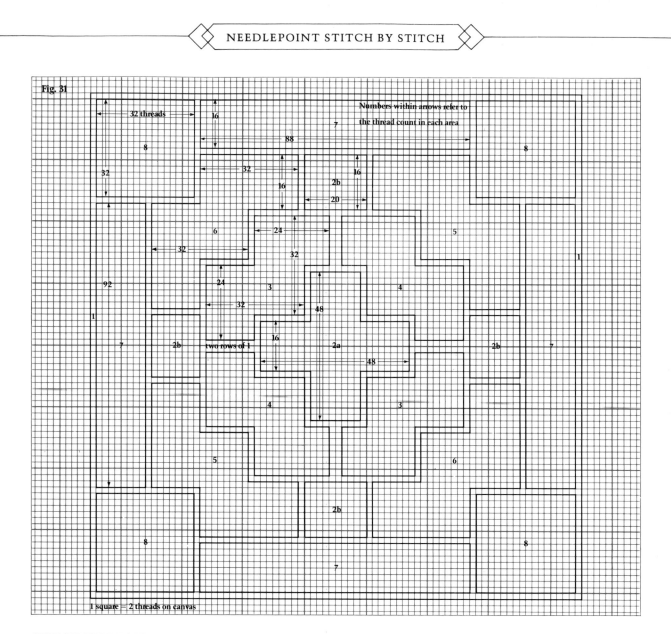

Fig. 31

Numbers within arrows refer to
the thread count in each area

1 square = 2 threads on canvas

STITCH SUMMARY

Number	Stitch	Colour	Number of plies
1	Cross stitch	American Beauty Pink (ABP) 901	2
2a	Rhodes (over 8 threads)	ABP 904 and Pearl Grey 212	2 of each colour
2b	Small-scale Rhodes (over 4 threads)	Pearl Grey 211	2
3	Crossed corners stitch (chequerboard)	ABP 905 and 903	2 of each colour
4	Smyrna stitch (chequerboard)	ABP 905 and 903	2 of each colour
5	Large and straight cross stitch	*Large crosses:* Pearl Grey 212. *Straight crosses:* ABP 905	2 of each colour
6	Vertical cross stitch	*Vertical crosses:* Pearl Grey 212. *Tie-stitches and small vertical stitches:* ABP 905	2 of 212 and 905 for Vertical crosses and 1 of 905 for small vertical stitch
7	Long-legged cross stitch	ABP 904	2
8 (see Figure 32 for more detail)	Leviathan	*Large crosses:* ABP 903. *Small crosses:* ABP 901	2 of each colour
	Rhodes	ABP 901	2
	Crossed corners stitch (tipped with contrast)	ABP 905 and Pearl Grey 212	2 of each colour

design, matching the spot in the diagram to the upper left-hand corner; this will ensure the stitches fit exactly.

Remember to work all the crosses with the same angled stitch on the top to give a neat appearance. You may find it easier to work the first stage of this stitch everywhere where necessary and only then complete the crosses with the second stitch as it is easier to check the angle of a single stitch. If all the first stitches, both across and down the canvas, are at the same angle, then the top stitch must also match everywhere!

◇

2a   RHODES STITCH

(See Stitch Glossary page 163)
Work the central cross-shaped area with Rhodes stitch, starting in the lower right-hand corner. Work the stitches in alternate colors. Be sure to work all the stitches in the same order so that the angle of the last stitch is always the same.

◇

2b   SMALL-SCALE RHODES STITCH

(See Stitch Glossary page 163)
Work Small-scale Rhodes stitch over 4 threads of canvas in the four areas. Start each area in the lower right-hand corner.

◇

3   CROSSED CORNERS STITCH

(See Stitch Glossary page 153)
Work Crossed corners stitch in the two areas diagonally across from each other. Work the stitches in alternate colors to give a checkerboard effect. Always work the base cross in the same order as the angle of these stitches shows. Start each area in

the lower left-hand corner.

It is possible to work a diagonal line of the Crossed corner stitches in one color before working a diagonal row of the contrasting color on either side; subsequently work alternate diagonal rows, using a different needle for each color. This is probably easier than working one color in horizontal rows and leaving gaps for the contrasting color to be stitched later.

◇

4   SMYRNA STITCH

(See Stitch Glossary page 166)
Work Smyrna stitch in the other two areas surrounding the central area. Work the stitches in alternate colors to give a checkerboard effect. Always work the horizontal stitch last.

Start in the upper left-hand corner and again work in diagonal rows as with the Crossed corners stitch.

◇

5   LARGE AND STRAIGHT CROSS STITCH

(See Stitch Glossary page 149)
Start in the upper left-hand corner and work the large Diagonal cross in horizontal rows back and forth across the area. Take care to work all the Diagonal crosses with the same angled stitch on top and work the whole area in this stitch before putting in the small Upright crosses. Only work these crosses in the full spaces between the Diagonal crosses. Do not work half crosses along the borders of the areas.

◇

6   VERTICAL CROSS STITCH

(See Stitch Glossary page 152)
The tall Vertical crosses are 4 threads high and 2 threads wide;

with this particular wool the small vertical stitch worked over 2 threads between each Vertical cross stitch was necessary for good coverage of the canvas.

The best order to work this stitch in is to start in the upper left-hand corner of each area; for the Vertical cross stitch, prepare two needles, one with 2-ply 212, and one with 2-ply 905; make the first Vertical cross in 2-ply 212, following the numbers in the diagram on page 152.

Then immediately work the tie-stitch in the contrasting color. The next Vertical cross starts down and across 2 threads to enable you to come up in an empty hole and go down in a busy one, i.e. one that already has wool in it; the tie is again worked immediately after the Vertical cross. The third stitch starts 2 threads up and across. Only when the area is completed are the small vertical stitches fitted in between the Vertical crosses.

◇

7   LONG-LEGGED CROSS STITCH

(See Stitch Glossary page 149)
Long-legged cross stitch is always only worked from left to right with a straight stitch behind the work; each line starts and finishes with a Basic cross stitch. In order to make the return trip from right to left a row of Continental tent stitch underneath gives a neat appearance.

In order for the rows to fit perfectly in these areas it is necessary to work both the first and last rows in Continental tent stitch. It will help to break the rule for once and turn the canvas a quarter turn when starting each new area so that the stitches run along the length of the area.

The first long-legged stitch

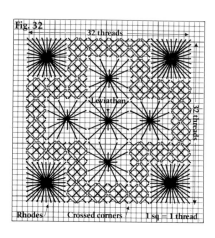

Fig. 32 — 32 threads — 32 threads — Leviathan — Rhodes — Crossed corners — 1 sq = 1 thread

should start at the spot in Figure a on page 149.

8 LEVIATHAN, RHODES AND CROSSED CORNER STITCHES

(See Stitch Glossary page 160 for Leviathan)
Each corner motif (see Figure 32) has two stitches that have been done before in this project, Rhodes in 2-ply 901 in all four corners, and Crossed corners but this time with the base cross in 2-ply 905 and the corner stitches in 2-ply 212. (This alternative way of stitching Crossed corners is shown on page 153 of the Stitch Glossary.)

The new stitch, Leviathan, is worked with 2-ply 903 for the first six stitches of the large diagonal cross and 2-ply 901 for the small upright cross.

Stitch the Rhodes in each corner first, remembering to always start and finish with the stitches on the same angle. Next, work the central Leviathan stitch over 8 threads; work four more Leviathan stitches, one on each side of the central one as shown in Figure 32. Finally, work the Crossed corners, using a separate needle for each color, so that each complete stitch can be worked in turn.

CHURCH KNEELERS

To work kneelers for a church can be an interesting alternative to making a pillow top. As a project it brings together all sorts of people; stitching can be done in small groups or individually with only occasional meetings in order to check on progress and to discuss problems. When the project is completed the church will look immeasurably more beautiful and cared for.

When working on the overall design for a group of kneelers, the most satisfactory plan is to have a small choice of appropriate designs for the top area. For example, various different shapes of religious cross can be worked in shades of old gold wool while all the background to the designs can be in a single contrasting color.

If the church has an interesting architectural detail, such as patterned tiles in the porch or an attractive plasterwork ceiling, motifs from these features could be incorporated into the designs for the kneelers.

You may also like to incorporate your initials and the date or possibly the initials of a person whom you wish to be remembered along one of the long sides. Alphabets to choose from are on pages 72, 73 and 74.

Any design incorporating Cross stitch is an excellent choice for a kneeler. Besides being so hardwearing, there are many different Cross-stitch designs that are easy to do but the end result is still good-looking. Everyone who participates can be proud of his or her finished piece. By using Cross stitch there will be minimal distortion of the canvas when it comes to making-up.

WORKING THE KNEELER

Figure 33 shows the pattern to use for any kneeler. Check the standard size of heavy density foam pads that are easily available to you (see page 130); these pads are far more satisfactory than using loose chips or Kapok as they will give better wear.

The central cross area and the next four areas immediately surrounding the cross are the same as the Simple Cross-stitch pillow on page 55, except that Small-scale Rhodes stitch (No. 2b in the pillow) would wear better than the large one and so would be more satisfactory for the central area. Work in groups of four stitches in one color.

Depending on the color scheme of the church, the outline Basic cross stitch would look good in the darkest shade; the Rhodes stitch in a bold, contrasting combination; and the Crossed corners and Smyrna stitches in two similar shades.

The design I have outlined for you will be approximately 16 cm (6¼ in) square if stitched on 14-mesh canvas. Measure and mark the canvas against your foam pad. Work a single row of Crossed corner stitch just inside the marked line on all four sides. This will outline the top of the kneeler and should be worked in the darkest shade.

Then fill in between this frame and the area already worked, using Large and straight cross stitch (No. 5 in the pillow). Use one mid-color for the whole stitch.

Work the four sides with Long-legged cross stitch and Continental tent stitch (No. 7 in the pillow), working along the length of each area as before. Use the darkest shade.

Fig. 33

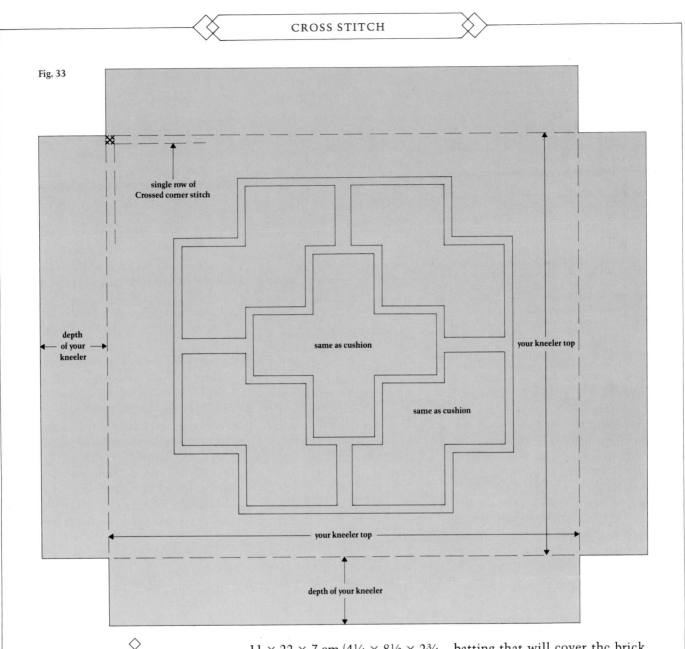

single row of
Crossed corner stitch

depth
of your
kneeler

same as cushion

your kneeler top

same as cushion

your kneeler top

depth of your kneeler

◇

DOOR STOPS

This is another attractive yet practical project that is not too large and for which Cross-stitch designs are particularly suited.

◇

WORKING A DOOR STOP

When planning to make a door stop, a brick is an appropriate size and weight but these vary in size. So measure yours carefully before finalizing the design.

Most bricks are approximately

11 × 22 × 7 cm (4¼ × 8½ × 2¾ in) so the thread count here is based on these measurements (see Figure 34).

Work a central area of 16 × 48 canvas threads with two rows of six large Rhodes stitches (No. 2a on the pillow). Work a border of Basic cross stitch around the central rectangle.

Now mark out 20 threads along both long sides and 32 threads along both short sides. Check carefully against your brick at this stage, and remember to allow for a thin wrapping of dacron

batting that will cover the brick under the finished canvas. It is imperative to get the top exactly the right size otherwise the sides will not fit.

As Crossed corners and Smyrna will be the stitches used it is simple to reduce or increase the dimensions of the top by 4 or even 8 threads. Both these stitches cover 4 threads of canvas, so calculate in units of four as you do not want part of a stitch. Remember that if 4 threads are too many a row of Basic cross stitch over 2 threads of canvas in

Fig. 34

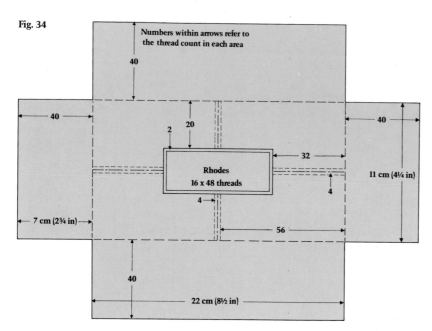

Numbers within arrows refer to the thread count in each area

40

40

40

2

20

Rhodes
16 x 48 threads

32

11 cm (4¼ in)

4

4

7 cm (2¾ in)

56

40

22 cm (8½ in)

could be worked as an outline to the top. Work Crossed corners and Smyrna stitches in diagonal corners as in the pillow.

When the top is complete, check again that your tension has not taken it up too much. Now work the sides with Long-legged cross and Continental tent stitch in horizontal rows (No. 7 in the pillow) to a depth of about 40 threads on each side. Do not work the corners.

◇

MAKING-UP THE KNEELER OR DOORSTOP

When either project is completely worked, the best way to make it up yourself is to wrap the brick or foam pad with thin dacron batting and stitch this in place with long, firm stitches, using a sharp needle and a cotton thread (see Figure 35). Block the canvas as instructed on page 124, damp and allow to dry naturally.

Fig. 35

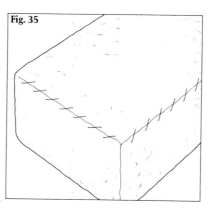

Trim the canvas in the four unworked corners to 8 threads of bare canvas and finger-press them in; use the Binding stitch (see Stitch Glossary page 143) in either matching or contrasting wool and stitch the two folded edges of the canvas together from the outside, making a decorative feature of the stitches.

Fasten the needlepoint cover in place over the chosen filling with long herringbone stitches, using strong buttonhole thread (see Figure 36).

Cut suitable fabric such as closely woven linen approximately 5 cm (2 in) bigger than the base on all sides, turn the edges under and pin in place. With a curved needle, stitch the base fabric to the needlepoint canvas on all sides (see Figure 37). Make sure that the canvas, and not just the needlepoint stitches, is caught with these stitches, otherwise the wool will just pull and the fabric will quickly start to come away. An alternative method of making-up is given in Finishing and Aftercare on page 130.

Fig. 36

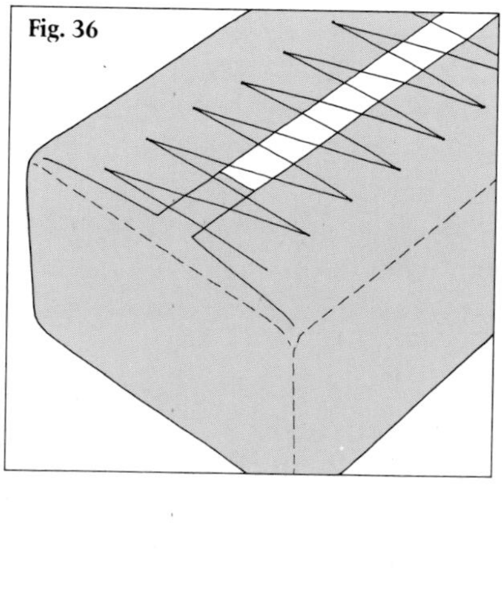

Fig. 37

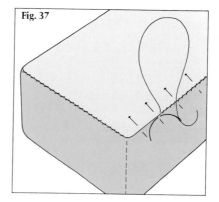

Advanced Project

P igs in Clover makes an amusing rug or wallhanging; on such large-mesh canvas it grows comparatively quickly and as each pig is worked in a different variation of Cross stitch it is fun to stitch.

Children will love the finished rug but it would look equally at home in a family room or country-style kitchen.

Paterna Persian wool has been used for this project – the same wool was used in the previous project, the Simple Cross-stitch pillow. On the coarser 7-mesh canvas more plies are used for each stitch but it illustrates how adaptable divisible wool such as Appleton's Crewel, Medici or Paterna Persian can be.

As so often with needlepoint designs, Basketweave tent stitch has been used in the wide border behind the pigs in order to offset their interesting stitches. The central area of the rug is worked in a fast-growing Cross-stitch variation called St George and St Andrew.

A template of an individual pig is given on page 63 to enable you to use it elsewhere, either by itself as a pillow, as one each on a series of chair cushions or in a single line as a valence for a window treatment. The pig could even be enlarged to a different scale to that suggested and used for many other projects.

◇ MATERIALS

1.60 × 1 m (5¼ ft × 40 in) 7-mesh mono rug canvas

Paterna Persian wool

American Beauty Pink:
  100 g (4 oz) 901
  200 g (8 oz) each 902 and 906
  175 g (7 oz) each 903, 904 and 905

Pearl Gray:
  50 g (2 oz) 211
  450 g (16 oz) 213

Hunter Green:
  50 g (2 oz) each 611 and 612

Daffodil:
  2 strands 762

Sunny Yellow:
  2 strands 772

Black:
  12 g (½ oz) 220

White:
  25 g (1 oz) 260

Additional wool for fringe
  200 g (8 oz) each Pearl Gray 211 and 213

1 packet Tapestry needles size 18

◇ MARKING THE CANVAS

Tape or machine stitch the edges of the canvas. Find the center of the canvas by folding and mark with a small cross, using a pencil. Following Figure 38 count out and mark a rectangle 100 threads across the width and 232 threads down the length.

Count out and mark a border on all sides 4 threads away. Count out and mark a further 78 threads on all sides. Finally, count out and mark 8 threads all round to make a border.

Straight lines on the canvas are best marked with a sharp pencil as the pencil point stays in the channel between the canvas threads.

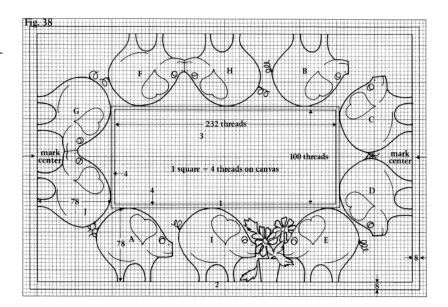

Fig. 38
232 threads
3
100 threads
1 square = 4 threads on canvas
mark center
4
78
mark center
8
2

STITCH SUMMARY

Number	Stitch	Colour	Number of plies
1	Broad cross stitch	American Beauty Pink (ABP) 902	4
2	Broad cross worked in groups of four	*Base stitches:* Pearl Grey 211. *Upper stitches:* ABP 901	4 of each colour
3	St George and St Andrew	*Diagonal crosses:* Pearl Grey 213. *Upright crosses:* ABP 906	5 of 213 and 4 of 906
4	Small-scale cross	Hunter Green 611 and 612	2 of each colour
Pig A	Webb variation	*Pig's body:* ABP 903 and 904. *Pig's ear:* ABP 905	4 of each colour
Pig B	Wicker cross stitch	*Pig's body, upright crosses:* ABP 904. *Wicker backstitches:* ABP 903. *Pig's ear:* ABP 905	4 of 904 and 3 of 903. 4 and 3 of 905
Pig C	Upright cross gone wrong	*Pig's body:* ABP 903 and 905. *Pig's ear:* ABP 903	3 of each colour
Pig D	Upright and diagonal cross *interlocked*	*Pig's body, upright crosses:* ABP 903. *Diagonal crosses:* ABP 905. *Pig's ear:* ABP 905	3 of each colour
Pig E	Tall cross stitch	*Pig's body:* ABP 903 and 904. *Pig's ear:* ABP 905	4 of each colour
Pig F	St George and St Andrew	*Pig's body, upright crosses:* ABP 903. *Diagonal crosses:* ABP 904. *Pig's ear:* ABP 905	4 of 903 and 5 of 904. 4 and 5 of 905
Pig G	Cross and Smyrna cross	*Pig's body, Smyrna crosses:* ABP 905. *Diagonal crosses:* ABP 903. *Pig's ear:* ABP 904	3 of 905 and 4 of 903. 3 and 4 of 904
Pig H	Reversed Smyrna	*Pig's body, upright and diagonal base crosses:* ABP 904. *Upper crosses:* ABP 905. *Pig's ear:* ABP 905	3 of 904 and 2 of 905. 3 of 904 for base crosses and 2 for upper crosses
Pig I	Staggered cross stitch	*Pig's body, large crosses:* ABP 905. *Small crosses:* ABP 904. *Pig's ear:* ABP 904	4 of 905 and 2 of 904 for pig's body. 4 and 2 of 904 for pig's ear
Pig J	Upright crossed corners	*Pig's body, upright crosses:* ABP 903. *Tipping the arms:* ABP 905. *Pig's ear:* ABP 905	4 of 903 and 3 of 905 for pig's body. 4 and 3 of 905 for pig's ear
	Pot of daisies	See stitch summary on page 65	
	Basketweave tent	Pearl Grey 213	3
	Chain stitch	ABP 903	3

Fig. 39

1 square = 65 mm

Take a large piece of paper the same size as the canvas (join two pieces together if necessary). Measure out and mark the same rectangles as marked on the canvas.

Make a tracing of the pig (see Figure 39) and enlarge it, either by using the grid method described on page 15 or by taking it to your local copy or photostat shop.

Cut out ten identical pigs in strong paper. Arrange the pigs between the two borders until you have got the positions you want. (By turning the tracing over you have a partner.)

Leave a space for the pot of daisies along one side. Along one end of the rug a pair of pigs have their tails entwined on the central line and along the other end, the pigs are snout to snout, again on the central line.

Trace off the pot of daisies (see Figure 39), and enlarge it the same amount as the pig. Arrange it on the paper layout.

When you are happy with the positioning, place the canvas on top of the paper, lining up the rectangles and making sure that the pigs' feet are resting on the inside edge of the outer border and that their backs are just touching the inside border.

Draw the design on to the canvas with a marker pen. Do not mark the clover; it is easier to count it out as a repeating pattern when stitching it.

◇

WORKING THE RUG

Mount the canvas on a large frame if you have one available or, as I did, a 45-cm (18-in) one that will have to be moved around, on the area being worked.

If you decide to use a smaller frame that has to be moved from pig to pig, remember that all the crosses must be stitched in the same direction. If you turn each pig to face you, the order of stitches will be the reverse on the sides to that at the ends. The same will have to be watched with the clover stitches. By working the central area and its border first you can then check on the angle of the top stitch when working each pig. By following the numbers below in order this will automatically happen.

◇

1   BROAD CROSS

(See Stitch Glossary page 147)
Work the inner border marked on the canvas over 4 threads. Work

all the stitches in the same order so that the top three stitches are always on the same angle.

◇

2   BROAD CROSS WORKED IN GROUPS OF FOUR

(See Stitch Glossary page 148)
Work the outer border marked on the canvas over 8 threads. Work these stitches in groups of four, only working the first three stitches in each group and angling them alternately so that they form a series of diamond shapes. When complete, work the upper stitches in the second color over each group on the other diagonal to the base stitches.

◇

3   ST GEORGE AND ST ANDREW CROSS

(See Stitch Glossary page 164)
Work the central area of the rug in this stitch. If working on a frame these stitches can be worked diagonally across the area; if you are not using a frame it will be more satisfactory to work in horizontal rows to avoid distortion.

◇

4   SMALL-SCALE CROSS STITCH

(See Stitch Glossary page 150)
Work the clover motifs in this stitch (see Figure 40). Start centrally down one of the long sides and follow the diagram. Count out the spaces between each leaf carefully. Look at the photograph carefully to see where the clover motif occurs. Remember to watch the angle of the second stitch of the cross if you turn the canvas 90 degrees to get at the working area more easily.

It is much easier to do the clover motifs now when this part of the canvas is blank and before stitching the pigs.

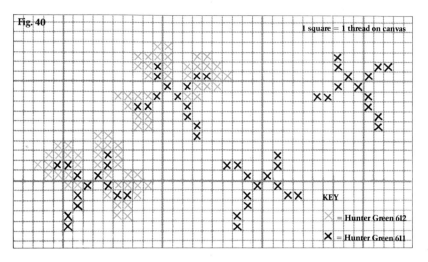

Fig. 40

1 square = 1 thread on canvas

KEY

= Hunter Green 612

X = Hunter Green 611

Now work the pigs. Each pig on the chart has a letter which refers to the stitch to work him in. In each instance the ear and the eye have been worked in exactly the same stitch. The shade to use for the ear has been given in each case and the eye is always white with one or two black stitches at the bottom of the area. The pigs can also be given 'toe-nails' with one or two stitches worked in black in the appropriate position.

It is important to maintain the pattern repeat from the body to these areas, so start stitching at the top of the pig's body and work the ear, eye and toe-nails when you reach these areas, not as a separate undertaking afterwards. Use two or three needles threaded with the different colors and correct number of plies.

◇

WEBB VARIATION (PIG A)

(See Stitch Glossary page 173)
Work the pig's two colors in alternate horizontal rows. Start at the top of the pig's back, and work down the area, working the first row from left to right. (It is impossible to work this stitch up an area.) When the ear is reached simply work that part of the row with a needle threaded with 905.

This can be worked backwards and forwards along the rows as it is only one color. The arrows in the diagram on page 173 show the direction of the stitches. As the two colors are being used for alternate horizontal rows in the pig's body it will be necessary to finish off each row and start again.

◇

WICKER CROSS STITCH (PIG B)

(See Stitch Glossary page 173)
Work both the pig's body and ear with the Upright crosses before starting the wicker backstitches following the arrows in the diagram on page 173.

◇

UPRIGHT CROSS GONE WRONG (PIG C)

(See Stitch Glossary page 151)
Work the two colors for the pig's body in alternate horizontal rows starting at the top. Work the ear as you reach the area in 903 only.

◇

UPRIGHT AND DIAGONAL CROSS INTERLOCKED (PIG D)

(See Stitch Glossary page 152)
Start with a horizontal row of

Upright crosses at the top of the pig's body. Work the rows of crosses alternately down the pig's back. While two needles will help with all the stitches, this pattern really does need to be worked row by row – it is extremely difficult to fit the Upright stitches into a completed area of Basic crosses or vice versa.

Again, work the ear when you reach the area, not afterwards.

◇

TALL CROSS STITCH (PIG E)

(See Stitch Glossary page 151)
Work the two colors for the pig's body in alternate horizontal rows, starting at the top of the body. The tie-stitch is worked in the same color as the Upright stitch. Work the pig's ear as you reach the area in 905, not afterwards.

◇

ST GEORGE AND ST ANDREW CROSS (PIG F)

(See Stitch Glossary page 164)
Start at the top of the pig's body, using two needles to stitch horizontal rows of Basic and Upright crosses alternately. On subsequent rows an Upright cross fits under a Basic one and vice versa.

Even though the ear is worked in a solid color you will need two needles, one threaded with 4-ply 905 and one threaded with 5-ply for stitching the two types of Cross stitch.

◇

CROSS AND SMYRNA CROSS (PIG G)

(See Stitch Glossary page 148)
Start at the top of the pig's body, alternating a Smyrna cross stitch and Basic or Diagonal cross stitch. On subsequent rows the Basic cross stitch fits under the Smyrna and vice versa.

REVERSED SMYRNA (PIG H)

(See Stitch Glossary page 167)
Start at the top of the pig's body. Work Upright and Basic crosses over 2 threads alternately across one row. Next work a Basic cross over the Upright and an Upright cross over the Basic cross in the contrasting color.

The second row has an Upright cross below a Basic one and a Basic one below an Upright.

STAGGERED CROSS STITCH (PIG I)

(See Stitch Glossary page 150)
Start off high up on the left-hand side that allows a good long run at the pattern. Use three needles, one with 4-ply 905, one with 2-ply 904 for both the pig's body and ear and one with 4-ply 904 for the ear. This will continue the pattern smoothly across the ear.

UPRIGHT CROSSED CORNERS (PIG J)

(See Stitch Glossary page 153)
Using two needles, start at the top of the pig's body, with a horizontal row of crosses. Tip the arms before starting the second row.

THE POT OF DAISIES

The pot of daisies (see Figure 39) uses stitches already known to you. Follow the Stitch Summary below for full details of these stitches. Start with the flower pot and stitch a row of Continental tent in between each row of Long-legged crosses. Work the stamens in two shades of yellow. Then work the daisy petals.

Work a vein of Hunter Green 611 down the center of each leaf before filling in the area with Hunter Green 612.

BASKETWEAVE TENT STITCH

(See Stitch Glossary page 168)
This is used for the background behind the pigs. Decide which way you would prefer to work the piece (ours was worked landscape). Start in the upper right-hand corner and do not turn the canvas. Use the weave of the canvas thread (as explained on page 20) to ascertain the up and the down rows and do not be tempted to jump around – it will show when the piece is finished!

CHAIN STITCH

(See Stitch Glossary page 145)
Work a short curved line of Chain stitch as a tail on each pig.

MAKING UP A RUG

When you have put so much effort into the stitching of a large piece it is even more worthwhile having it made up professionally. However, there are special tips to bear in mind if you want to do this job yourself.

Block the piece as you would do any smaller project but use a large piece of masonite or insulation board as a base. Square the corners and straighten the sides with a large T-square. Sometimes this process has to be repeated before leaving the rug to dry.

Industrial felt is best for interlining; cut it 2 cm (¾ in) smaller on all edges than the finished measurement of the rug.

Lay the interlining over the back of the rug (still on the blocking board) and pin in place every 10 cm (4 in). Use a curved needle and invisible thread to baste the interlining with running stitches – try to catch only the back of the rug with the stitches. Work from end to end and then from side to side to form a cross hatching to hold the interlining firmly in place.

Miter the corners of the canvas. Turn the unworked edges of the canvas over the edge of the interlining and secure with herringbone stitches, using ordinary carpet thread. Steam the edges flat.

Irish linen Holland is best for lining. Cut it 3 cm (1¼ in) larger than the rug on all sides. Lay the lining over the underside of the rug, right side up, fold the edges under and pin in place. Using a curved needle and invisible thread, blind stitch the lining to the edge of the rug. Be sure that you pick up the needlepoint canvas threads and not just the wool when you make the stitches.

Needlepoint rugs are usually laid over a non-slip padding if they are to be laid on a fitted wall-to-wall carpet.

For making this piece into a wallhanging see Finishing and Aftercare on page 131.

STITCH SUMMARY for Pot of Daisies

Number	Stitch	Colour	Number of plies
1 (Flower pot)	Long-legged cross stitch	American Beauty Pink 902	4
2 (Stamens)	Smyrna over 2 threads	*Base diagonal crosses:* Daffodil 762. *Upright crosses:* Sunny Yellow 772	2 of each colour
3 (Daisy petals)	Upright cross gone wrong	White 260	3
4 (Leaves and stalk)	Small-scale cross stitch	*Leaves:* Hunter Green 611 and 612. *Stalk:* Hunter Green 611	2 of each colour

Inspirational Projects

C ross stitch was a favorite stitch used for sampler work from earliest recorded pieces and so I have chosen two very different samplers, both from the Victoria and Albert Museum, London, to inspire you to make not only your own commemorative samplers but also to be able to adapt some of the traditional designs for present-day pieces.

Samplers fall into two distinct categories, those that were purely a convenient form of stitch and pattern record and those that were for display; we have one of each type here and although only separated by approximately fifty years, they are very different in style.

The earliest samplers were records for marking household linen, darning patterns and patterns for adorning clothing; in the seventeenth and eighteenth centuries young ladies worked decorative samplers in school. The Danish one dated 1795 (see facing page) is a beautiful mellow-colored example following a very typical format; a large house, which might have been the girl's school or a local landmark, alphabets and numerals, Adam and Eve and other religious items and a large bowl of fruit.

The English Victorian one below (from the middle nineteenth century) was worked for reference and would have been rolled up, not framed and put on display. It was most probably worked by a married lady and has motifs copied from friends as well as patterns that appeared in the magazines of the period.

The Victorian sampler has coarser canvas than the Danish one but the most dramatic difference is the colors – much gaudier with a great deal of black used in the designs and for backgrounds. Analine dyes were first introduced in 1856, about the time of this sampler and, therefore, these bright colors became available. They became popular with the nouveau riche who had the time to embroider.

Even though the ground fabric of both these pieces is far finer than a needlepointer of today would be used to working, samplers are a wonderful source of design material; their interesting alphabets can be used both to identify your own pieces and also to personalize a gift and their motifs will give you ideas.

Both the samplers shown on the previous pages are so full of wonderful motifs that I had a problem choosing which ones to chart for your use; the closer I looked at each area, the more interesting detail I found. I longed to settle down with some canvas immediately as I could see so many things that sparked off my imagination.

In the Danish sampler I particularly liked the right-hand alphabet worked in Cross stitch; I have graphed this together with the left-hand numbers on pages 72–74. It could equally well be scaled smaller simply by working in Tent Stitch or scaled larger by working in a stitch such as Crossed corners.

I decided to chart the garland of flowers that is repeated halfway down both sides (see Figure 41) as it could be so attractive mounted on a small pill-box or within the lace circle as on page 49. On the

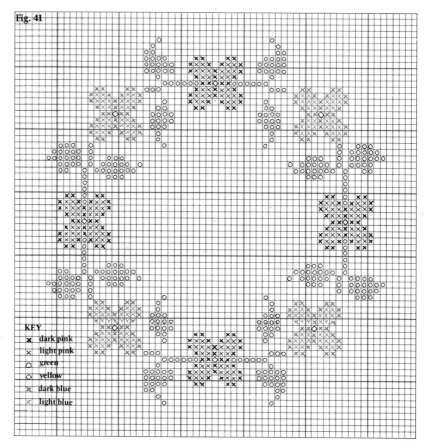

Fig. 41

KEY
x dark pink
x light pink
○ green
◇ yellow
x dark blue
x light blue

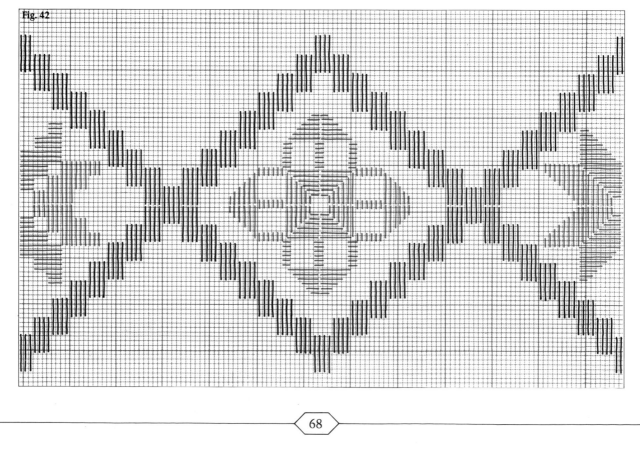

Fig. 42

original it is worked in Tent stitch but it would be equally satisfactory worked in Cross stitch – simply copy each stitch symbol with a Cross rather than a Tent stitch. One of the letters from the Alphabet on page 72 could be worked in the center. Each flowerhead is stitched in two shades of a color – the outline in the deeper shade and the filling in in a mid-shade.

The star border, which is worked across the top in varying sizes of stitch (see Figure 42), would make a dramatic border to a rug or an all-over trellis and star design for a stool, chair or pillow. Note the varying patterns between the stars. When charting it I realized that if there had been a group of five stitches (instead of four) at the top and bottom points of the diamonds it would mean that the stars could be absolutely central instead of one thread off; I have charted it exactly as the original

and you can decide whether to have five or four stitches.

Finally, from the bottom of the Danish sampler, I have charted the fruit basket (see Figure 44). Worked in Cross stitch on 14-mesh canvas, it would make a lovely pillow front.

Even the narrow Satin and Cross stitch border immediately below the star border would be useful for a belt, a shoulder strap to a purse or for something that needs an unfussy pattern.

Moving on to the Victorian piece on page 67 I quickly realized that selection was going to be even more difficult. The crude colors that the Victorian needleworker loved so much make pieces like this a little vulgar to our eyes, but there are literally masses of pretty designs that, worked in colors of your choice, would make beautiful projects.

The pink and white flowers towards the right in the lowest

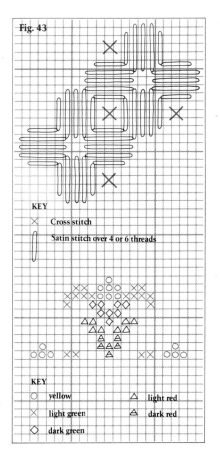

Fig. 43

KEY

× Cross stitch

▯ Satin stitch over 4 or 6 threads

KEY

○ yellow   △ light red

× light green   ▲ dark red

◇ dark green

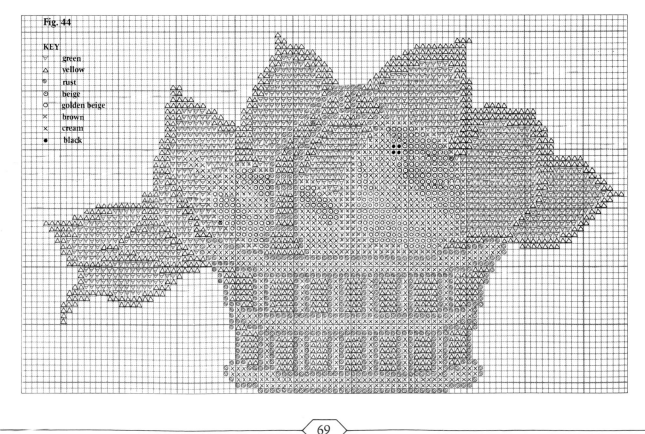

Fig. 44

KEY

▽ green
△ yellow
◉ rust
⊙ beige
○ golden beige
× brown
× cream
• black

panel (see Figure 43 above) are a potential design for almost anything, large or small. I have seen the flowerheads worked before but the dark burgundy cross between them makes the design really special. Use Florentine or Satin stitch over 4 or 6 threads with Cross stitch in between.

Another design I particularly like in this sampler is the yellow, green and red stylized flower motif worked on a black background right next to the pink flowers (see Figure 43 below). It instantly said evening slippers, worked in similar colors if your man is adventurous or in blues if he is more conservative. Any small item such as an eyeglass case or checkbook cover would also be successful.

Sadly, there is not space to chart more motifs; but look at the three lacy patterns worked with black wool, particularly the scalloped border on the red and white diagonal pattern in the top panel and the all-black one on the right of the third panel. Would it not be attractive to work a similar idea with the ecru pearl cotton and brown canvas used for the small scissor case shown on page 109?

◇

EARLY SAMPLERS

Samplers tend to follow certain design formats, based largely on the period when they were worked, the purpose for which they were stitched and the age of the stitcher. So, before we look at ways of designing samplers yourself for special occasions, it will be helpful to look briefly at the story of the sampler and of the people who stitched them.

Throughout the centuries, Cross stitch has been the most universally popular single stitch for English, Dutch, Danish and later, American samplers.

The earliest known English signed and dated sampler was worked in 1598 by Jane Bostocke (it is now on display in the Victoria and Albert Museum, London). It includes a typically wide range of stitches including Two-sided Italian cross stitch. The Bostocke sampler is unusual for its period in both its dimensions, 43 × 38 cm (17 × 15 in) and the fact that it was stitched by Jane Bostocke to commemorate the birth of her sister, Alice Lee. Other samplers surviving from the beginning of the seventeenth century are all long and narrow and intended only as a reference for future projects – the idea of a celebration sampler is unknown elsewhere at that time.

Other contemporary samplers are long and narrow as that was the normal width of the fabric available. The simple, one-color designs consisted of horizontal rows of different alphabets, sometimes with small self-colored borders in between each band; frequently, there is no border around the piece; the letters and motifs are always closely packed so as to waste no space.

These pieces were stitched by young girls as a record of different alphabet or monogram styles, to be used when marking their linen when they were grown-up and running their own home; as lady of a house they were expected to supervise the servants with the household sewing or, if they themselves went into service, they had their own reference sampler from which to work. These pieces were never designed to be decorative or to be put on display.

Samplers with a series of techniques, such as cutwork or white and black work were considered more advanced and would have been worked as a secondary project – but these were also only used for reference.

Towards the end of the seventeenth century samplers became part of the school curriculum for young ladies. It would appear from the way schools advertised their curriculum that needlework was considered the most essential part of a girl's education, certainly more necessary than reading and writing.

Around the end of the seventeenth century linen became available in wider widths and so the samplers became less exaggeratedly long and thin. Alphabets were still popular but frequently there was a pious verse and various flower or fanciful animal motifs copied from the newly available herbals and bestiaries. As they were taught in class to a group of girls the designs became more stereotyped and one frequently sees the same border or motif – obviously copied from one of the many pattern books of the period. The range of stitches used was very much reduced although Cross or Two-sided Italian stitch appear regularly.

Later on, map samplers were popular with the teachers, if not with the young girls – it enabled them to 'learn' geography at the same time as stitch!

In the nineteenth century the quality of almost all needlework was extremely low. However, the idea of a sampler for reference purposes only re-emerged and it is still possible to find long strips of canvas, frequently 60 or 90 cm (2 or 3 ft) long and only 10 cm (4 in) wide. These are bound on all edges with satin ribbon, and running down the length, are interesting Cross-stitch designs, sometimes repeating patterns, sometimes individual motifs and usually separated by narrow borders. The one I have chosen from the Victoria and Albert Museum on page 67 is a particularly fine example. I find these samplers extremely interesting and, worked in contemporary color combinations, they are among my favorite designs.

In the twentieth century needleworkers have again discovered the pleasure of both collecting samplers (escalating wildly in price now) and stitching them. In recent years there have been a number of samplers designed and marketed to record events such as royal weddings and Queen Elizabeth II's Silver Jubilee in 1977. I have one that was obviously started in mid-1936 in preparation for the Coronation of Edward VIII which, in the December when he abdicated to wed Mrs Simpson, had to have the royal monogram in the center changed to 'G & E', for King George and Queen Elizabeth. Samplers of this period again rely on simple Cross or Tent stitch.

◇

WORKING YOUR OWN SAMPLER

Although early samplers were worked on fine linen and are not strictly within the realms of needlepoint and this book, the counted-thread stitches lend themselves so well to being worked by needlepointers on their favorite ground fabric, canvas, that such a small deviation can surely be forgiven.

If you become interested in samplers and want to try working on evenweave linen (which is widely available in 26 and 29

threads to the inch) all the principles of working are the same as on canvas. I have recently written a book *Samplers for Presents* and so I had the opportunity of trying canvas, congress cloth, evenweave linen and even the recently reintroduced perforated paper much loved by the Victorians. I found them all to have certain advantages and each had its place. General techniques varied hardly at all.

I am so enthusiastic about stitching samplers today because first, they make a personal present; second, they do not take long to stitch as much of the area can be left unstitched; and third, they do not cost a great deal – a wonderful present made with love but little expense.

To achieve an attractive result there are just a few things to remember when planning and working a sampler that differ from other needlepoint projects – all the other materials, tools, techniques and tips remain the same.

◇

DESIGNING A SAMPLER

This need not be too daunting a task; for example, the flower garland shown on page 68 could be worked to a fairly large scale with one of the initials from pages 72 and 73 in the center and then you have your own original.

There are three main formats to samplers; first, early ones were pure records of lettering to be used later for marking linen; they were never intended to be decorative and so, when choosing an overall plan for a contemporary sampler, these samplers do not concern us.

The second type of sampler has bands of designs, usually three, as, broadly speaking, the one

shown on page 67 has. The third format has one large central motif such as a monogram, a family tree or a house.

It is the last two ideas that you should be guided by when planning a design; study as many as you can either in books (see the suggestions on page 174 for particularly good ones) or in a museum.

Notice that if there are bands of design the heavier or denser motifs look best low down (in the Danish sampler on page 66 the fruit bowl is treated more dramatically than the house at the top). The other trick is to balance motifs – either repeat (the flower garland), reverse (the angels) or choose two motifs of approximately the same scale (the Crucifixion and Adam and Eve are much the same height).

With a single, large motif, remember that simple things translate on to canvas best, whether you work them in Cross, Tent or any other stitch. The straight-on view of a house in a 'Moving House' gift would look better – and be infinitely easier to graph and work – than an angled perspective with roofs, windows and other features of the house running off at odd angles.

◇

CANVAS

As with any project, the amount of detail required balanced against the approximate final size required will guide you to the right canvas mesh to use. If you want a simple name set in a stylized flower garland such as the one on page 68 a 16-mesh canvas would be suitable. If you are uncertain about which mesh to use, refer to page 10 in Materials and Techniques. If, on the other hand, you plan a sampler

Fig. 45

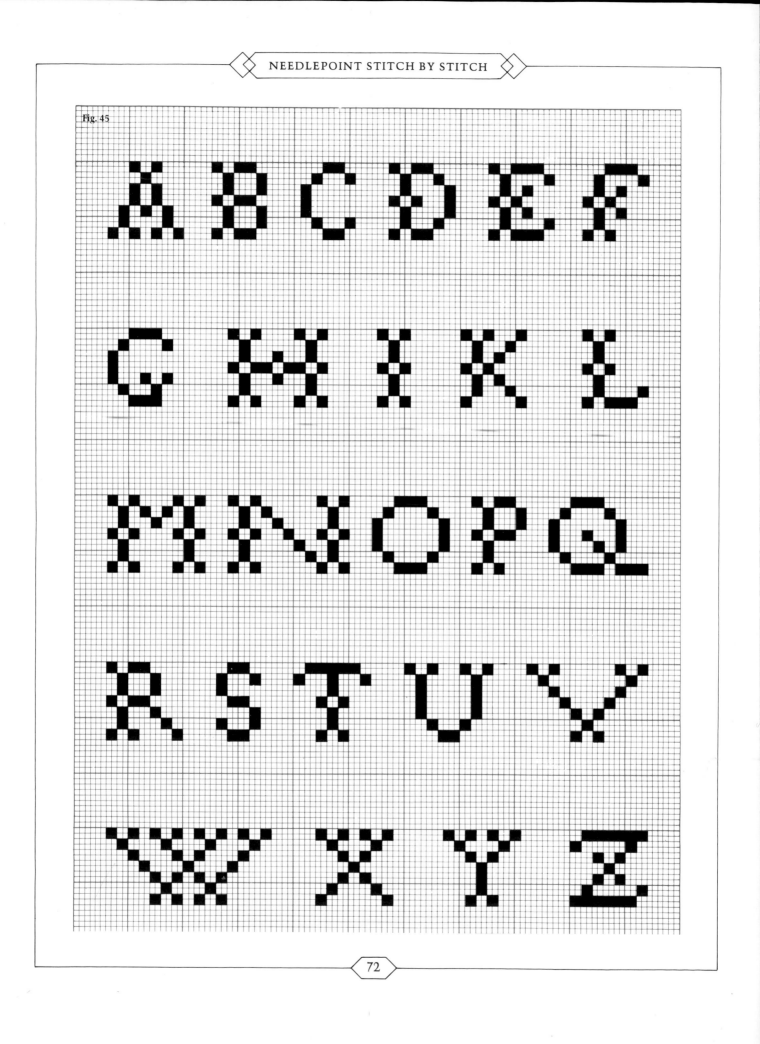

Fig. 46

Fig. 47

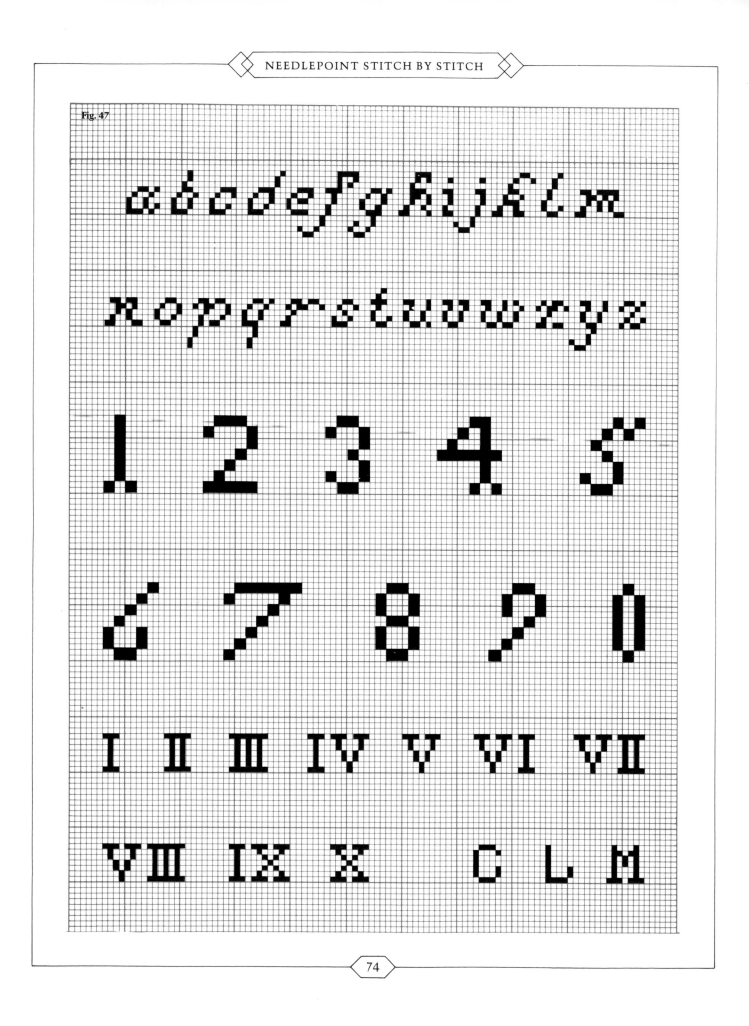

with a similar number of motifs as the one shown on page 66 the canvas or linen would have to be extremely fine or else the final size would be enormous.

Choose a natural-colored canvas as dead white can look very harsh, and brown or the bright yellow often available is not generally very attractive when used for samplers. The only acceptable alternative I propose is 24-mesh congress cloth which comes in lovely pastel shades, in Christmas Red and Green as well as in white; if the color can be used to good effect and enhances the theme of the design, for example, soft blue for a boy's birth sampler, red for a Valentine, green or red for a Christmas gift, so much the better.

◇

PREPARATION OF GROUND FABRIC

As with all needlepoint projects, first tape and mount the canvas or linen. However, as parts of the canvas will be left unstitched, use only running stitches in a contrast thread to mark the center of the fabric; mark guidelines for important motifs to help you position things accurately. Do not make any pencil or pen marks on the canvas.

◇

SPECIAL WORKING TECHNIQUES

When there is no previous stitching in the area to use for anchoring, use a long 'away' knot (see page 16). When the motif is complete, snip the knot, pick up the thread in a sharp needle, and anchor it firmly in the back of the stitches.

Do not trail any thread from one area to another as it will show through to the canvas front.

When some stitching is already worked, use the back of these stitches to anchor new threads; use existing stitchery to get from area to area; in the case of an isolated motif, start and finish all threads within that motif.

To end a thread, weave in and out of the back of previous stitches, working a back stitch or two for extra security.

When following a chart, either one prepared by you or from a book, it is usually easier to start in the center, then work any borders running across the piece, then the outer border and finally position the individual motifs in each section. This method of working a 'skeleton' first avoids many major unpicks that can easily happen through miscounting.

◇

ALPHABETS AND NUMBERS

One of the greatest charms of working a sampler as a gift is to stitch the recipient's name or initials (and also the stitcher's name) on it with the date of the special occasion such as a wedding or birth.

Cross-stitch pattern books are a good source of reference for a great many styles of lettering as they can be copied in Tent stitch over 1 thread or in something larger, such as Crossed corners over 4 threads. You can also needlepoint handwriting, such as your own signature to personalize a present.

Use the alphabets and numbers on pages 72 to 74. The alphabet on page 72 and the Arabic numerals were taken from the Danish sampler on page 66. Plan out the letters you want on graph paper before stitching. If a name is very short you can plan extra threads between each letter. If you have two names, one extremely long and one short, again you can 'cheat' by adapting the thread count between letters.

Do not get caught, as I have been, by letters that 'hang down' below the line, for example, 'p' and 'q', bumping into the row below. This is quick and easy to see if you spend a short while planning on graph paper beforehand.

In addition to regular or Arabic numbers there are also Roman numerals. You may consider these to be more appropriate for some projects — not too many girls want the whole world to see at a glance when they were born, but knowing the date of a wedding does not seem to offend!

The general principle of Roman numerals is that a smaller letter before a larger one subtracts from its value and a small letter after a larger one adds to it, i.e. IV = 4 and VI = 6. The roman numerals for 1987 would, therefore, be MCMLXXXVII.

CHAPTER FIVE

STITCHERY

Simple Project

T his Simple Stitchery project is based on diamonds and diagonals, unlike the Simple Cross stitch project on page 55 which is based on square and rectangular shapes.

For the purpose of this book the Cross stitch and its variations, has been separated from other stitchery, remember that for future projects they can be used together very successfully. It is for this reason that I have chosen a diamond-based pattern here. The Cross stitches you have mastered earlier on will be useful for square areas and all the stitches in this chapter fit well in both diamond and diagonal areas.

I find needlepoint designs in many sources. The original design of this project comes from one of my favorite ones, Chinese lattice designs. This early twentieth-century one is from Yunnan. These lattice patterns were constructed in wood for window grilles; individual patterns are very regional as the skilled craftsmen who planned and supervised their construction had seldom traveled more than a few miles and had little or no access to other craftsmen's patterns. Each window grille was made individually on site and it was common, when the especially skilled man came to work, that he would bring his canary in a cage so that it could sing as the work progressed. My radio is my greatest companion when I work but a song-bird does sound rather more romantic.

◇
MATERIALS

14-mesh evenweave, mono canvas
Cut size: 45 cm (18 in) square
Frame: 45 cm (18 in) square
Paterna Persian wool
  Copper:
    40 g (1½ oz) 864
  Salmon:
    25 g (1 oz) 845
  Beige Brown:
    25 g (1 oz) 462
    25 g (1 oz) 463
  Cream:
    50 g (2 oz) 263
2 Tapestry needles size 20
1 Tapestry needle size 22

◇
MARKING THE CANVAS

Bind the edges of the canvas with masking tape or machine stitch them as explained on page 15.

Find the center of the canvas by folding (the exact thread does not matter) and make a small mark.

Mark also the central point on all four sides, right on the edge of the canvas (this will be very helpful later on). With the selvedge of the canvas to either the left or the right, mark the top of the canvas.

Figure 48 showing the design is slightly different to some of the other project charts. Diagonal lines are a little more difficult to mark on to canvas than horizontal and vertical ones. Therefore, the Straight Gobelin stitches are graphed full size in Figure 50 so that if you prefer to count and stitch these outlines you can. Otherwise, mark them with either a pencil or a contrasting basting thread which is removed just ahead of the work as it progresses.

If using a pencil, it is easier to mark the canvas before mounting it on the frame. Basting or actual stitching is better done after mounting the canvas on the frame. When mounting the canvas on to the frame pull it as taut as possible.

◇
WORKING THE PIECE

1 STRAIGHT GOBELIN STITCH OVER 2 THREADS

(See Stitch Glossary page 158)
Use the size 20 Tapestry needle. Work the inner and the outer diamond shapes, not the middle one, in Beige Brown 462. Start with the inner diamond and count up 24 threads from the center of the canvas. The bottom of the first Straight Gobelin stitch will be in this hole. Subsequent stitches jump down 1 thread each time as shown in Figure 50.

To find the starting-point of the outer diamond, count up 66 canvas threads from the top of the first stitch made in the central diamond and this will be the bottom of the top stitch of the outer diamond.

Work the middle diamond and other outlines in Beige Brown 463.

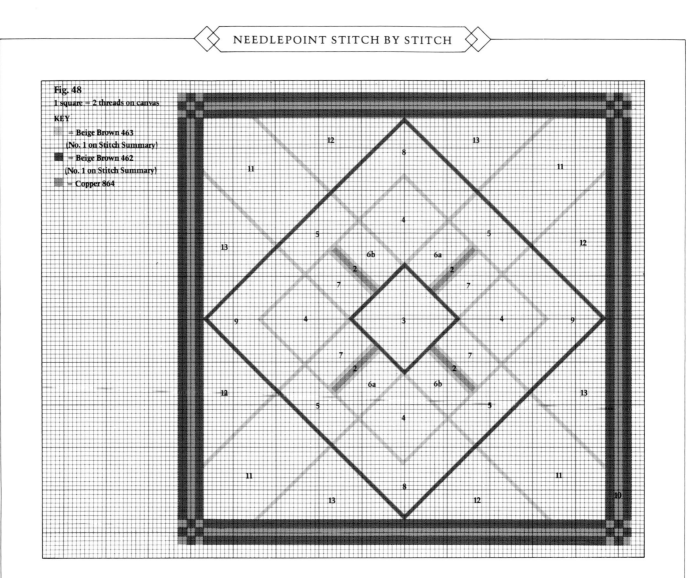

Fig. 48
1 square = 2 threads on canvas

KEY

▨ = Beige Brown 463
(No. 1 on Stitch Summary)

▨ = Beige Brown 462
(No. 1 on Stitch Summary)

▨ = Copper 864

STITCH SUMMARY

Number	Stitch	Colour	Number of plies
1	Straight Gobelin stitch over 2 threads	*Inner and outer diamonds:* Beige Brown 462. *Other outlines:* Beige Brown 463	3 of each colour
2	Straight Gobelin stitch over 4 threads	Copper 864	3
3	Star with 4 rings of colour	*Central star:* Copper 864. *Second star:* Cream 263. *Third star:* Salmon 845. *Outer star:* Copper 864	2 of each colour
4	Star with 3 rings of colour	*Central star:* Beige Brown 462. *Second star:* Cream 263. *Outer star:* Copper 864	2 of each colour
5	Star with 2 rings of colour	*Central star:* Copper 864. *Outer circle:* Beige Brown 463	2 of each colour
Background to 3, 4 and 5	Basketweave tent stitch	Cream 263	2

Number	Stitch	Colour	Number of plies
6	Mosaic with tent stitch	*Mosaic stitches:* Salmon 845. *Tent stitches:* Cream 263	2 of each colour
7	Mosaic variation	*Diagonal stitches:* Salmon 845. *Upright crosses:* Cream 263	2 of each colour
8	2, 4, 6, 4, 2 with backstitch	*Upright stitches:* Salmon 845. *Backstitches:* Copper 864	3 of 845 and 1 of 864
9	Eggs in a basket	*Baskets:* Copper 864. *Eggs:* Salmon 845	3 of each colour
10	Main border (Straight Gobelin over 4 threads and Cushion stitch)	Beige Brown 462 and Copper 864 for each stitch	4 of each colour
11	Byzantine variation with boxes	*Tent stitches:* Copper 864. *Byzantine steps:* Beige Brown 463. *Boxes:* Cream 263	2 of each colour
12	Brick stitch	Cream 263	3
13	Double brick stitch	Cream 263	3

2 STRAIGHT GOBELIN STITCH OVER 4 THREADS

(See Stitch Glossary page 158)
Fit these stitches between the two rows of Straight Gobelin already stitched between areas 6 and 7.

Now the lattice design is stitched on the canvas work the individual areas. These stars are versatile, quick to work and dramatic looking. The Vest on page 40 has a large star with an initial worked in the center.

When stitching the stars in the following numbers, 3, 4 and 5, note that it is easier to work a first circuit of horizontal and vertical stitches before a second circuit of diagonal ones. All the horizontal and vertical stitches are over 4 threads of canvas and all the diagonal ones over 3 threads. Leave the background to the stars until later.

3 STAR WITH 4 RINGS OF COLOR

Use the size 20 Tapestry needle. Start by working the central star of 8 stitches down in to the middle hole (see Figure 49). Next, work the second star of 24 stitches. The third one has 40 stitches and the final one 56 stitches.

4 STAR WITH 3 RINGS OF COLOR

Use the size 20 Tapestry needle. There are four of these areas. Start with the central star of 8 stitches worked in to the middle hole (see Figure 49). The second star has 24 stitches and the outer one 40 stitches.

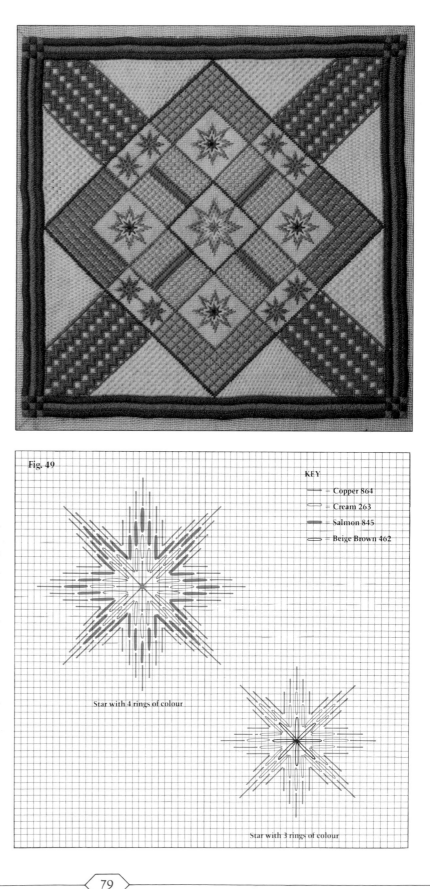

Fig. 49

KEY

— = Copper 864
— = Cream 263
— = Salmon 845
— = Beige Brown 462

Star with 4 rings of colour

Star with 3 rings of colour

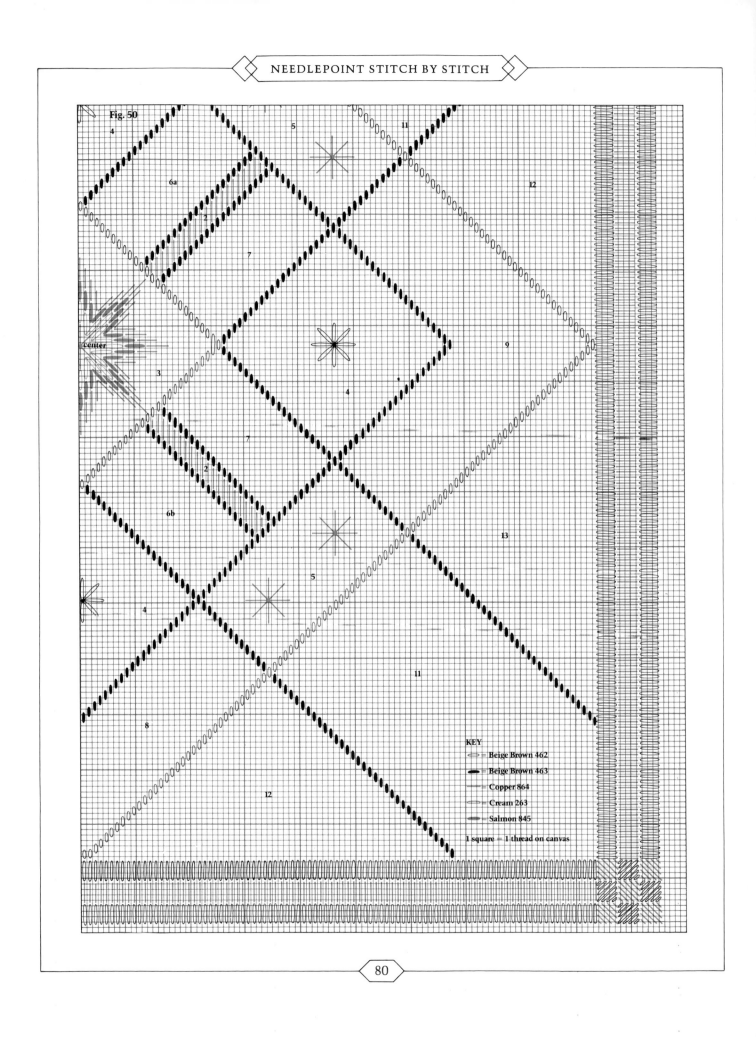

Fig. 50

4   5   11

6a

2

7

12

center

3   7   9

4

7

2

6b   13

5

4   11

8

12

KEY

◯ = Beige Brown 462

⬤ = Beige Brown 463

— = Copper 864

⬭ = Cream 263

⬛ = Salmon 845

1 square = 1 thread on canvas

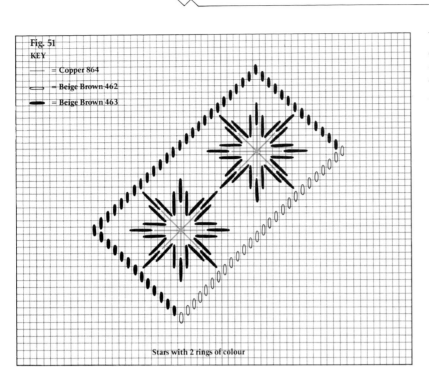

Fig. 51
KEY

— = Copper 864
⊏⊐ = Beige Brown 462
⬤ = Beige Brown 463

Stars with 2 rings of colour

5 STAR WITH 2 RINGS OF COLOR

Use the size 20 Tapestry needle. There are four of these areas. Two small stars are worked in each one (see Figure 51). The Straight Gobelin already stitched is shown outlining the area of the stars. The central point of each star is shown with a black dot in both Figure 50 and 51.

Start with the central star of 8 stitches and then work the outer star of 24 stitches.

BASKETWEAVE TENT STITCH

(See Stitch Glossary page 168)
Use the size 20 Tapestry needle. Work the background behind all the star areas (3, 4, and 5) in this stitch.

Look at 'Reading the grain of canvas' on page 20 beforehand to help work out whether the first diagonal line of stitches should be ascending or descending.

Work round the stars rather than trailing the wool behind each one. Do not be tempted to turn the frame on its side when working the different areas, otherwise the angle of the stitches may vary. Upsidedown does not change the visual angle of the stitch, but can give a nap-like effect.

6 MOSAIC WITH TENT STITCH

(See Stitch Glossary page 161)
Use both the size 20 Tapestry needles, one for each color. There are four of these areas.

Area 6a is below and to the left of the central star. Follow Figure a on page 161; all the stitches are worked from the lower left to the upper right. Work exactly the same stitch in the area diagonally opposite, above and to the right of the central star.

Area 6b is below and to the right of the central star. Follow Figure b on page 161; the Mosaic stitches slope on the other angle.

Work the same stitch in the area diagonally opposite, above and to the left of the central star. The Tent stitch is always stitched in the same direction.

7 MOSAIC VARIATION

(See Stitch Glossary page 161)
Use the size 20 Tapestry needle. There are four of these areas in the design, all worked exactly the same.

Work all the diagonal stitches over 2 threads of canvas first. In order for the pattern to fit exactly, start with one sharing with the bottom hole of the top Straight Gobelin stitch.

Fill in the area with the small Upright crosses with the horizontal stitch last.

8 2, 4, 6, 4, 2, WITH BACKSTITCH

(See Stitch Glossary page 172)
Use the size 20 Tapestry needle for the 2, 4, 6, 4, 2 stitch and the size 22 Tapestry needle for the Backstitch. Work the top area first.

Work the upright stitches over 2, 4, 6, 4, 2 threads. Position the first stitch over 6 threads sharing with the bottom of the top stitch of the outer diamond outline in 462 which you have already stitched. This will make the pattern fit exactly.

Work backwards and forwards in horizontal rows across the area until you reach the top point of the middle diamond in 463. Then work down the left-hand leg, still in horizontal rows. When complete finish off and stitch the right-hand leg.

When the whole area is complete work Backstitches between the diamond shapes. Remember the size 22 needle! Do not work a

Backstitch between the 2, 4, 6, 4, 2 stitches and the Straight Gobelin surrounding the two areas. Turn the canvas 180 degrees and repeat for the lower area 8.

◇

9   EGGS IN A BASKET

(See Stitch Glossary page 155)
Use a size 20 Tapestry needle for each color. Work a basket first and then the 'eggs' that fit in it.

Before starting the first area be sure that the canvas is the right way round and not on its side, otherwise the 'eggs' will not be in the basket! For the second area, you may prefer to turn the canvas completely upside-down.

The best place to start this stitch is with the top stitch of a basket (over 6 threads) sharing with the side point created by the Straight Gobelin outline in 463 already stitched.

◇

10   MAIN BORDER

(For Straight Gobelin see Stitch Glossary page 158 and for Cushion stitch see page 154)
This border has Straight Gobelin over 4 threads (already used in this Simple project) and Cushion stitch.

Follow Figure 52. Start in the top center sharing with the outer diamond already stitched. Work

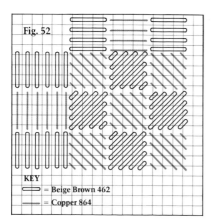

Fig. 52

KEY
⊏⊐ = Beige Brown 462
— = Copper 864

the Straight Gobelin over 4 threads towards a corner, working each color in turn so that there is always an empty or clean hole for you to come up in. When the corner is reached work the Cushion stitches, using both needles and completing each box in turn.

◇

11   BYZANTINE VARIATION WITH BOXES

(See Stitch Glossary page 145)
This is worked in the four corners of the design. Use both size 20 Tapestry needles.

Work the upper right-hand corner first (see the diagram on page 145), starting with the Continental tent stitch. The Straight Gobelin border already stitched is shown at the top right-hand corner of the diagram.

When working subsequent corners turn the canvas round so that it matches the stitch diagram. If this is done, each of the patterns will radiate out from the central star and will balance in the area. The Continental tent stitch will lie the same way as the boxes and on the opposite angle to the Byzantine steps.

◇

12   BRICK STITCH

(See Stitch Glossary page 143)
Use the size 20 Tapestry needle. This stitch is worked in four triangular areas. Two of these, the upper and lower ones, have vertical stitches and the two side ones have the same stitch but lying horizontally.

The simplest way to achieve this is to have the canvas the right way up when working the upper and lower areas. Turn the top to the side when working the side areas in order to make the stitches lie horizontally.

If you prefer to turn the stitch diagram on page 143 on its side rather than the canvas the result is the same but always start the first row along the long side of the triangle sharing with the Main Border already worked. This will allow you to establish the pattern most easily.

Work the stitches over 4 threads of canvas, leaving 2 threads between each stitch. The second row fits half-way down in to the spaces left.

Compensation stitches over 2 threads of canvas will be needed to get a straight edge sharing with the border. Work these after completing the second row. Vary stitch lengths along the diagonal edges to compensate for the design. The second and subsequent rows fit half-way in to the spaces left by the previous row.

◇

13   DOUBLE BRICK STITCH

(See Stitch Glossary page 144)
Use the size 20 Tapestry needle. Work this stitch in the last triangular areas. Again the upper and lower triangles are worked with vertical stitches and the two side ones with horizontal stitches. Turn the canvas as for Brick stitch above.

Work a pair of stitches side by side and then leave 3 threads of canvas before starting the next pair.

Start the first row along the long straight edge sharing with the Main Border so that the pattern can be established before any compensation stitches have to be worked.

The second and subsequent rows fit half-way in to the spaces left by the previous row.

Advanced Project

This Country Cottage explores the use of some exciting and unusual fibers and techniques on canvas. As well as how to copy this cottage exactly, this section shows you how to plan and work your own house in needlepoint for either a picture, wallhanging, doorstop or large paperweight or purely as a decorative object.

When it comes to the flowers and bushes round the cottage I make no apologies for the across-the-calendar selections; I love wisteria, hyacinths, and cherry blossom and when I found some small red beads that cried out to be pyracantha berries I had no choice other than to let a bush 'grow' in profusion.

However, if you prefer a more accurate seasonal range of plants it is perfectly possible, using the techniques and ideas explained fully here, for you to create a true spring, summer or fall garden.

◇ MATERIALS

18-mesh evenweave, mono canvas.
   Brown or ecru is preferable to white
   for this project.
Cut size: 50 cm (20 in) square.
Finished free-standing cottage is
   approximately 16 cm wide × 22 cm
   high × 11 cm deep
   (6¼ × 8½ × 4¼ in).
Frame: 50 cm (20 in) square.
Yarns for the cottage:
Rowan Aran
   1 skein 752 brown. This is the
   thick wool used for the roof thatch.
   You may well find it in a knitting
   shop but you can always substitute
   it with any thick, tweedy-looking
   yarn and either use singly as here or
   2 or more ply together.
Appleton's Crewel
   25 g (1 oz) Off-White 992
   15 g (½ oz) White 991
   25 g (1 oz) Black 993
   Flame Red:
      15 g (½ oz) 204
      15 g (½ oz) 206
   Biscuit Brown:
      15 g (½ oz) 763
Medici wool
   Dark browns:
      3 small skeins 500
DMC Floss
   4 skeins 318
   1 skein 939
Yarns for flowers and bushes: This is
a good opportunity to use up small
amounts of yarns left over from other
projects.
I used:
DMC Floss
   1 skein each DMC 352, 700, 727,
   754, 799, 3078, 3345 and 3347
DMC Pearl Cotton
   1 skein each 351, 799 and 826
Beads
   Small red beads for pyracantha and
   small quantities of any other
   'flower' shades you like
1 packet size 10 or 12 beading needles
1 packet size 22 Tapestry needles

◇ WORKING THE PIECE

I have made this Country Cottage a three-dimensional piece. (If you are making a picture or wall-hanging you need only stitch the prettiest side). When working the Cottage it is necessary to work the front, roof and back elevation all in one piece. It is also easier for matching the various details to work the two side elevations alongside the main house. Refer to the photograph above which was taken after the work was complete but before the canvas was cut up for making-up. (Please note that the chart of the Cottage has had to be divided between Figures 53 and 54 because of its size.)

Following Figures 53 and 54 and the photograph, mark the canvas. Leave approximately 7 cm (2½ in) between the main house and the side elevations and leave the same again between the top points of the side elevations. Mine was a little too close which made the making-up more difficult.

The flowers and bushes are worked on top of the stitchery; therefore, work the house first, leaving no gaps for foliage or flowers. The thatch is couched on to the roof area after the walls are complete and the thick wool hangs over the walls. Bind the edges of the canvas with masking tape or machine stitch them before mounting on the frame.

◇ 1 STRAIGHT GOBELIN OVER 3 THREADS

(See Stitch Glossary page 158)
This is used for the front door. Turn the canvas on its side and work seven rows over 3 threads of canvas. This will give a door with rough-looking vertical planks of dark timber.

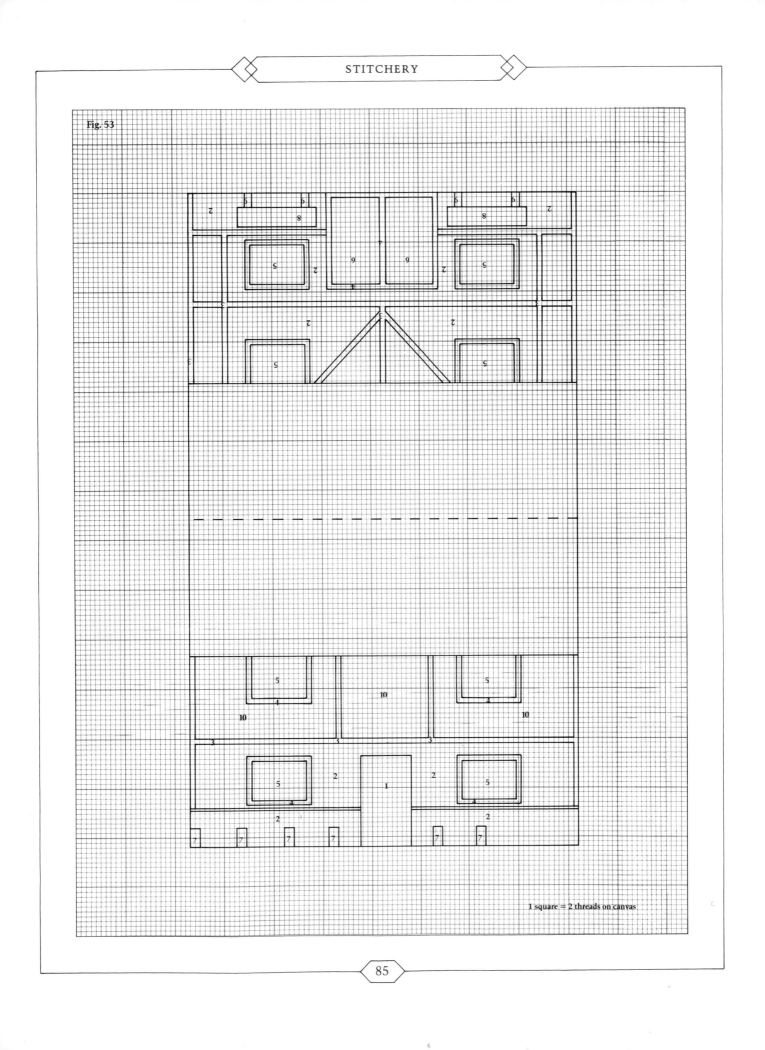

Fig. 53

1 square = 2 threads on canvas

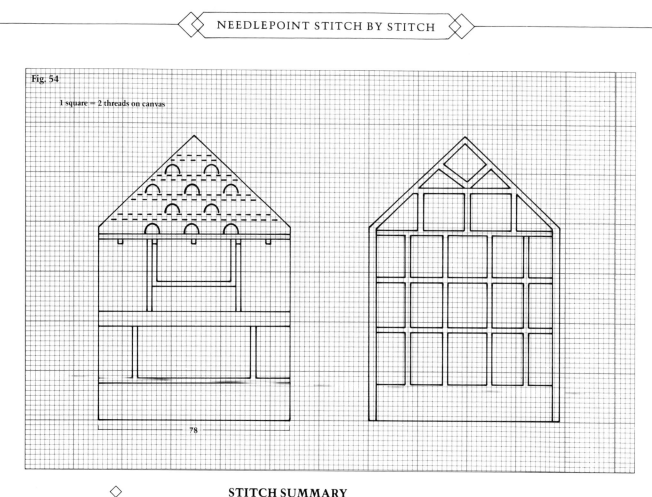

Fig. 54

1 square = 2 threads on canvas

78

STITCH SUMMARY

Number	Stitch	Colour	Number of plies
1 (Front door)	Straight Gobelin over 3 threads	Appleton's Crewel Black 993	3
2 (Plasterwork)	Parisian stitch	Appleton's Crewel Off White 992	3
3 (Beams)	Satin stitch	Medici Brown 500	3
4 (Window frames)	Straight Gobelin over 2 threads	Appleton's Crewel Black 993	3
5 (Window panes)	Hungarian with backstitching	*Hungarian:* DMC Stranded Cotton 318. *Backstitching:* DMC Stranded Cotton 939	6 for the Hungarian and 2 for the backstitching
6 (French windows)	Sloping Gobelin with Continental tent stitch	*Sloping Gobelin:* DMC Stranded Cotton 318 *Continental tent stitch:* Appleton's Crewel Black 993	6 for the Sloping Gobelin and 2 for the Continental tent stitch
7 (Garden posts)	Sloping Gobelin	Appleton's Crewel White 991	3
8 (Flower troughs)	Cushion stitch	Appleton's Crewel White 991	3
9 (Legs of the flower troughs)	Sloping Gobelin	Appleton's Crewel White 991	3
10 (Brickwork)	Sloping Gobelin with Continental tent stitch worked horizontally	*Sloping Gobelin:* Appleton's Crewel Flame Red 204 and 206. *Continental tent stitch:* Biscuit Brown 763	Mix 1 ply of 204 and 206 together to give 2 ply for the Sloping Gobelin. 2 of 763 for the Tent stitch
11	Basketweave tent stitch	Appleton's Crewel Black 993	2

◇

2   PARISIAN STITCH

(See Stitch Glossary page 162)
This is used for the plasterwork. Turn the canvas on its side to do this stitch. On the front of the house work the first floor level to just above the front door. On the back of the house work both the first and second floor. On both the front and back of the house leave the necessary threads for the beams, windows, the garden posts in the front and the flower troughs on the back. Do not work any compensation stitches at the edges as the beams, which are worked next, will dovetail in for a rustic look.

BEAMS: Work the horizontal and diagonal beams on the front and back of the cottage. These are worked in random Satin stitches. The vertical beams are worked in

Parisian and fit into the Off-White Parisian already worked.

◇

4 STRAIGHT GOBELIN OVER 2 THREADS

(See Stitch Glossary page 158)
This is used for the window frames. Work the frame to each window over 2 threads of canvas. Anchor the wool in itself carefully and do not trail behind the Off-White. Check the stitch diagram on page 158 carefully when turning the corners to get really neat-looking ones. Work the frame of the French windows and the central door jamb in the same stitch and wool.

◇

5 HUNGARIAN

(See Stitch Glossary page 160)
This is used for the panes of glass in the mullioned windows. Look at the photograph on page 84 and balance the stitches as much as possible.

When a window is complete, the Hungarian stitching can be backstitched over 1 thread with the black floss.

◇

6 SLOPING GOBELIN WITH CONTINENTAL TENT STITCH

(See Stitch Glossary page 159)
This stitch is used to fill in the French windows. With two needles work the window panes and glazing bars (to work the two at the same time is easier than trying to fit the Tent stitch in afterwards). Work each window pane and then surround it with Tent stitch. The Sloping Gobelin is worked over 1 and 2 threads, three of 3 threads, 2 and 1 thread of canvas to form vertical window panes 3 threads wide and 5 threads deep. The Continental

tent stitch is worked over 1 thread. There is a row of Tent stitch either side of the central door jamb.

◇

7 SLOPING GOBELIN

(See Stitch Glossary page 159)
This is used for the garden posts on the front of the house. It is similar to the stitch used for the French windows but here it is worked over 1, 2 and 3 threads, four stitches of 4 threads, 3, 2 and 1 thread to form a vertical post 4 threads wide by 8 threads deep.

◇

8 CUSHION STITCH

(See Stitch Glossary page 154)
This is used for the flower troughs on the back of the house. Each square consists of seven stitches worked over 1, 2, 3, 4, 3, 2, and 1 threads. Start in one corner and work two rows of

eight cushions as shown in the diagram on page 154.

◇

9 SLOPING GOBELIN

(See Stitch Glossary page 159)
This is used for the legs of the trough and is similar to the two variations of Sloping Gobelin already worked. This time it is worked over 1 and 2 threads, four stitches of 3, threads, 2 and 1 thread to give a vertical upstand 3 threads wide by 6 threads deep.

◇

10 SLOPING GOBELIN WITH CONTINENTAL TENT WORKED HORIZONTALLY

(See Stitch Glossary page 159)
This is used for the old brickwork and is worked on the second floor level on the front of the house. It is another scale of the versatile Sloping Gobelin worked horizon-

tally over 1 thread, three of 2 threads and 1 thread to look like bricks. Bricks, especially old ones, are seldom one uniform color so I mixed two colors together for this stitch (see Stitch Summary on page 86).

Now work the side elevations. Once the thatch is couched on the piece it becomes a little more difficult to work on. Similarly, it is fun to 'plant' the garden all at the same time at the end.

◇

SIDE ELEVATION WITH DOVE COTE

The plasterwork up to the 6-thread pantile roof is worked in Parisian stitch, using 3-ply Off-White 992 as before. Remember to turn the canvas on its side for this stitch. The beams are stitched as on the front and back of the cottage, the horizontal beams in random Straight Gobelin and the vertical beams in Parisian stitch. Work also the two vertical beams either side of the upper window. The pantile roof is three rows of Sloping Gobelin over 2 threads, using the Appleton's Crewel Flame Red mixture as in the brickwork. Stitch the brickwork and the window, using the same stitches and threads as on the front and back of the cottage.

◇

DOVE COTE

It is easiest to start this area at the bottom with the 2-thread channel immediately above the window. Work a row of Straight Gobelin over 2 threads in 3-ply White 991. Then work the five supports for the dove cote – these are two Straight Gobelin stitches over 2 threads.

Then plan out and work the three entrances in Basketweave

tent stitch. These are stitched in Appleton's Crewel 2-ply Black 993. Work the central one first and then one on either side (mine is 13 threads away).

Then work three rows of Straight Gobelin in 3-ply Off-White 992. Continue up the area, working a White beam, the entrances and then the three Off-White beams. Shorten each line by 1 thread of canvas to get a smooth diagonal edge to the area.

◇

SECOND SIDE ELEVATION

Using two needles, stitch the plasterwork and surrounding beams panel by panel. Remember to turn the canvas on its side for the Parisian stitching used for the plasterwork and the vertical beams. The diagonal and horizontal beams are worked in random Straight Gobelin as before. Use 3-ply Off-White 992 for the plasterwork and Medici brown 500 for the beams. By stitching the plasterwork and beams in turn as you go both colors will fit together. On the corners of the house work the Parisian over 2 and 3 threads on the front and back of the cottage.

◇

COUCHING

(See Stitch Glossary page 146)
This is done for the thatching on the roof. Use the Aran wool straight from the ball. Hold the piece sideways with the front door on the left. Start at the upper left-hand corner of the roof and leave a 10-cm (4-in) tail hanging over the front. Lay the wood down with the ball of wool over the back of the house.

With a single ply of the dark brown Medici 500 make a small, vertical stitch over 1 thread of canvas over the thick wool every

4 threads working towards the right.

Look again at the photograph on page 84. I couched a second layer just over the central area, working as before and leaving a loop on each turn.

When the back is reached, leave a long loop (about 6 cm/2½ in) and work back across the roof with the thick wool, laying it right beside the first piece and the couching stitches lining up with those already worked.

However tempted you are to trim the thatch now, it is much wiser to do this after the piece is made up!

As everyone has his own favorite plants and trees, or has some thing growing in his garden that would be nice to represent on his own piece, I have explained fully below the stitches and techniques to make tree trunks, thick stems, large and small leaves and blossom. I have described also the flowers and shrubs used in this Cottage on the facing page. In this way you can adapt these techniques for your own choice of plants.

As explained in Materials on page 84 this is a good opportunity to use up threads left over from other projects. Use either pearl or floss.

I have given the number of plies I used in the Stitch Summary on the facing page but as well as following my suggestions experiment until you achieve the desired effect.

◇

CHAIN STITCH

(See Stitch Glossary page 145)
Thick tree trunks, the main stem of a bush, even a branch of a small plant can be worked in Chain stitch. Always start at the base of

STITCH SUMMARY for flowers and plants

Stitch	Thread and number of plies
French knots	Stranded cotton (6); Pearl cotton (1)
Raised Needleweaving	Stranded cotton (4); Pearl cotton (1)
Split stitch	Stranded cotton (4); Pearl cotton (1)
Detached chain	Stranded cotton (4); Pearl cotton (1)
Chain stitch	Stranded cotton (4); Pearl cotton (1)
Satin stitch	Stranded cotton (6); Pearl cotton (2)

the plant or tree. Always have sufficient thread to complete the required line and always turn the canvas so that the Chain stitch is coming towards you.

FOR TREE TRUNKS: use a number of rows of Chain stitch worked in a thick thread, possibly with rows in different shades to indicate light and shade. Leave the chain loops fairly loose at the base of the tree and pull them tighter as the trunk ascends and gets slimmer.

FOR BUSHES: use a single row of Chain stitch but pull each loop slightly tighter as the stem gets higher.

◇

DETACHED CHAIN STITCH

(See Stitch Glossary page 145)
This is a single Chain stitch which can be worked at various angles to form leaves. Large-scale stitches can be laurel or rhododendron and large-scale stitches with a single Straight Gobelin worked inside can be a variegated leaf. Small-scale stitches can be yew or rose-bush leaves.

◇

SPLIT STITCH

(See Stitch Glossary page 168)
Split stitch is a good choice if a very fine line is required for a delicate plant or at the very top of a bush or tree. It resembles a very neat Chain stitch.

◇

FRENCH KNOTS

(See Stitch Glossary page 158)
Worked with a thickish thread, these make good single blooms. Worked in clusters they make multiple flowerheads such as wisteria.

◇

FRENCH KNOTS ON STALKS

(See Stitch Glossary page 158)
These can radiate, either loosely or packed tight, from the end of a stem to indicate a puffball-type flowerhead or can be used around a central cluster of French knots. The 'Flowers of Elizabeth I' purse front illustrates this combination well on page 109.

◇

RAISED NEEDLEWEAVING

(See Stitch Glossary page 163)
This is good for important tall single flowers or leaves that you really want to stand out. It was also used in the 'Flowers of Elizabeth I' purse front photographed on page 109.

◇

BEADS

The generally accepted size for beads is to choose one that sits comfortably in the mesh of the canvas being used. It helps to try a number of shades on the worked area as the stitching and the surrounding colors do affect how they look.

Always sew each bead on individually. In Victorian pieces they were frequently sewn on in multiples, five or six on one stitch and this is why so many of them have now fallen off.

For sewing beads use a fine thread – 2-ply of floss in a matching color is good. Make a Tent stitch over 1 thread of canvas, picking up a bead as you stitch. If you wish an area to be filled smoothly with beads stitch them individually in a row. When the row is complete bring the needle up at one end, run through all the holes of the beads, lining them up and take the needle down through the canvas at the other end. This ensures that the beads all lie the same way.

Clusters of beads can also look good, simply go on piling them (still stitched individually) on top of each other until you have the desired effect.

◇

THE PLANTS AND FLOWERS ON THE COTTAGE

THE FRONT: The low flowers are French knots and French knots on stalks; the pink hyacinths are Raised needleweaving; the hollyhocks are pink French knots clustered around a single yellow French knot on a Split stitch stalk.

The link chain between the garden posts was worked in 3-ply black floss in Chain stitch.

THE BACK: In the flower troughs are Detached chain leaves, multicolored beads and French knots. The cherry blossom on the right is French knots on a Chain-stitch stem. The dense green tree to the left is closely packed Straight Gobelin stitch worked at random.

SIDES OF THE HOUSE: The wisteria has a trunk of Chain stitch, the leaves are in Detached chain stitch and the flowers are in closely packed French knots.

The pyracantha has detached Chain-stitch leaves and red glass beads for the berries. The hostas below it have larger Detached chain stitch worked in green with a single cream Straight Gobelin inside each one for the variegated leaves.

◇
PLANNING AND STITCHING YOUR OWN HOUSE

The simple geometric lines of any house make it a perfect project for canvas work. The different textures of bricks, slates, windows and plaster lend themselves to stitchery as we have seen from the Cottage.

Planning your own house and drawing it on to canvas is not too difficult and the actual stitching is great fun; no area to be stitched is too big and you can add details such as window boxes or increase the size of the bushes as you wish.

All styles of architecture seem to work; I have had a number of classes when students have worked their own home and I have stitched the following myself – Georgian brick, clapperboard, town or mews houses, English Edwardian, San Francisco Gingerbread, ski chalets and English Country cottages; they all have their own character, are rewarding to stitch and make a great conversation piece when finished.

I made this Country Cottage into a three-dimensional piece which could be a door-stop, book-end or purely decorative.

◇
PREPARATION

All you need to work from is a simple straight-on photograph of the view or views you wish to stitch. Angled views of houses make charming water- or oil-colors but they are no good when it comes to working on canvas. If available, a good alternative is an architect's elevation, which is drawn to scale.

It is important to look really hard at the photograph (and the house too if necessary) to assess the scale and relationship of the various features. The simplest way to do this is to take a ruler and ask yourself the following questions:

WHAT MESH CANVAS DO YOU WISH TO USE? This depends largely on the finished size required and the amount of detail you wish to show. For example, I wanted the cottage to be quite small but I also wanted mullioned windows and brickwork so that 18-mesh canvas was necessary to show all the detail. It follows that the finer the canvas the more detail you can show. If you want to make a large wall-hanging use a relatively coarse canvas.

DO YOU WISH TO WORK A FLAT PICTURE OR A THREE-DIMENSIONAL PIECE? It is only fairly regular houses that lend themselves to the free-standing approach. The house can be either large or small but the ground plan should be square or rectangular. Single-story back extensions, sloping roofs to a conservatory, and towers or turrets could be difficult to fill! Any house with or without a garden makes a good picture.

WHAT COLOR CANVAS TO USE? Use a white canvas for a light modern house and a brown or ecru one when there are areas of brickwork or stone.

WHAT ARE THE DIMENSIONS OF THE HOUSE? With the ruler check the relative height and width of the house. If it is tall do you wish to widen it with trees and bushes to the sides? If it is wide will you add some sky or grass, paths and hedges to the foreground?

WHAT SIZE DO YOU WANT THE FINAL PIECE TO BE? Having decided this roughly, work out the relationship between the dimensions in the photograph and the planned piece. Keep the same proportions. For example, if the front elevation is 10 cm (4 in) high and the roof is 5 cm (2 in) deep on the photograph and the finished piece is to be 150 cm (60 in) high, then the roof will be 50 cm (20 in) and the front elevation 100 cm (40 in).

Many houses such as the Cottage have roofs which add tremendously to the character of the house so watch the proportions carefully.

WHERE IS THE FRONT DOOR? Doors can be central and very grand with pillars or porches or very insignificant. Is the door panelled or plain? Does it have a knocker or are you about to repaint it another color?

Does the door align with other features such as the top of the windows on the same floor or is there a window immediately above it?

WHERE ARE THE WINDOWS? Are they all the same shape and do they align? Frequently, windows are smaller on upper floors; sometimes windows in extensions that have been built later have different glazing. Are the individual panes square or rectangular? Is there any surface decoration that will affect the thread count? For example, if the windows have shutters, they must 'fit' the windows, in other words each side should be half the thread count of the complete window.

Windows always have frames that are wider than the glazing bars. If the window is three panes wide with a glazing bar between each one, then the area you allow has got to be a number from which you can subtract 2 (1 thread for each glazing bar) and divide by 3 – so that each pane is the same width.

ARE THERE ANY PLANTS YOU WISH TO INCLUDE? Most flowers, climbing plants and small bushes are best worked as surface decoration on top of the stitched house. There are only a few of these that are extremely dense and so should be stitched directly on the canvas, not as surface decoration.

ARE THERE ANY OTHER DETAILS YOU WISH TO ADD? Flower boxes, planters either side of the door: now is your opportunity for showing how nice they could look!

◇

CHOOSING THE MATERIALS

CANVAS

I have already talked about selecting canvas. The important features are what you are happy working on and how much detail you want to stitch. For three-dimensional pieces such as the Country Cottage use 18 to 24-mesh canvas and for wallhangings or large pictures use 10 to 12-mesh canvas.

◇

YARN

As you will see from the Materials list for the Cottage on page 84, almost anything that gives the right texture is suitable. Wool is probably the best choice for the house itself as neat stitches are needed. Rug thrums, weaving or knitting yarn can all be experimented with for thatch, paths and brickwork. Silks, chenilles and beads can be used for flowers and foliage.

◇

MAKING-UP YOUR PIECE

I recommend professional help for making-up both pictures and three-dimensional houses. However, if you have an attractive frame you would like to use for making a picture, stretch the finished canvas over a piece of board cut to fit the frame, lace it in place with strong stitches across the back of the board and put it in the frame. I never recommend putting glass on top of the stitches as this tends to flatten the work (see Finishing and Aftercare page 130).

In the case of the Cottage and making other three-dimensional pieces, at least get your carpenter to cut you the correct size piece of wood, allowing for the sloping roof. Trim the three pieces of canvas to 6 threads of unworked canvas. Fingerpress the bare canvas behind the work, miter all the corners and trim away any excess canvas. Baste the canvas to the back of stitchery.

Starting with the top point of a side elevation, match it to the central point of the main cottage roof. Work down one side, stitching canvas thread to canvas thread with 2-ply Medici wool in dark brown (500) to match the stitching on the already worked canvas so that it is invisible. Return to the central point and stitch down the second side.

Attach the other side elevation in the same way. Ease the canvaswork on to the wood shape. Turn any spare canvas under the wood and either use clear glue or lace in place with strong thread. Cut a piece of self-adhesive felt to the same size as the base and fit in place. Then trim the thatch (see also page 130).

Inspirational Projects

This group of needlepoint projects shows some of the exciting things that can be worked with Stitchery. The pillow stitched in apricot colors is worked almost entirely in concentric squares of Straight Gobelin stitch with a row of canvas left bare between each row to give a light look. This is an extremely simple idea to copy, but it does rely on the individual stitches being laid smoothly.

The soft pink and green pillow is worked in wool, floss and pearl cotton. The original design came from the table carpet depicted in the Dame au Licorne tapestries in the Cluny Museum, Paris. The design is more complicated than that of the little pillow and relies on only a few different stitches being used but this time planning and working them so as to give interesting light reflection and texture.

The evening purse was designed as a class project so that it incorporates a great many interesting fibers, silk, cottons, metallic blending filament and wool. It has been finished also as a jewelry roll, with internal pockets to take bracelets, necklaces and rings, and also as a pillow front for a rectangular pillow.

Finally, the picture with the two butterflies is by far the most ambitious of these stitchery pieces. Besides using more than thirty different fibers and both traditional canvas work and embroidery stitches, the areas to be worked are both curved and irregular. Even so, there are some stitches here that you have already learned: Brick stitch, Basketweave tent, and Ribbed spider. The Chinese knot border is graphed on page 95 as it is easily adaptable and can be used on the corners of many other designs.

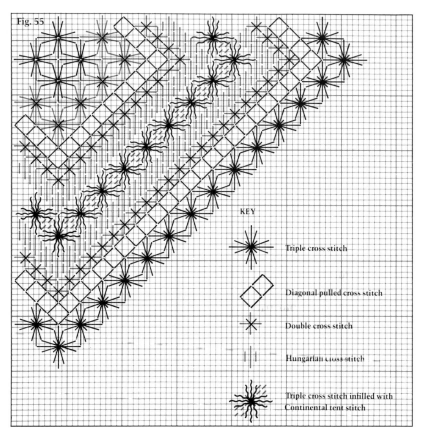

Fig. 55

KEY

✳ Triple cross stitch

◇ Diagonal pulled cross stitch

✳ Double cross stitch

❘❘❘ Hungarian cross stitch

✳ Triple cross stitch infilled with Continental tent stitch

Starting with the simplest design, the apricot pillow, it is interesting to see how two stitches already used in other projects can make such an attractive pillow. In the center is a Rhodes stitch (see the Simple Cross Stitch project). This is surrounded by rows of Straight Gobelin (see the Simple and Advanced Stitchery projects), worked over 2, 4, 6 and 7 threads of the canvas. Between each row 1 or 2 threads of the white canvas have been left exposed to give an overall light look. There are two bands of other stitches; 2, 4, 6, 8 Stitch worked both horizontally and vertically (which is an adaptation of the 2, 4, 6 stitch used in the Simple Stitchery project) and Reversed eyelet stitch. Rhodes stitch worked in the same square shape as the Reversed eyelet would look equally good.

This pillow would make a perfect present as it does not take too long to make or, if you wanted a slightly larger one, the canvas could easily be mounted on an existing pillow when some of the pillow fabric would show on all sides and form an attractive border to the stitched canvas.

As already explained, the design of the second pillow comes from the Cluny Museum, Paris. I love to find designs when traveling and never worry if they come from architectural detail, embroidered or woven textiles or any other likely or unlikely source. Train yourself to look at things around you as a possible source of design for needlepoint. My first attempt to copy this design was in deep-colored crewel wools and it was lovely. I then became interested in using fibers other than wool for needlepoint projects and re-did the design, finishing up with this very delicate piece worked in floss and pearl cotton on 18-mesh canvas. There are only a few different stitches in the design, including Pulled diamond eyelet, 2, 4, 6, 8 Stitch worked in two directions to catch the light and Satin stitch (all of which are in the Stitch Glossary on page 142).

The design of the evening purse is from an antique rug I saw once in Madison Avenue, New York. There are many interesting fibers, and both Pulled thread and Stitchery in this piece but one of the main reasons I think it is so visually successful is that all the stitches echo the shape of the area in which they are worked. For example, the central diamond shape is filled with only diamond-shaped stitches — of various sizes but each one forming a diamond on the canvas. In the rectangular outer border all the stitches are square, surrounded by an outline of Pulled thread to make them stand out well. As with all my geometric pieces, the stitches are designed to fit the area; the mathematics are worked out at the outset, with each stitch allowed to form its own pattern and texture within an area with no half or compensation stitches to worry about.

I have charted the central diamond for your own use (see Figure 55). As a single motif it would make an attractive pinpillow or herb sachet. Three diamonds linked together (as stitched on the purse) would make a rectangular panel for a pillow front or with a half-drop pattern repeat it would make an intricate all-over design.

One final tip to note here is the two rows of dark Tent stitch that are worked on all sides of the design – this allows the maker-up to machine neatly around the edge when attaching the lining. If the piece was multi-colored on the edge he or she would have to choose one color for the machine-stitching and it would consequently show up far more.

Finally, the Butterfly picture is a very exciting piece for me to be able to include in the book as I worked it with two great teachers, DeDe Ogden and Sue Strause, in a four-day workshop. Therefore, all the stitches, techniques and fibers used were unusual in order to let the students have experience working them.

There are some old friends in this picture: Brick stitch (from the Simple Stitchery project), Basketweave tent in the butterflies, and Straight and Sloping Gobelin and Mosaic stitch in the border (all found in the Stitchery projects).

The Or nué couching on the upper wings of the lower butterfly is a very grand version of the couching you have already done with the thatched roof of the Country Cottage (see Advanced Stitchery). With Or nué the couched thread is traditionally gold and the couching thread colored silks stitched either close or far apart to form a pattern.

A finishing tip to note is to mount the finished canvas of a piece such as this one on a soft batting fabric before framing. This soft fabric will absorb some of the ends of the thicker threads rather than allow them to form bumps behind a canvas mounted tight down on to a board (see page 129 for further instructions on how to do this).

Finally, I think that the professional mounting used here pays dividends; there are three different frames fixed together and

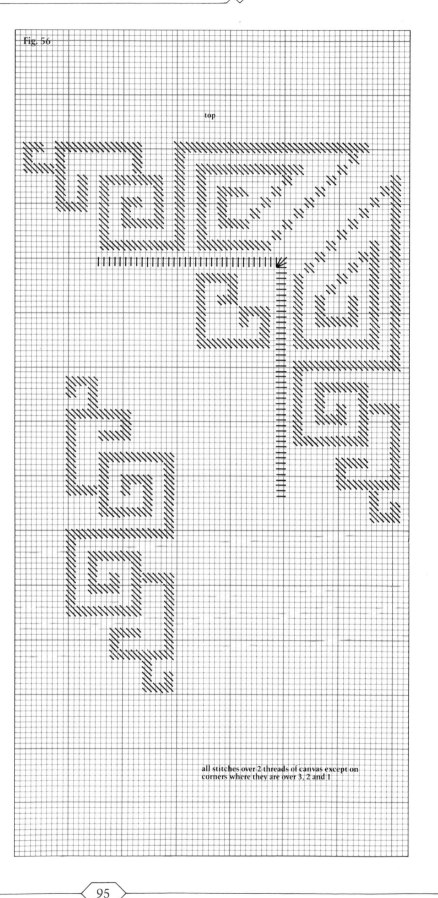

Fig. 56

top

all stitches over 2 threads of canvas except on corners where they are over 3, 2 and 1

hand-gilded to give a spectacular finish to such a beautiful piece.

If you are planning to frame a piece of needlework it is wise not to work a linear border around the piece. The framer then has an almost impossible task of lining up the weave of the canvas with the sharp edge of the frame. The Chinese-knot adaptation from the Butterfly picture shown here (see Figure 56) is a good compromise; it is sufficiently bold to 'hold' the design but it is only on the inside edge that there is a continuous line of stitches.

I have charted it for you as it is, a simple border to adapt for other projects, with a corner motif and two motifs placed centrally on the two long sides. If adapting this you may prefer to invert one of the central motifs or, with a square panel you might like to use the motif on all four sides. If making a pillow you may like to include as well a row of stitching such as Straight Gobelin on the outer edges.

◇

BORDERS

I find borders possibly the most exciting part of a design. Most of the stitching of the piece has been accomplished and hopefully during the stitching some border ideas have presented themselves, waiting to be tried.

If you try one or two borders for a piece, I suggest you work them first as a piece that can be mounted in your Reference Collection (see page 140) for future use even if you decide against them on this occasion.

The depth of a border can vary from a simple one worked in two or three rows of Straight Gobelin and covering under 3 cm (1 in) in all, to a very dramatic one which

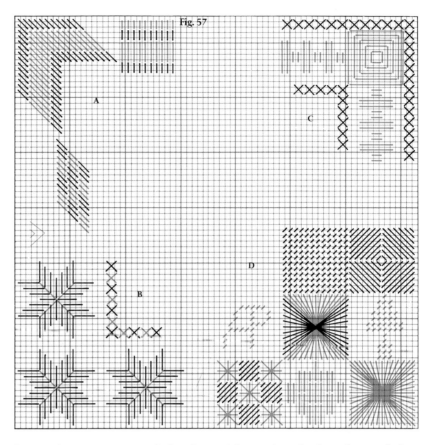

Fig. 57

forms the major part of the design. An example of this would be the wide Florentine border worked on the Yellow Rug (see Inspirational Florentine page 48) with a single initial worked in the middle. With the 'Pigs in Clover' rug (see Advanced Cross Stitch page 61) the center of the design is extremely simple and it is the pigs around the border that give the interest.

Border designs can also be used most successfully for belts, bell-pulls, suspenders, luggage-rack straps, curtain trims and tie-backs, and book markers, all with the added advantage that these items do not have corners around which the design has to be planned!

The colors used in a border depend on how important you want the final effect to be. Two combinations I find that work are either using shades of one of the colors used in the main design, generally working from light out to dark on the outer edge, or using the strongest shades of two color families already used in the design and mixed with white or cream.

If you marked the center of the design on each side of the canvas before stitching, now is the time that it will really pay off and make any counting or planning needed for the border much easier and more accurate. It is almost always best to start with the innermost row of the border; complete that and then move outwards in stages.

Shown above in Figure 57 are some ideas for you to experiment with; they also demonstrate four very different types of planning needed for successful borders.

1. These three borders are the simplest ones of all. They will fit any thread count that you have already stitched on the canvas. The Straight Gobelin (upper right in this group) is worked here in horizontal rows over 2, 2, 4, 2 and 2 threads of canvas. It would be worth trying the first and last rows in one color family, the second and fourth in the contrasting color and the long stitches in the third row in either white or cream. Experiment also with the white or cream colors in the second and fourth rows and the contrasting color in the center row. This design can also look good with a row of fine backstitching worked along the top and bottom of the long stitches, possibly using a pearl cotton in a soft shade to echo the color in the two outer rows.

The Sloping Gobelin border (shown turning the corner) will also fit any size. Starting as usual with the innermost row, which is over 2 threads, simply reverse the direction of the slope of the stitch when you reach the center of each side. Work compensation stitches in the triangle created by reversing the direction. When working the second row over 4 threads use either one color or, as shown here, two colors alternately. Again, when the center of a side is reached, reverse the stitches and work the same number on either side of the central point – in this way all the corners will be identical. Work compensation stitches in the triangle created by reversing the direction.

The third border in this group resembles a twisted cord. The groups of three stitches in alternate colors could be enlarged to five or even seven stitches or a third color could be introduced. Again, reverse the color and the

stitches at the center of each side and then the corners will match.

2. This shows a 'spot' motif as it does not interlace or need to touch the adjoining motif. The motif can either be carefully counted out and the number of threads between each 'spot' carefully assessed or, much more simply, work one motif in each corner, one in the center of each side and then plot out how many more motifs you want along each side. Sometimes it is impossible to have exactly the same number of threads left between each motif. If this is the case, make a positive feature of the central motif and have the extra thread or two on each side of the central motif – in this way it will look as if it was deliberate.

The four stitches worked down into the center of each flower are only shown on two of the three flowers to enable you to copy the base stitches more easily.

3. This shows a pattern that is impossible to swing round a corner and so a complimentary motif is worked in each corner. The Straight Gobelin over 2 and 6 threads could be replaced by Upright cross and Basic cross stitches worked alternately and the inner and outer rows of Basic cross stitch could be Long-legged cross stitch. The stitches left void on the chart would normally be filled in with white or cream in either the same Gobelin or else in Basketweave tent stitch.

4. This shows a number of ideas for a more dramatic checkerboard border – not all to be used at once but to give you some ideas to play with.

Any stitch can be worked checkerboard fashion in two col-

ors or any two stitches (of the same scale) can also be worked in alternate colors. If the individual border stitch is over 2 threads (for example Basic cross stitch) the thread count along the side of the work already completed must be divisible by two. If the stitch is over 4 threads (for example, Smyrna and Crossed corners) the thread count must be divisible by four. With the Rhodes stitch, shown here, each one is over 12 threads so it may be necessary to 'increase' the size of the completed design by adding a row of either Continental tent stitch (as this is worked over 1 thread each side it will add 2 threads on to the count) or Basic cross (2 + 2 = 4) or even Straight Gobelin over 3 (3 + 3 = 6).

Charted here are two sorts of Rhodes stitch, one worked in a single color, the second worked with a change of color after the first 13 stitches; a variation of Cushion stitch worked over 6 threads but in a group of four to bring it up to the same scale as the Rhodes; and Smyrna and Cushion stitches worked alternately, again forming a square 12 threads by 12.

In the squares between plain Basketweave would be effective to show off the raised texture of the Rhodes; the Christmas Tree would be fun on a seasonal piece; the Strawberry could be attractive if the color fitted in with the overall scheme of the piece; and a monogram (I have used my initials AP) would be nice worked in each Basketweave square as an overall motif or just in one of the corners.

When searching for interesting border ideas look also in the other Inspirational sections of this book.

CHAPTER SIX
PULLED THREAD

Simple Project

Pulled thread was worked traditionally on finely woven linen and there are many excellent examples of eighteenth-century German and Danish Dresden work as it came to be known. Originally, it was used for women's caps, fichus and aprons as it was more practical and quicker to make than the true laces which were made without a ground fabric. Recently, Pulled-thread work has proved extremely popular with needlepointers as the final effect is very pretty, the evenweave, open-mesh canvas makes an excellent foundation fabric and it does not take too long to complete.

With most of the Pulled-thread patterns a great deal of the canvas is left unworked, it is only certain threads that are stitched or 'bound' tightly together and so this creates patterns both in the positive (stitches) and negative (holes) spaces. Therefore, the most satisfactory color schemes for Pulled-thread projects are natural-colored canvas and self- or soft-colored threads.

The Simple project shown here is worked on 13-mesh linen canvas with two self-colored threads of different weights.

◇ MATERIALS

13-mesh linen canvas
Cut size: 50 cm (20 in) square
Finished size: 36 cm (14¼ in) square
Frame 50 cm (20 in) square
11 skeins DMC Floss 712
1 ball Twilley's Stalite Pampas 21
Tapestry needles sizes 18 and 20

◇ SPECIAL TIPS FOR WORKING PULLED THREAD

As you can see from the photographs in this chapter not all the canvas is covered. When doing Pulled-thread work you are making two sorts of pattern, one with the stitches, getting them smooth and satiny, and one with the holes that are made by pulling firmly and not allowing any stray threads to pass behind the holes. If you look at the made-up pieces on pages 108 and 109 carefully you

will see that a deep contrasting lining is used immediately behind the finished canvas to accentuate this 'negative' pattern.

In order to get the very best results remember the following tips.

It is impossible to work Pulled thread without the correct size of frame. The piece cannot be moved around on a small frame or a roller frame.

Use a contrast thread for marking any design on the canvas which can be pulled out later on just ahead of your stitching. Marks from a pencil or marker pen could well show when the piece is finished.

Use the 'away' knot technique described on page 16 for starting threads if there is not any surrounding stitchery to use.

If there is stitchery, anchor the new thread particularly firmly as you will be pulling quite hard on the thread and you do not want it to come out.

Finish the thread carefully in the back of the stitches; threading it into a sharp needle for this process might help.

Use a needle at least one size larger than you would normally for the mesh of canvas – this will automatically make the hole larger as you stitch.

Two pulls at the threads you wish to distort are far better than one – this is called 'double-wrapping'; in order to do this only use half the number of plies that each stitch recommends and work each stitch twice, immediately after one another, getting two wraps in the process. For example, for an 8-ply covering, thread your needle with 4 plies and make each stitch movement twice.

All the stitches in the Pulled-thread section of the Stitch Glossary on page 142 have detailed numbers and/or arrows. By following these you will get maximum pull when needed.

If your pulled areas are not as lacy as those in the photographs do not worry, the important thing is to keep the tension in each area constant.

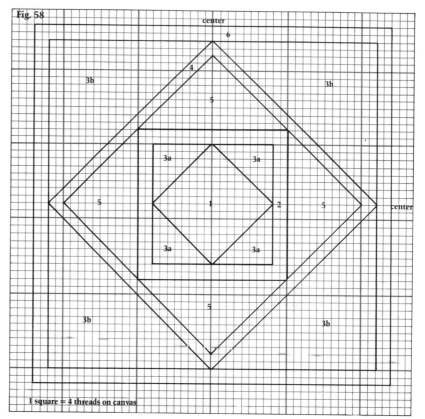

Fig. 58

1 square = 4 threads on canvas

◇

WORKING THE PILLOW

Mount the canvas on the frame as tautly as possible.

Mark the design in Figure 58 on to the canvas with a contrasting thread. This can be pulled out as you work.

The numbers in Figure 58 and in the Stitch Summary refer to the stitches to be used in each area. It is easier to work in the order suggested.

◇

1 DIAMOND EYELET

(See Stitch Glossary page 155)
Work this stitch in the central diamond area using the size 18 Tapestry needle. Each eyelet is double-wrapped.

Start the first eyelet matching

the spot in the diagram on page 155 to the top of the central diamond area – then the pattern will fit exactly. There are 16 stitches down into the central hole; follow the numbers given on the diagram, working counter-clockwise round each eyelet. Start subsequent eyelets at the top and continue to work counter-clockwise. Work from the upper left of the area diagonally to the lower right; turn the canvas upside down and work back on the next diagonal row; this will ensure that there will be no trailing threads behind the holes.

◇

2 SQUARE EYELET

(See Stitch Glossary page 156)
Work the first square eyelet marked over 8 threads of canvas, using the size 18 Tapestry needle.

This stitch is single-wrapped as

STITCH SUMMARY

Number	Stitch	Colour	Number of plies
1	Diamond eyelet	DMC Stranded Cotton 712	4, double wrapped to give 8
2	Square eyelet	Twilley's Stalite Pampas 21	1, single wrapped
3 a and b	Spaced satin	DMC Stranded Cotton 712	6, double wrapped to give 12
4	Diamond eyelet	Twilley's Stalite Pampas 21	1, single wrapped
5	Honeycomb	Twilley's Stalite Pampas 21	1, single wrapped
6	Cushion variation	Twilley's Stalite Pampas 21	1, single wrapped

it would be too thick worked twice. Start in the top left-hand corner of the area, follow the numbers in the diagram on page 156 and work clockwise. By following the numbers you will make two trips round the eyelet, the first time missing out alternate holes and then filling them in on the second trip. In this way the thread is more evenly distributed in the central hole.

◇

3a   SPACED SATIN

(See Stitch Glossary page 166)
This is worked in the four triangular areas inside the Square eyelet frame, using the size 18 Tapestry needle.

This is worked in horizontal rows in groups of 6 stitches with 7 threads of canvas between each group. When working the second row the group of 6 stitches fits below the unstitched area immediately above. The third row of stitches lines up below the first row.

Look at the photograph on page 99 carefully; start the first row along the longest line immediately below or above the Square eyelet framing the area. The first group shares with one of the side points of the Diamond eyelet already worked – this will

balance the pattern and give a group of only five stitches instead of the usual six on the side margins of alternate rows.

At this point do not work 3b, it will be easier to work it later on when the surrounding stitchery is in place.

◇

4   DIAMOND EYELET

(See Stitch Glossary page 155)
You have used this stitch already in this project.

Start at the top point of each eyelet, matching the spot in the diagram on page 155 to the upper point of the area. Work down to the right-hand turning point, quarter turn the canvas and still following the stitch order continue down to the bottom point. Turn the canvas one quarter each time you round a point.

◇

5   HONEYCOMB

(See Stitch Glossary page 159)
Work this stitch in the four triangular areas between the square- and diamond-shaped frames already worked, using the size 18 Tapestry needle.

As you work each area turn the canvas so that the first horizontal row can fit along the long wall of the triangle (sharing with the

Square eyelet). Just for this project it will be easiest to turn the diagram on page 159 upside down so that you can follow and work towards the sharp point of the area. Follow the arrows – a back stitch is taken over all the horizontal threads. When working the second row a second wrap is worked on the lower horizontal stitches of the first row.

When an area is complete, fill in the combs with Basic cross stitches as shown in the Stitch Glossary. Use the same thread but a size 20 Tapestry needle. Work these crosses in diagonal rows so as not to trail behind the holes already made.

If you incorporate Honeycomb stitch into another project it is best to use a substantial thread as it looks more decorative.

◇

6   CUSHION VARIATION

(See Stitch Glossary page 154)
Work this in the outer square border marked over 8 threads, using the size 18 Tapestry needle. Start in a corner so that the pattern fits exactly.

Groups of seven stitches are worked into boxes in groups of four on alternate diagonals to form a larger box over 8 threads.

◇

3b   SPACED SATIN

(See Stitch Glossary page 166)
You have already used this stitch in this project.

Study the photograph again and note how a group of stitches fits either side of the top Diamond eyelet; if you start sharing with a Diamond eyelet and work outwards the side margins on all four areas will match up. This will make these four areas balance well like the first Spaced satin triangles (3a).

Advanced Project

Soft colors in floss and pearl cotton and three different widths of ribbon combine to make this lovely piece that would make a beautiful table top or wallhanging as well as the pillow front shown here.

The original geometric design has been adapted from a complex Chinese octagon-square wooden grille found in a Buddhist temple in Sichuan and dated 1875.

Looking at this and the other geometric designs in this book I think it becomes obvious that I see possibilities for needlepoint in the most unlikely places! Wrapping paper, greeting cards, tiled floors, manhole covers, wrought-iron panels and treasure after treasure in Islamic, Japanese and Chinese decorative motifs. The only two things I warn you against unless you are feeling strong are circles (as each thread has to be counted out) and angles that are not 90 degree right angles or 45 degrees; it is very difficult to fit any stitch other than Tent stitch in to a steep or shallow angle and for the finished piece to look good.

◇

MATERIALS

17-mesh linen canvas
Cut size: 55 cm (20 in) square
Finished size: 40 cm (15 in) square
Frame: 55 cm (20 in) square
Floss
   7 skeins DMC 712
   9 skeins DMC 754
Pearl cotton
   9 skeins DMC 948
Offray double-sided Satin Ribbon
   7 m (7½ yd) × 3 mm (⅛ in) Cream
   6 m (6½ yd) × 1.5 mm (1/16 in)
Peach
   2 m (2¼ yd) × 6 mm (¼ in) Peach
1 each Tapestry needles sizes 20 and 22

Use the size 22 for all ordinary stitching and the larger size 20 for the Pulled-thread stitches since you want the holes to be bigger.

◇

WORKING THE PIECE

Mount the canvas as tautly as possible on the square frame. A roller frame or small frame that you move around will not be suitable.

◇

1 DIAGONAL CROSS STITCH OVER 4 THREADS

(See Stitch Glossary pages 146–7)
Following Figure 59, lay horizontal rows of the 3-mm (⅛-in) cream ribbon across the canvas and pin in place on both sides. Start with the central ribbons and work outwards; this ensures that your piece will be centralized.

Each ribbon covers 4 threads of the canvas (Tent stitch worked later on the two outer threads will give complete coverage) and there are 34 threads left in between each row. Couch in place with the Diagonal cross stitch over 4 threads, using the size 22 Tapestry needle.

Couching means laying a thick thread, cord or ribbon that would be too thick to stitch with comfortably on the surface of the work, holding it in place with stitches worked through the canvas and only taking it down through the canvas at either side of the work – this is called 'plunging' and is done later on.

Turn the canvas a quarter turn and then, in the same way, lay rows of the same 3-mm ribbon at right angles to those already in place, weaving them over and under the horizontal rows already there. Again, hold the ribbon in place with pins at either end.

Couch in place as before with the Diagonal cross stitch over 4 threads. Do not plunge at this stage. Check now that you have at least 22 threads of canvas beyond all your outer ribbons.

◇

2 BASIC CROSS STITCH

(See Stitch Glossary page 147)
Next, lay the 1.5-mm (⅛-in) narrow peach ribbon, first horizontally and then vertically as shown in Figure 60. Couch each ribbon in place as you position them, using Basic and Upright crosses and the size 22 Tapestry needle. Thread the peach ribbon under the cream ribbon at each intersection (see Figure 59 for correct threading). Follow Figure 60 carefully when couching the diagonal sections of this ribbon. The Upright crosses are stitched on the diagonal sections and Basic cross stitch on the straight lines. Do not plunge at this stage.

Now we come to the Pulled-thread stitches. As suggested in the Simple Pulled-thread project you get a much better pull on all the stitches if half the required number of plies are used first. Each stitch is then repeated as a double wrap. Refer to the Stitch Summary on page 105. Use the size 20 Tapestry needle for these stitches to make each hole larger as you stitch into it.

3a SATIN STITCH WORKED HORIZONTALLY

(See Stitch Glossary page 165)
Work this Stitch in all the horizontal areas between the peach and cream ribbons. Use the back of existing stitches for anchoring the thread or use the 'away knot' described on page 16 and anchor it in the stitches.

3b SATIN STITCH WORKED VERTICALLY

(See Stitch Glossary page 165)
Work exactly the same stitch as 3a with the same color but in vertical bands. You may find it even easier just to turn the frame a quarter turn and do the horizontal version as in 3a. Either way is fine.

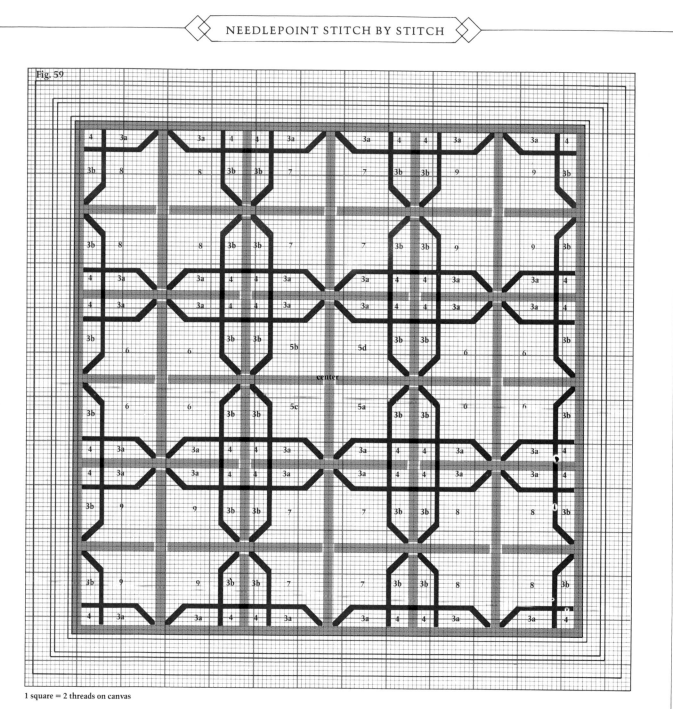

Fig. 59

1 square = 2 threads on canvas

4 SQUARE EYELET WITH TENT

(See Stitch Glossary page 156)
This is worked in the small 8-thread squares that the ribbons have formed on the canvas. Work the line of Tent stitch first and use the remainder of the thread to work the eyelet (this saves anchoring a new thread). This stitch was also used in the Simple Pulled-thread project on page 100. Make two trips round the square, missing alternate holes on the first time and filling them in on the second trip to get the neatest effect.

5 TRELLIS

(See Stitch Glossary page 170)
Trellis is worked in the four quarters of the central area of the design. The diagram on page 170 shows how to set up the diagonal radiating out from the center in area 5a. When this is complete, turn this book upside down and work area 5b.

Then, following Figure b (the right way up again) work area 5c. Turn the book again and work 5d! Each of the patterns will radiate out from the central point.

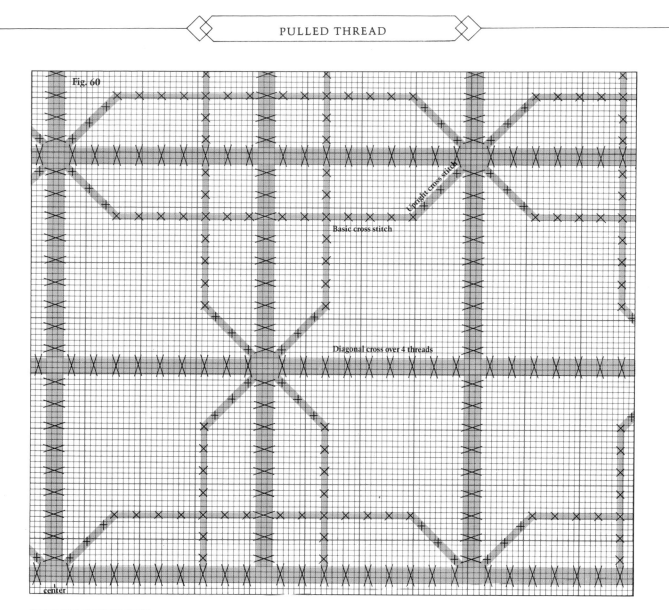

Fig. 60

Upright cross stitch

Basic cross stitch

Diagonal cross over 4 threads

center

STITCH SUMMARY

Number	Stitch	Colour	Number of plies
1	Diagonal cross stitch over 4 threads	DMC Stranded Cotton 712	2
2	Basic cross stitch	DMC Stranded Cotton 712	2
3a	Satin stitch worked horizontally	DMC Pearl Cotton 948	1, double wrapped to give 2
3b	Satin stitch worked vertically	DMC Pearl Cotton 948	1, double wrapped to give 2
4	Square eyelet with tent stitch	DMC Pearl Cotton 948	1, double wrapped to give 2
5	Trellis	DMC Stranded Cotton 754 and 712	3, double wrapped to give 6
6	Framed cross	DMC Stranded Cotton 712	4, double wrapped to give 8

Number	Stitch	Colour	Number of plies
7	Cobbler filling	DMC Stranded Cotton 712	4, double wrapped to give 8
8	Trellis bars with cross variation	DMC Stranded Cotton 754	Trellis: 6 (not pulled). Cross variation: 3, double wrapped to give 6
9	Trellis bars with diamond eyelets	DMC Stranded Cotton 754	Trellis: 6 (not pulled). Eyelet: 3, double wrapped to give 6
10 (Border)	Continental tent stitch	DMC Stranded Cotton 754	4
11	Spaced Cretan stitch	DMC Stranded Cotton 712	4
12	Lacy edge with four-sided stitch	DMC Pearl Cotton 948	1

6 FRAMED CROSS

(See Stitch Glossary page 157)
There are two areas where Framed cross is worked – the center of each of the side columns.

Start in a right angle (either formed by the peach or cream ribbon), not in one of the more difficult sloping areas. Work all the upright pairs of stitches first. Each pair is side by side with a gap of 4 threads before the next pair. When the whole area is complete, turn the frame a quarter turn and work the other pairs in the same way.

7 COBBLER FILLING

(See Stitch Glossary page 146)
There are two areas where this stitch is worked, the central top and bottom. Work both areas, starting in a right angle and work all the vertical stitches first. These stitches have a pattern of 2 and then 4 threads between each one. When complete turn the canvas a quarter turn and work the stitches in the same way.

8 TRELLIS BARS WITH CROSS STITCH VARIATION

(See Stitch Glossary page 171)
This is worked in the remaining two corners of the design above right and below left. The Trellis stitch is not pulled. The diagram on page 171 shows the upper-righthand quarter of one of the areas with the right angle formed by the cream ribbon (as with the previous stitch). Follow the diagram carefully so that the pattern fits exactly. Turn the diagram so that it matches up with each area.

9 TRELLIS BARS WITH DIAMOND EYELETS

(See Stitch Glossary page 171)
This is worked in two diagonally opposite corners of the design above left and below right.

The Trellis stitch is not pulled but the Diamond eyelets are. If you work the upper right-hand quarter of one of the areas first, the diagram on page 171 shows the right-angled corner formed by the cream ribbon on the canvas and will help you fit the stitch in to the area. Turn the diagram so that it matches up with each area as you come to it.

Now plunge both the peach and cream ribbons. It is easy to thread the peach ribbon through the size 20 needle and stitch down through the canvas but it will be necessary to enlarge a canvas hole before taking the cream ribbon through it. Pull all the ribbons firmly as the canvas will have been taken up slightly with the Pulled-thread stitches. Stitch in place with a sharp needle and 1 ply of floss back on itself.

10 CONTINENTAL TENT STITCH

(See Stitch Glossary page 169)
Immediately beyond and sharing with the Diagonal cross stitch over 4 threads which is couching the outer cream ribbon in place, work two rows of Continental tent stitch on all four sides of the completed design. Leave 6 threads of canvas bare for the peach ribbon and work a further 2 rows of Continental tent stitch with the same thread round the whole design.

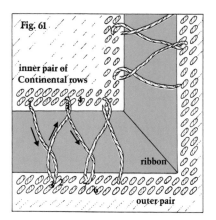

Fig. 61
inner pair of Continental rows
ribbon
outer pair

11 SPACED CRETAN STITCH

(Stitch Glossary page 167)
Lay the 6-mm (¼-in) peach ribbon along the channel between these rows of Tent stitch, over the bare threads of canvas. Leave an end of ribbon about 10 cm (4 in) long before taking the first stitch (it will be needed when finishing).

Follow Figure 61 and couch this ribbon in place with Spaced Cretan stitch. The stitch goes down in a hole that already has a Tent stitch in it and comes up one thread immediately inside it. The needle comes up behind the previous stitch to lace it in an 'S' shape. Hang on to the thread on the right side of the work until the needle comes up again and it is easy to place the thread in front of the needle point.

When turning a corner it will be necessary to catch the ribbon in place with a few stitches in 1 ply of the matching floss and a sharp needle. Follow the diagram and finish off the thread and start again on each corner. To finish the ribbon overlap about 10 cm (4 in) of ribbon with the tail you started with.

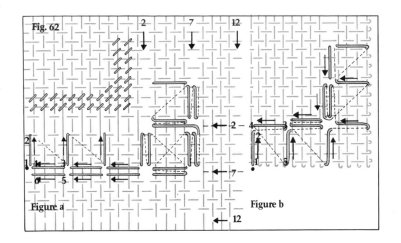

Fig. 62

Figure a

Figure b

12   LACY EDGE WITH FOUR-SIDED STITCH

(See Stitch Glossary page 157)
Working out from the outer rows of Tent stitch and with the canvas still on the frame, remove the second, seventh and twelfth threads on all sides. Do this by snipping the necessary canvas threads with a pointed pair of embroidery scissors about halfway along each side, then with the point of a needle pick the thread out completely.

Work the stitches shown in Figure 62a. Work from left to right, following the arrows; the vertical stitches are wrapped once and all the horizontal stitches are worked twice. Work the extra vertical wrap on the corners as shown where the canvas thread has been withdrawn.

Remove the canvas from the frame. Turn back the spare canvas (miter the corners) and finger press, aligning the canvas elements of both layers. Work a

second trip of this stitch where you started the first, following Figure 62b. Both the vertical and horizontal stitches are double-wrapped this time. At the corners be careful to line the threads up.

◇

MAKING-UP THE PIECE

Whip any spare canvas to the back of the canvas behind the ribbon and trim any excess. Do not damp and block as a normal pillow as the ribbons tend to **stretch** to a different amount from the cotton threads.

Mount the canvas on to an existing pillow front or piece of fabric of your choice which is cut about 10 cm (4 in) larger on all sides and make into the front of a pillow.

If a wallhanging or tray top is preferred allow a little extra space on all sides of the stitched piece with a mount or fabric-covered board so that the lacy edge can be appreciated.

Inspirational Projects

T his is a glimpse at some of the beautiful projects that lend themselves to Pulled thread and hopefully will inspire you to try some designs with the stitches you have become acquainted with in the previous two projects.

As with many of the Inspirational sections in this book, most of the pieces here have Pulled-thread stitches used with other canvas-work techniques. This makes the choice of stitch, whether it is a geometric area or a curved shape, easier and the stitch that looks good in the shape is the one to use. It does not matter whether the stitch is a traditional canvas one or whether it has its origins in embroidery.

The two pillows both have geometric designs. 'Islamic Tiles' is worked in off-white and 'Victorian Rose Trellis' in soft apricots. Geometrics are always a good choice for the first few projects in a new technique; compensation stitches or trying to decide what part of a stitch to do or not to do to get a pleasing curve is something that comes with experience. Generally speaking, the more comfortable one is with a particular stitch before attempting curved shapes the better. The other reason that geometric designs are so high in my popularity list is there usually is no boring background!

'Islamic Tiles' was originally designed as a multi-colored sampler until I realized that with so many different stitches it would look far more sophisticated in one color. It is worked on 18-mesh regular canvas with Appleton's Crewel wool and floss; four star shapes worked in Florentine stitches are surrounded by linked squares and diamonds worked with traditional canvas stitches and it is only the background that is worked with Pulled thread, a small scale stitch as each area is not large.

The 'Victorian Rose Trellis' design came from an early twentieth-century wind wheel found in Sichuan, China. The center is four-way Florentine and the border a small Florentine scallop pattern. The wide ribbon has been stitched to the canvas rather than cutting canvas threads to plunge the ends. Either side of the ribbon Cross stitch is worked over 2-ply Appleton's Crewel wool to give it extra bulk.

Spaced Cretan stitch, as used in the border in the Advanced Pulled-thread pillow, is used over all the ribbons, but with a gap of 6 threads between the stitches. Among the other stitches you will already be familiar with are the two areas of the Trellis, and Trellis and Diamond Eyelet worked in all four corners. However, any of the stitches you enjoyed working in the previous Pulled-thread projects would fit well.

The Scissor case is exposed canvas rather than Pulled thread but it is so charming I wanted to include it; it also gives you a very pretty idea for a small gift for a fellow stitcher, and they are the people who really appreciate something stitched as they know how long it takes! This was worked by Mrs Julie Houser and given to me while I was at Woodlawn Plantation in Virginia in 1986; it is now a kit available from the gift shop at the house. The case is ecru pearl cotton and seed pearls on brown canvas and has totally changed my mind about disliking brown canvas – I cannot wait to use it for something.

The inspiration for the flowers in the two small pieces, the purse and the picture, worked on congress cloth, comes from Elizabethan embroideries; flowers appear countless times on pillows and items of women's dress. The purse has the background worked with a small Florentine stitch and the picture was worked on a pale blue canvas which was left unworked.

In these two pieces floss was used for Pulled thread, traditional canvas and embroidery stitches, including variations of Chain stitch, French knots and Bullions.

You will notice that the framed piece has, in fact, got glass covering it and in Finishing and Aftercare on page 130 I recommend not covering your work; in self-defence this piece was a class project and needed protection as it was to be handled frequently. However, the bevelled mount is extremely thick so it holds the glass well away from the stitching.

What can be said about this wonderful mirror worked in one of my classes by Joan Downes, except to say that a friend of hers got married especially so that she could have a similar one made as a wedding present!

A number of the motifs from the mirror are diagrammed in Figure 63 for you to use when planning something for yourself. Refer to the enlarging and marking techniques on page 15. Unless you plan to work the background with solid stitching make as few marks as possible on the canvas and keep a drawing by you for the fine-line detail such as the stalks.

When planning something like this my favorite way is to make a number of tracings of each motif, cut them out and arrange them on a sheet of paper the same size as the proposed project and move them around until I am happy with the way they look. Stick them down and only then mark the canvas. You may remember that this is the way I designed the Hydrangea Rug on page 28 and it works well, whatever the scale.

By studying the photograph of the mirror on page 108 you will see how each flower is balanced with some petals in solid stitchery and some in Pulled thread. In almost all cases the outlines of the motifs are defined with Couched thread, Split or Outline stitch.

The border of the mirror is Cushion stitch in isolated boxes with a single row of Continental tent around each one. It is wise not to have too strong a border on

Fig. 63

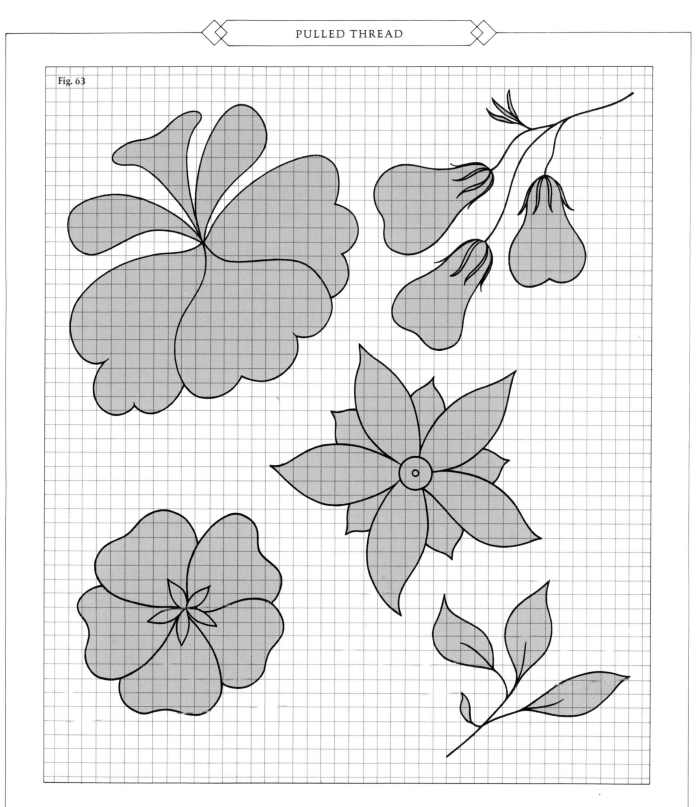

a framed piece; first, the mount or decorative wood of the frame sets it off and second, since canvas is a natural fabric it is almost impossible to get it sufficiently straight alongside the hard edges of the metal or wood frame.

The background is Skip tent, which is Tent stitched worked with a fine thread close to the same shade as the canvas, on alternate canvas threads only.

Up in the left-hand corner the stitcher's initials are worked in the same fine thread but in ordinary Continental tent stitch, a very nice subtle finishing touch.

CHAPTER SEVEN

A LOOK AT HISTORY

The painting 'The Quilting Party' sets the scene for this glimpse at the history of embroidery and, in particular, needlepoint.

Plain stitching has always been used to make and mark household linen and to remodel and reutilize worn garments, while fancy stitching was worked when a community became more leisured. At all times needlework has been a social pursuit.

The unveiling of a new quilt, like the one above, was frequently the equivalent of the announcement of an engagement according to Susan Burrows Swan, the associate registrar of the Winterthur Museum; this painting clearly shows the guests, including the future bridegroom, arriving in their hats at the very moment a young girl is easing the quilt off the frame; a musician has started to play, the table is set and tea things are ready in preparation for the celebration. The hastily swept floor, the broom left out and the

ABOVE: *Needlework of all kinds and especially quilting was a social occasion. In the geometric designs all the seams were straight and so anyone who could thread a needle could help stitch. This American painting attributed to John Lewis and painted in 1813 depicts the completion of a quilt. The design of the quilt is 'Double Wedding Ring' which indicates, with the young gentleman being guided by the girl, that this is indeed an engagement party. From the Henry Francis du Pont Winterthur Museum, Delaware, USA.*

FACING PAGE: *An English double casket dated 1650–1700. It is stitched mainly in Satin stitch with Outline stitch around the figures and French knots for the lady and gentleman's hair. The ground fabric is silk satin on a wooden core and the stitching is in brightly colored silks and silver plate. From the Burrell Collection, Glasgow, Scotland.*

needlework baskets not yet cleared away amuse me – it reminds me of how often I have finished things at the eleventh hour.

Museums with collections of needlework are wonderful places to study the designs, techniques and threads that were available at different periods. I have given a list of some of the more important collections on page 174, but here I should like to explore briefly the people, their conditions and surroundings, and their choice of projects and show how many aspects of needlepoint are the same today.

To make the history of stitching come alive and to put it in its context of a woman's life, I have described important periods in detail: the sixteenth and seventeenth centuries in Europe, the mid-eighteenth century in the United States and finally, the similarities and differences between needlewomen on both sides of the Atlantic in the nineteenth century.

◇

ELIZABETHAN NEEDLEWORK

We start our look at needlepoint with Elizabethan England for many reasons; first, the strong rule of the Tudors had put an end to the unsettled years of the Wars of the Roses and had led to increasing prosperity of many landed and merchant-class families. This in turn meant more comfortable homes. Second, the dour asceticism of Henry VII had been replaced by the flamboyant style of Henry VIII, which reached its zenith with the long reign of his daughter, Elizabeth I, who lived from 1533 to 1603.

Elizabeth I loved both working embroidery (though she was not as prolific as her cousin Mary, Queen of Scots) and wearing richly embroidered and decorated clothes; she believed in being seen by her subjects and made constant 'progresses' around the English countryside.

The Broderers Company was granted its first charter in 1561 and while many of the professional embroiderers among its members were employed on banners, coats of arms and hangings for the livery companies, many of the greater households had one or more professionals (frequently men) to help with the larger pieces of embroidery and overall designs for the home.

Tent stitch became popular as a stitch to copy the earlier imported tapestries and table carpets. The construction of this stitch gives a larger proportion of thread on the reverse of the ground fabric and so it is extremely hardwearing. Therefore, many more Tent stitch pieces of needlework have survived.

Good steel needles became more widely available and imports of silk and metal threads increased. In fact, Continental influences were extremely important: Elizabeth I's predecessor and half-sister, Mary I, was half-Spanish and married a Spaniard; Mary, Queen of Scots was herself half-French and was brought up in the French court. She had also been married to Francis I of France before his early death.

Printed books became more accessible; most manor houses, however modest, would have had their library, so the needleworker would have been able to refer to illustrated herbals and bestiaries for plants and animals of which they had no personal knowledge. Specific pattern books began to appear, expressly for the guidance of the gentlewoman and her needlework.

Young girls were taught needlework by their mothers or, in some instances, they were sent to another family, possibly with a slightly higher social status, to learn to stitch and generally prepare to become a good wife. Early samplers, as we have seen in the Cross stitch chapter (see page 70), were purely worked as a record for lettering and household linens. Even when girls were sent away to another family or to a small organized group outside the house this was the type of work that they would have tackled first. It was not until later on with the introduction of dame schools and then boarding schools that more ambitious pieces were attempted.

Therefore, while the Elizabethan canvas worker, made beautiful things, these were all extremely practical and were sorely needed in the house of the time. As explained, Tent stitch was much favored and as it is hardwearing a comparatively large number of pieces have survived. Much information about needlepoint comes to us through wills and inventories of the period, where it features prominently – and shows how important it was.

Furniture was very plain and simple, chairs hardly existed and most people would sit on wooden stools and benches so that pillows were necessary to make them more comfortable; tables and side cupboards (later sideboards) were plain and therefore covered with richly patterned table carpets; rooms were draughty (glass in the windows, having only recently been introduced, was extremely costly) and beds were found in most rooms (specific rooms set aside as bedrooms came much later); therefore, wall- and bed-hangings were much needed for both warmth and privacy.

During the period designs changed due to both fashion and the materials that became available. The earlier Elizabethan pieces had stiff, formal motifs from the Eastern table carpets the needleworkers set out to copy. Gradually, the English love of naturalistic flower forms and being able to refer to the many herbals of the period led to more freeflowing flower designs; improvements in linen weaving resulted in wider ground fabrics so that the need for patterns which masked frequent joins became less important. Rich woven velvets started to be imported from Italy – thus a fashion for needlepoint 'slips' grew; these slips were individual motifs, frequently flowers, stitched on fine canvas, trimmed and applied on velvet panels, usually with a couched thread around the edge to hide the raw canvas edges. These became very popular for bedhangings as they were so much faster to finish than completely stitched work and also draped better as hangings.

◇

THE SEVENTEENTH CENTURY

The photograph on page 112 shows an embroidered casket produced between 1650–1700. This is the date quoted by the Burrell Collection in Glasgow, Scotland, where it is on show; however, I doubt that it was made during the Cromwellian period (1649–60) as such a flamboyant piece would have been considered very decadent during the years of Puritan rule in England.

This double casket shows a very interesting development in the short period since the end of the Elizabethan era: although the interior of the casket was fitted out to take writing materials, jewelry or needlework, it is far less utilitarian than the items discussed so far.

Frequently these caskets, although not this one, had raised or stump-work decorations; this is embroidery with a three-dimensional effect made by covering small wooden figure

A George I wing chair c. 1720. This is a particularly fine example still glowing in its original colors. It is interesting how carefully the needleworker planned the motifs for each area, including matching the large blue flower that runs over the front seam on the chair seat but did not mind that the background color varied here and there from ginger brown to creamy yellow.

shapes with stitchery and then applying them to the surface of the work. Themes for these caskets are generally taken from the Old Testament and, as in this example, the biblical figures are frequently modelled on Charles I and his Queen, Henrietta Maria of France. Although Charles I was beheaded by Cromwell, the royal couple were much revered for the rest of the century by the type of lady who would have done this fancy work.

The unrecorded stitcher of this piece would probably have worked a few less ambitious samplers beforehand and this would have been the final piece worked under supervision.

The reasons for the popularity of these charming (and in this instance superbly worked) decorative pieces as opposed to the practical pieces worked only a few decades previously are many. Woven fabrics became far more available, furniture became ornate, decorated with marquetry, veneer and gesso and did not need to be covered, and there were tremendous advances in house-building (aided by the Great Fire of London in 1666 when a large proportion of the City was totally destroyed and had to be rebuilt).

Upholstered chairs were gradually introduced and by the reign of George I at the beginning of the eighteenth century, wing chairs such as this one on page 115 with contemporary needlepoint covers worked in wool on fine canvas were the fashion. This design was worked in Tent stitch but Florentine was also a popular choice for upholstered chairs.

◇

THE EIGHTEENTH CENTURY IN THE UNITED STATES

In the early days of the American colonies the women, especially in rural areas, had to produce the fabric and yarn before they could even sew; they had to rear sheep for wool or grow flax for linen thread and then spin it. Frequently, it was then sent out to professionals to weave and dye but only then did the making of garments or household items take place. Little wonder that worn clothes were constantly repaired or remodelled, then cut down into smaller garments, using all the bits that were still all right, and finally they were cut into patches for bed quilts.

Even in the towns cotton was very expensive as it was not until the mid-nineteenth century that it was successfully grown in the United States. Silk was even more expensive; although some families did have mulberry trees and reared silkworms it was too time-consuming to be commercially successful.

The upbringing of girls was not that different from English girls of the same period: they were prepared for marriage. Girls were frequently sent away to another family but, unlike Britain where they would have joined the family as an equal, more often in the United States they were indentured for a set number of years; it relieved the girl's family of a person to support and gave a relatively cheap servant to the other family.

For girls staying with their own families there would be local classes held by a woman in her own home, where they would practise needlework and knitting and in some instances, reading and a little arithmetic. After attending this dame school (there was no set length for the course) young ladies could proceed to sewing classes, more formal and frequently situated in town; out-of-town girls would either stay with relations or even sometimes with the teacher's own family: besides learning more advanced needlework, staying in the city enabled a young girl to enlarge her circle of acquaintances, and especially to meet young men.

After 1750 some sewing schools began to offer dancing, drawing and occasionally English and French. Samplers of increasing complexity were the normal project for the young ladies and, as in Britain, were long and narrow and worked on linen. All looms of this period were narrow and therefore only produced narrow fabric.

The period of the finest American needlework was from 1700–1780, worked by women from the prosperous classes who enjoyed canvas work, crewel, lace and silk embroidery; embellishment for clothing and pocket books or purses were very popular and chairs and upholstered pieces appealed to the even more ambitious.

Most businesses were situated very close, if

not in or under the living quarters; frequently a merchant would invite a customer into his private rooms to take some refreshment during negotiations and so the furniture and interior decoration were very important. Married women seldom ventured out alone except to church, on a rare shopping expedition for things she did not produce in the home, or to visit friends or nearby relations. Reading both American and English authors such as Jane Austen, the Brontë sisters and Harriet Beecher Stowe it becomes apparent how so much recreation took place in the home or at the house of a friend. So a wife could add immeasurably to the comfort and style of the house with her needlework. It was one of the few ways a wife could help convey the level of her family's prosperity and social standing.

Canvas work was done in all the colonies during the seventeenth and eighteenth centuries; Tent stitch was popular for scenes, most famous being the Fishing Lady pictures done in the Boston area in the mid-eighteenth century.

Judging by the number of surviving pieces, the Florentine or Irish stitch was the most common canvaswork stitch, no doubt popular as it worked up so quickly, covering 4 or 6 threads of canvas rather than the single one covered by Tent stitch. Pocket books (see below) were a particular favorite; both men and women tended to carry their valuables around with them; men used them for money, wills and promissory notes and women used them for jewelry and sewing items. Florentine or Irish stitch was also used for upholstered chairs, fire-screens and wall-pockets.

Cross stitch was widely used for marking linens but infrequently for canvas work as it was considered gross compared with Tent-stitch pieces.

Queen stitch or Rococo was also used even though it was difficult to execute well and looked best in the costly silk; it was, therefore, used only on small items such as pincushions and small purses. (For those of you who would like to try this stitch I have graphed it on page 162 even though it is not used in any of the projects in the book.)

As with plain sewing for the ordinary woman, fancy sewing afforded the wealthy woman some relaxation as she could supervise children and servants and continue to stitch herself. However, unlike plain sewing, fancy work could not be done at night as neither candles nor firelight could produce enough light by which to do the fine work. In

Four American pocket books stitched in Florentine or Irish stitch and showing popular designs all dated between 1740 and 1790. The pocket book on the far right is one of the most simple zigzag designs with only the elongated V-shape in the centre to add interest. The 'Flame' and 'Diamond with Diamond' designs (below and left) both have random use of color combinations, whether for reasons of economy or whether intended to add sophistication is not clear. The 'Carnation' design (center) is a fairly complicated traditional design.

Being eighteenth-century pieces, they are all worked in soft shades. I have charted both the 'Flame' and the 'Carnation' design for you to stitch in your own color schemes (see pages 118 and 119). From the Henry Francis du Pont Winterthur Museum, Delaware, USA.

fact, a woman was frequently forced to stop this sort of stitching around the age of forty to forty-five as eyeglasses were uncommon and anyway, were not effective enough for this type of work.

Social visiting, leaving one's visiting card, taking tea and playing cards became fashionable in Britain about the mid-eighteenth century and in the United States shortly after. In the well-to-do circles where these ritualized get-togethers took place, it was important to appear relaxed and at ease; if people dropped in it was smart to be seen to be doing embroidery, sketching or painting and for the household to be running efficiently.

One of the sidelines of the social stitching that I find fascinating are the beautiful workboxes and needlework tools, ivory and silver needlecases, intricate clamps and inlaid pinholders that the ladies were able to show off. Much interest has recently been shown in these items and I have included some suggestions on page 174 for further reading.

Towards the end of the eighteenth century the position of women in the United States underwent a dramatic change; women were encouraged by their menfolk to be lavishly self-indulgent, but at the same time their intellectual awareness increased – they attended lectures, wrote poetry and published articles and books. The boarding schools that had formerly taught needlework realized the need for more academic subjects.

The English feminist Mary Wollstonecraft's writings were read by a wide and intellectual readership; Benjamin Franklin and other men encouraged women to prepare themselves to be intelligent, responsible citizens of the new republic.

These newly aware women had different ideas about their handcrafts and what they wished to achieve with their needlework; they wanted bright silky effects but they were not prepared to devote the many hours that women in previous generations had done; frequently skies, faces and water were painted on the ground fabric and it was only the clothes and plants that were stitched.

◇

THE VICTORIAN ERA

Moving on to the second quarter of the nineteenth century, the industrial revolution in Britain brought wealth to a far wider group of people (but abject poverty to many more); however, these newly rich had little or no taste, and fashions for various types of needle- and fancy work came and went with great speed.

The dawning of the industrial age on both sides of the Atlantic had an immediate effect on most men and a more gradual one on their womenfolk. Whereas in the past, men frequently worked close to or even within the home, involving their wives with entertaining customers, the need for automation and machinery moved the place of employment away, removing any partnership or sense of equality; the system separated the home from the business, the husband from the wife. The man was the earner and the wife the homemaker.

Servants were cheap to employ and were necessary to impart a sense of affluence to even a modest family; therefore, Victorian housewives had time to fill and so became zealous needleworkers, making accessories, both practical and ludicrous.

Berlin work became popular about 1830; the original designs were hand-painted and used attractive shades of wool. However, the idea of Berlin work became so popular that coarser canvas than the original was used, colors became more gaudy and, after the introduction of analine dyes around 1856, frankly lurid. Subjects became sentimental and a vogue for Turkey work, long loops of thread stitched and trimmed into a pile were great dust catchers.

Associated with the popularity of Berlin work there was a craze for beadwork mantel hangings, pillows, firescreens and other items such as this well-preserved pair of tie-backs. During this period the beads were frequently sewn on, four or five at a time, on one stitch rather than each bead on an individual stitch, so that now many Victorian beaded pieces are in a poor state of repair with a lot of beads missing.

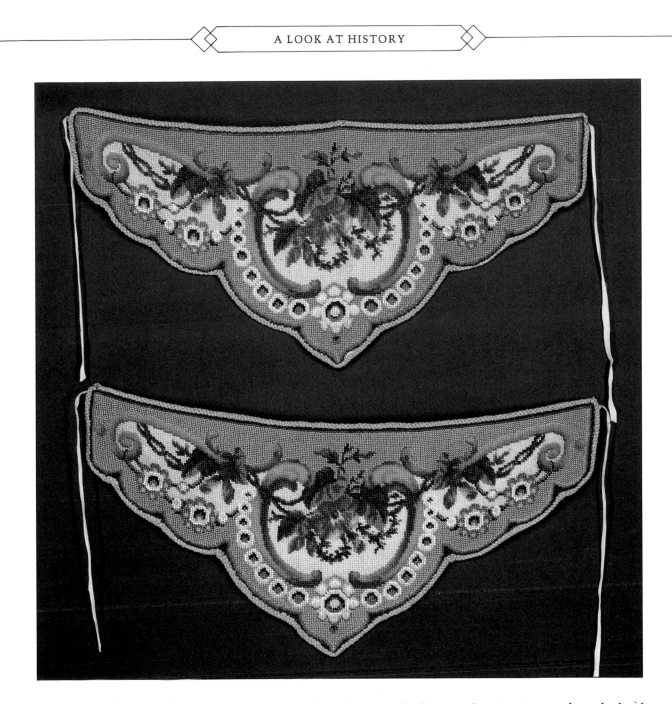

A pair of mid-nineteenth-century English beadwork curtain tie-backs with a finger-knotted cord around the edge.

I have adapted two of the Florentine patterns from the pocket books at the Winterthur Museum (see page 117). Pattern One is the 'Flame' design and Pattern Two the 'Carnation' design.

◇

PATTERN ONE

(See Figure 64)
This is an interesting design because the 'candleflame'-shape outline is in a very deep shade of gray blue or even black and each area is filled in with random combinations of copper rusts and golden yellows with a little gray blue at the base of each area.

Whether the stitcher simply had small quantities of wool left from other projects to use up or whether it was planned, it makes a handsome piece. Unusual color combinations set in a framework such as this are discussed in more

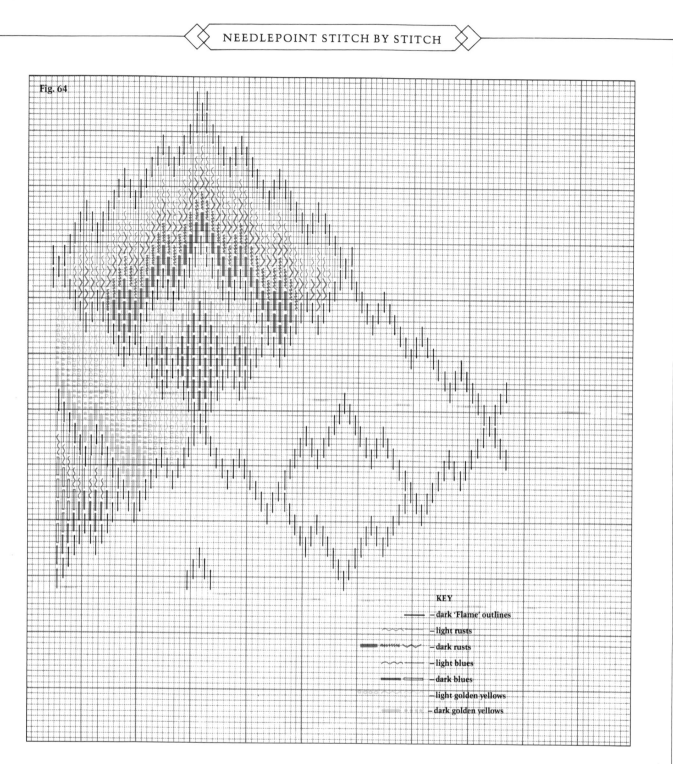

Fig. 64

KEY

——————— – dark 'Flame' outlines

∿∿∿∿∿∿ – light rusts

▬▬▬▬ ∿∿∿∿∿ ∿∿ – dark rusts

∿∿∿∿ —— – light blues

▬▬▬▬ ▬▬▬ – dark blues

—————— – light golden yellows

————— – dark golden yellows

detail in the Florentine chapter on page 51.

To copy the design, start in the center of the canvas and set up the dark 'flame' outlines. All 'flames' have a four-stepped point and an inner two-stepped point worked in the same dark colour. All stitches are over 4 threads of canvas. When the outlines are complete, fill in each area in a combination that pleases you. On the chart I have shown some ideas. If you want to echo the colors used in the original pocket book I suggest Blue Spruce (530) for the outlines and Rust and Tobacco shades for filling in from the Paterna Persian range; and Peacock (647) for the outlines and Flame and Honeysuckle shades from the Appleton's Crewel range for filling in.

For a stool top or chair cover I suggest using a limited range of shades as in the original pocket book. For a pillow that will sit on a plain sofa it would be a wonderful way of using any harmonious scraps of wool you may have — even with this scheme, the outlines should all be one colour.

◇

PATTERN TWO

(See Figure 65)

This is a large design based on a carnation flower; all the stitches are over 4 threads. The design is a half-drop pattern. To work the design start in the center of the canvas so that the pattern balances. Set up the lozenge shapes in a deep color and then work the outline for the flower in the same color. In the original pattern the flower is filled in with three shades of rose pink, two above the central dark line of the flower already worked and a deeper one below. The 'shadow' behind the flower is soft blue; there is a single row of cream immediately inside the lozenge and the rest of the background between the cream and soft blue is in shades of yellow.

If you want to echo the colors, I suggest Old Blues (510) for the outlines and Rusty Rose and Old Gold for filling in from the Paterna Persian range; and Mid-Blue (158) for the outlines and Honeysuckle and Bright Terracotta for filling in from the Appleton's Crewel range.

This design would lend itself to large-scale pieces such as a duet stool, a wing chair or, if you were very brave, a headboard for your bed.

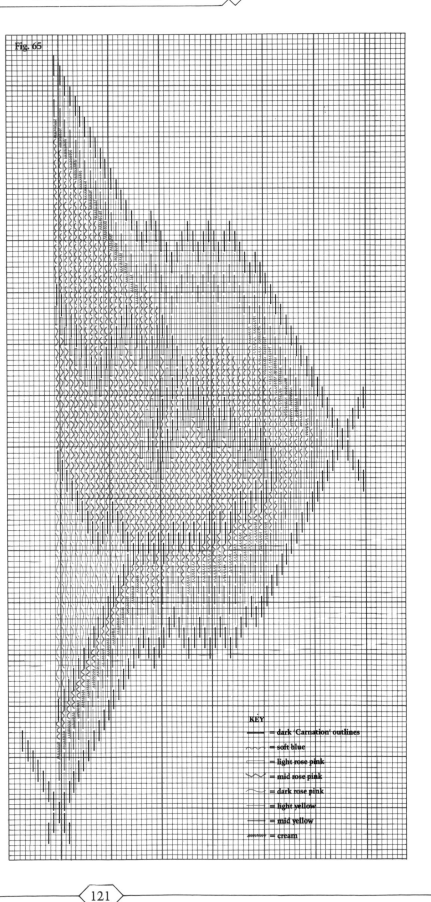

Fig. 65

KEY

= dark 'Carnation' outlines
= soft blue
= light rose pink
= mid rose pink
= dark rose pink
= light yellow
= mid yellow
= cream

CHAPTER EIGHT

*F*INISHING AND *A*FTERCARE

◇

FINISHING

Throughout this book professional finishing has been recommended. However, knowing the principles of how various items should be made up will help a great deal at the stitching stage and, if you wish to make things up yourself, all the necessary information is here.

Remember that there is a major investment in the stitched piece – your time. Any help that you can enlist to make the finished piece look wonderful is worth it. One golden rule is to never even start an unusual project without either knowing how to finish it or knowing someone who will do it well for you and at a reasonable price.

Therefore, the main aim of the finishing section of this chapter is to acquaint you with suitable projects to work in needlepoint, what finishing touches are appropriate, how to prepare templates, and to make cords, fringes and tassels, besides the basic blocking and making-up techniques for needlepoint in general.

Aftercare of your own needlepoint is explained in the second part of this chapter on page 132 – the day-to-day maintenance, cleaning and storage of your pieces. Restoration of valuable antique pieces has to be done by professionals and therefore, is not covered in this book.

All the instructions given in this chapter refer only to projects made with evenweave canvas. Plastic canvas, which really is designed to be home finished, is used in the Simple Tent stitch project on page 21 and full making-up instructions for it are given with the project. Interlock canvas has not been used for anything in the book as it is not so versatile and should not be treated in the same way as evenweave canvas.

◇

PLANNING THE WORK

Before starting to stitch any piece of canvas make a note of the overall measurement of the canvas. In the case of an irregular shape such as an upholstered-over chair or a curved stool, make an accurate template of the area to be stitched.

Even if the project is circular or curved in shape, always stitch on a square or rectangular piece of canvas (see Figures 66 and 67). It is easier to mount on the frame and also to block when stitched if the canvas is rectangular or square in shape.

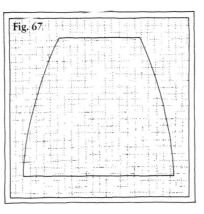

Fig. 66

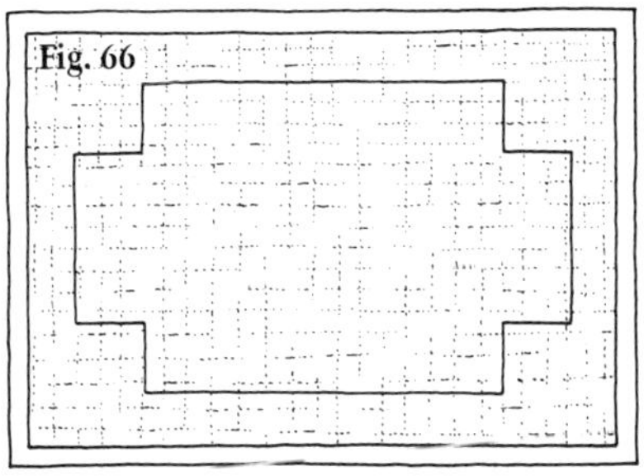

Fig. 67

◇

TEMPLATES

As part of your planning for any upholstered piece or a drape tie-back it is wise to make a template in fabric. Even with a simple chair cushion the measurement across the front is frequently wider than at the back and a template will be useful.

Upholstered-over chairs and stools often have corners where the canvas will be turned in and therefore, it is not necessary to stitch that area. Sometimes chairs have a central back post and two flaps of canvas need to be planned and worked to go either-side of this post and down to the back-rail.

Take into account the condition of the upholstery. If the cushion sags and needs extra stuffing before you re-cover, allow an extra inch or two on the canvas as the stitched area over the new stuffing will be larger.

Your working template can simply be the old piece of fabric that you take off the chair (it will be easy to see any areas that were turned in – the colors here will still be fresh). You can make one too from calico or old sheeting.

For drop-in seats make a template by laying old sheeting over the seat and mark all round where the wooden part of the seat begins (see Figure 68). Add 1 cm (½ in) extra all round. Cut out the pattern marked on the sheeting and mark the outline on canvas, leaving an extra 5 cm (2 in) all round. Do not cut it out (see Figure 69).

For upholstered-over chairs spread the fabric over the cushion area and pin it along the front edge with dressmaker's pins. Then smooth it out, straight along the grain of the fabric and

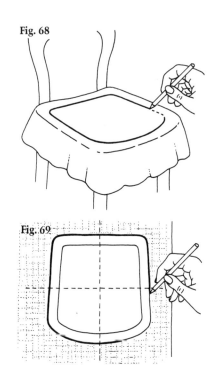

Fig. 68

Fig. 69

pin along the back, taking it through any decorative posts on the back of the chair (it might help to cut some of the excess fabric away at this stage). Smooth it out to the sides and again mark with dressmaker's pins. Tuck any excess fabric in on the corners and indicate with a line of pins. Also mark the 'flat' area of the cushion so that any motif does not fall over the edges!

If the chair is a complicated shape or needs complete re-webbing and new upholstery you may like to enlist at this stage the help of the upholsterer who will eventually mount the work for you.

Templates are also essential for drape tie-backs; the length of the tie-back depends so much on the number of widths of fabric used in each drape; whether the drapes are interlined; whether you want the tie-backs curved or straight and how looped back they need to be. An existing fabric tie-back can act as a pattern or try different shapes made from calico.

◇

BLOCKING

Always remember that silk must never be wet, congress cloth that is not completely covered with stitchery will watermark and any painted canvas you may have bought should be tested first to prove that the paint used is waterproof. Satin-faced ribbons appear to stretch more than other fibers, so avoid dampening them. In each case, it is better to be safe than sorry. I always label a piece with silk in it before handing it over to my finisher and you may well find some shops declining to make up a piece they did not paint themselves – they cannot be held responsible for the quality of the paint that is under your stitching and which they cannot see!

◇

MATERIALS NEEDED FOR BLOCKING

Have a thick board large enough to take the flat canvas. If it is wood it must not be painted, stained or varnished. ('Cellatex' or 'Gold Bond' board are fibrous, easy to push pins into and good for this job.) You can buy special blocking boards ready-marked with squares and rectangles which you may wish to get if you plan to do a lot of finishing.

You need also rust-proof thumb tacks or stainless-steel push pins; old sheeting; cheesecloth or muslin; a small hand spray and clean water, distilled if necessary; and a steam iron for steam pressing.

◇

DAMPENING METHOD

This is usually the most effective way to block needlepoint unless you are in any way uncertain of the fastness of any of the materials used, for example, the silk thread or painted canvas.

Cover the board with the sheeting and fasten it securely. Draw a pencil outline of the original canvas measurements on the sheet, making sure that the corners are square. Leaving the binding tape or stitched edges of the canvas intact, gently spray the back of the work with clean water using a hand-spray. Wet only the yarns, not the canvas; turn the work over and mount on the board. It will be necessary to pull and then pin the four corners of the canvas to the four marked corners, face up.

With an irregular design check the shape of the worked area as the blocking proceeds. It must match the template or pattern you made before the stitching. You may have to remove and reset some of the thumb tacks; and they may cause slight waves between each thumb tack along the edge of the canvas where they pull. This does not matter as this will be excess canvas that is cut off later.

When satisfied, allow the piece to dry naturally for a day or so in a horizontal position.

◇

STEAM-IRON METHOD

This is the alternative method to use if you are nervous of anything that might not be colorfast. Cover the board with the sheeting, fasten it securely and draw a pencil outline of the original canvas measurements on the sheet. Leave the binding tape or stitched edge intact and pull and pin the four corners of the canvas to the four marked corners on the sheeting, face up.

Wet a piece of cheesecloth or

muslin, wring it out and place it on top of the canvas. Fill the steam iron and allow it to reach the correct temperature for the yarn being used, hold it over the work and get as much steam into the piece as possible, barely touching the work at all. Pull the edges straight, working from one corner along to the next, basting the canvas through the tape or hem.

Never let the weight of the iron rest on the stitches as they would be crushed flat. The steam will dampen the piece slightly, softening the dressing that is put in during manufacture, allowing the canvas threads to be re-aligned back into shape. Leave the muslin in place and allow the piece to dry naturally for a day or so in a horizontal position.

Only when the piece is completely dry (whichever method has been used), remove it from the board and trim off the tape and excess canvas to about 8–12 threads.

After blocking, the following techniques are general to many projects.

◇

HEMMING CANVAS

This method applies to square and rectangular pieces of work such as rugs or bell pulls. Trim the excess canvas to approximately 8 threads and turn this excess canvas under. Use a sharp sewing needle and strong thread to hem this to the back of the work and pierce the canvas threads that are at right angles to the edge, not through the canvas holes as this will simply strip off the few remaining threads from the piece (see Figure 70).

With a large piece of work on coarse canvas (such as the

Fig. 70

'Pigs in Clover' rug) you may prefer to cut the binding tape and excess canvas off just ahead of the hemming in order to avoid the large-mesh canvas fraying.

◇

MITERED CORNERS

This will give a crisp square corner. Cut off the binding but leave 2 cm (¾ in) minimum of canvas for the stitching. Fold the corner diagonally so that you can

Fig. 71

Fig. 72

Fig. 73

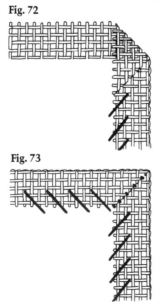

just see the corner needlepoint stitch (see Figure 71), and finger press firmly in place. As the hemming is worked up to the corner fold first one side in (see Figure 72) and then the other. Sew the two bias folds together to prevent fraying (see Figure 73).

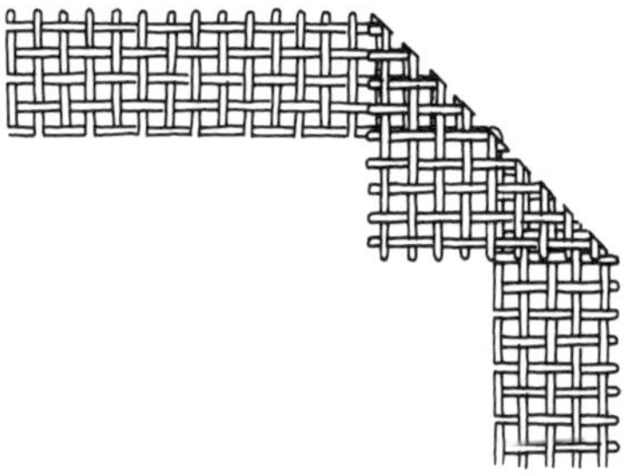

Fig. 74

Fig. 75

Fig. 76

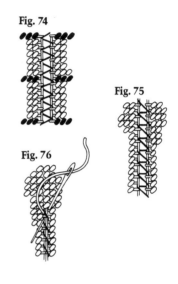

◇

JOINING CANVAS

Miter the corners and hem each piece as explained. Then, using heavy thread for coarse canvas and a finer one for finer canvas, stitch the two pieces together with a zig-zag stitch. Use alternate canvas threads on each piece (see Figure 74). If a horizontal stitch is worked over each pair of canvas threads one side would tend to slide up and offset any needlepoint pattern that repeats across the join (see Figure 75).

Make sure that the canvas threads are used for the joining stitches, not just the thread itself as this would quickly pull and there would be no strength in the stitches. Cover the seam with a row of Continental tent stitch in either a matching or contrasting color (see Figure 76).

◇

DECORATIVE FINISHES

CORDS

Cords made in the same yarns used to stitch the needlepoint add greatly to the custom look of a piece. In different thicknesses they can be used for so many things; fine ones can edge tiebacks or ties of the vests, medium-thick ones look great as an edging for pillows or to attach them to the back posts of chairs, and really thick ones can be used for suspending a wallhanging from a decorative pole.

It helps to have two people when making a cord; small hand machines do exist and you can also use a large hook on the wall for holding one end but a second pair of hands is best of all.

Measure the length of cord needed; for example, measure the four sides of a pillow. Multiply this measurement by three. Cut two pieces of yarn this length; these can be two different colors or both the same. If the yarn is thin you may wish to cut four lengths and treat each pair as one; for example, two blue and two yellow lengths. Knot both ends together and trim the knots neatly. Place these knots in a central position and both you and your friend place a pencil or long smooth stick in the loops at either end. Holding the yarn taut at all times, twist the yarn by rotating the pencils clockwise, both at the same speed. When it is twisted quite tight, still holding it taut, one person should grab the knot in the center and give the other person their end. Gradually release the cord at the middle knot, the non-pencil end. Twist the first 5 cm (2 in) counter-

clockwise, then hand over hand release it 5 cm (2 in) at a time, smoothing down the length. It will twist itself into a cord ready to be used.

◇

TASSELS

Simple tassels are quick to make and can be used for pillow corners, bell-pull ends and even belt closures (with a cord caught inside).

Uncut yarn is needed and it can either be wrapped around your fingers or a piece of card. If you want a number of matching tassels, for example, for the four corners of a pillow, use a card so that each tassel is exactly the same length. The bulk of the finished tassel will depend on the number of wraps around the card so, again, if you want the tassels to match, count the number of wraps in each tassel. Always make the tassel at least 1 cm (½ in) longer than you wish the finished one to measure – it can then be trimmed to the exact measurement.

Tassels in either a single color or in a mixture of shades used in the needlepoint piece look good. Pearl cotton, metallics and even the narrow double-faced satin ribbons used in the Advanced Pulled-Thread project would be suitable, depending on the effect you want.

Once you have wrapped the required fullness around a card of the right size slip another length of yarn (approximately 5–8 cm/2–3 in long) in to gather the loops together (see Figure 77). Tie this thread a number of times to hold the yarn securely. Cut the loops at the other end of the card (see Figure 78).

With another length of yarn (approximately 25 cm/10 in),

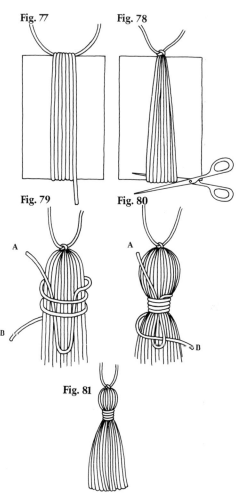

Fig. 77   Fig. 78

Fig. 79   Fig. 80

Fig. 81

wrap the tassel, about one-fifth to one-quarter-way down to form a neck. Leaving short length A lay a loop of yarn face down flat on the prepared tassel. Wrap over the two strands that form the loop and go round the tassel twice (see Figure 79); put the working end B through the loop; pull up at A to secure the loop and thread the end inside the neck (see Figure 80). Trim off the ends.

The finished tassel can be trimmed straight or rounded to the exact length required (see Figure 81). The skirt of the tassel can be combed gently with a large-toothed comb. Paterna Persian yarn fluffs up beautifully.

FRINGES

As with cords and tassels commercial fringes can be purchased ready made but frequently they are made in a blend of synthetics that is not compatible with your work, let alone the right color. Making your own fringe, using the yarns used in the piece, is obviously the perfect answer. Uncut yarn has to be used for the plain, knotted and alternate knotted fringes.

PLAIN FRINGES: To make a plain one, make a length of card about 15 cm (6 in) and to the depth of the proposed fringe plus 1 cm (½ in). Place the card up against the edge of the piece where the fringe will be added, loop the wool over the card and take a stitch into the canvas (not just the stitchery). Then make a small holding stitch to anchor the previous long one (see Figure 82).

Continue in this way, one loop

Fig. 82

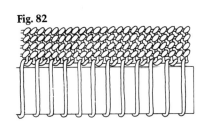

Fig. 83

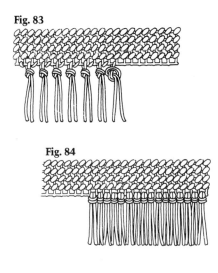

Fig. 84

round the card, one holding stitch, one loop round the card and so on. If the fringe is to be cut, do this before removing the card. Give the fringe a final trim.

This plain fringe can then be knotted in groups with an overhand knot (see Figure 83). It can be knotted in equal numbers of loops, or to make a more sophisticated fringe, alternating groups can be knotted.

LOOPED FRINGES: Ready-cut yarn may be used for this fringe. Cut lengths of yarn to a little more than double the length needed for the fringe. Use a needle with an eye large enough to take the ply or plies of wool that will form one loop.

Take a stitch through the needlework, close to one corner and from the right side of the work, leaving a tail on the front. Leave a loop on the back and come back to the front through the same hole. Bend the loop down and thread the two ends through it – they should be approximately the same length (see Figure 84). Figure 85 shows the same fringe hooked with a crochet hook. It is easier, when knotting to start at the left-hand side and work towards the right. A bodkin, large needle or crochet hook helps the tail through the loop.

This is the fringe that was worked on the ends of the pink and green Hydrangea Rug (see Inspirational Tent stitch page 29). By taking a number of threads together for each loop and coming

Fig. 85

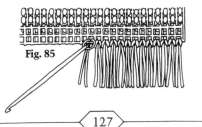

back through the canvas in the neighboring hole it was possible to make them cover 4 threads of canvas which was the same size as the blocks of Satin stitch worked immediately next door on the canvas edge.

SOME IDEAS FOR NEEDLEPOINT

Knowing the best way to make up some of the more popular items that can be stitched in needlepoint will help enormously even if you give your finished canvas work over to someone else to finish. Even at the design stage you will be able to allow for sufficient canvas, choose suitable fabric for mounting at the same time as the yarn (rather than afterwards and have difficulty finding a good match) and choose stitches that will wear well. When finished you will be able to select a professional person to make up your work by asking the 'right' questions or even suggesting finishing techniques and making custom details yourself.

Here are two important tips to bear in mind: one is to keep a scrap book with any ideas for finishing projects in an unusual way (these do not have to be needlepoint items – just things that look nice). Before starting a project find someone who is prepared to finish the project for you if you are nervous of doing it yourself. For a long time I knew of no one who would undertake leather-lined canvas work shoes at a reasonable price and not take too long, as needless to say, this was not something I felt happy to make up myself! Therefore, not until I tracked a craftsman down did I even design any slippers to offer to my customers.

PILLOWS

These are probably the most popular single items to make in needlepoint. They are not too large to stitch comparatively quickly and the materials are not particularly costly. If you work in the color scheme of your sitting-room you will be able to show it off to friends and enjoy their compliments on your new skill.

All the Simple projects in this book would make nice pillows – yes, even the shaded apple in the Simple Tent stitch section, worked on evenweave canvas instead of plastic, would make a charming panel for a small pillow.

However, even a simple pillow has many ways in which it can be made up. To give you a few ideas of the technical terms, and how pillows are constructed, here are some suggestions as to which methods suit particular designs.

PANELLED FRONTS: these are excellent when you have a small piece of needlepoint and want the pillow to be quite large. The easiest, quickest and most probably cheapest way is to buy a ready-made pillow – shops frequently have a good range with piping already attached in plain moiré or dupion that are zipped or have a flap at the back to slip the down interior in and out.

When the needlepoint is completed, block the work as usual, trim the canvas to about 8 threads and remove the canvas thread right next to the worked area on all four sides. Finger press the spare canvas to the back of the work and slip stitch it to the back of stitching (see page 125). Remove the interior from the ready-made pillow cover and slip stitch the canvas centrally in place.

Replace the interior and it's finished!

If you cannot find a matching ready-made pillow, you can make it yourself and then apply the panel. However, do not be tempted, in order to save a small amount of money, to attach fabric to each side of the canvas with mitered corners rather than mount the canvas on one piece of fabric – it can look very messy.

A really small piece of needlework might need an edging to add to its importance. The round pillow photographed in the Inspirational Florentine on page 49 has a circular panel approximately 9 cm (3½ in) in diameter. I found a lacy doily, removed the linen center and surrounded the needlepoint with the lacy edging. Lacemakers could of course make an even more beautiful edging but this simple method gave the effect I wanted. If working the Apple design on regular canvas I would suggest mounting it in this way.

Fine hand-made cords would also look good trimming the edge of a mounted piece of canvas or thicker ones would be perfect for a knife-edge pillow.

PIPED PILLOWS: generally my designs have an interesting border worked around the edges of the needlepoint and so I seldom consider piping necessary. Piping also requires a special attachment on your sewing machine.

TASSELS: these look good attached to each corner of a dramatic pillow or extra large ones look very oriental on a floor pillow. Look in home decoration magazines for interesting ways to make these useful floor pillows (extra seating at little cost). They can simply be an overlarge pillow

design with a firm interior or a stack of two or three pillows sitting on top of each other to make them more like pouffes; obviously the lower pillows would be made in a regular fabric and only the top one would have the needlepoint on the top and tassels in each corner.

KNIFE-EDGE PILLOW: this is the term used when the front and back of any pillow are sewn together with no decoration or gusset. One side only is needlepoint. For this you need the completed canvas, blocked and trimmed to approximately 3 cm (1 in) on all sides; a piece of backing fabric the same size as the canvas; a feather and down interior ready-made about 4–5 cm (1½–2 in) larger than the worked area of the canvas (canvas-work pillows need to be packed firmly, especially in the corners, to look good); and matching sewing thread.

With the right sides together baste the backing to the canvas on three and a half sides (if the design on the canvas is directional leave the unstitched area at the bottom – this side will never show when completed). Machine stitch as close to the needlework as possible (by machining with the needlepoint side uppermost this will be easy to see). Hem the excess canvas to the back of the stitchery, mitering the corners.

Turn the canvas inside out, insert the interior and hand stitch the opening as neatly as possible. If you wish, stitch cord over the seams and/or tassels on the corners.

BOXED PILLOWS: these are very tailored looking and can have just the front panel in needlepoint with the sides or upstands, generally about 5 cm (2 in) deep, the back and any piping in a fabric. More ambitiously, the up-stands can also be in a needle-point design. A simple one-color cord would be a good alternative to piping but something always has to mask the join between two pieces of canvas.

SQUAB PILLOWS FOR COUNTRY-STYLE CHAIRS: these are made like boxed pillows and tied in place with cords round the tops of the legs or round the two back posts.

There are many other shapes of pillow which can look good; for example, circular or octagonal ones in a group on a small bedroom chair, rectangular ones for the center of a long sofa or a pair of cylindrical-shaped ones at either end of a heavily-padded or high-armed sofa.

◇

UPHOLSTERED PIECES

A great deal has already been said about choosing suitable needlepoint for hard wear as upholstery in the Florentine section (see page 53). Florentine is a popular choice for chair cushions and stools but care must be taken when selecting a particular pattern so that there are not too long stitches in the repeat that will catch or snag. Any design worked in Basketweave tent will wear extremely well even if it does take a long time to stitch in the first place. A combination of small decorative stitches (for example, Cross stitch and some of its variations) with a background of Basketweave tent stitch would be suitable also.

Cushions are comparatively easy for a handy person to fix themselves. However, worked canvas is frequently thicker than regular fabric and it may be necessary to shave a minute amount of wood off each side of the cushion frame before fixing the needlework.

Having checked the snugness of the fit, center the worked canvas on the cushion (making sure any central design is optically in the middle), nail under the front rail of the cushion frame, pull firmly and nail along the back. Tuck in and trim any excess on the corners. Nail the sides (see Figure 86).

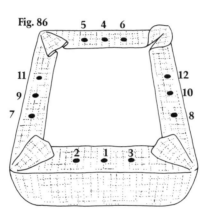

Fig. 86

An upholstered-over piece is best left to the professional; sometimes the excess canvas can be taken under the frame and fixed out-of-sight; other chair designs have a show-wood frame and the canvas has to be taken up to and fixed neatly with either braid or preferably antique-headed nails to give an authentic look.

◇

PICTURES

There is an enormous range of frames; modern, traditional and authentic antique. Look at stitchery exhibitions and consult a professional framer for suggestions. However, if he has not had previous experience with needlepoint it would be wise for you to mount the piece on stretcher bars yourself before handing it over to be framed.

This is one instance where binding the cut edges of the canvas before stitching with a cloth binding rather than masking tape works best. Machine stitch a 2–3 cm (¾–1 in) cloth binding on all cut sides of the canvas. Work the piece as usual, taking particular care not to run threads behind any area that will be left unworked. Allow 4 cm (1½ in) bare canvas on all sides of the design.

Block the piece as already explained on page 124, paying particular attention to obtaining accurate 90 degree corners. Purchase four artist's stretcher bars to form a frame the same size as the worked canvas. Cover this stretcher-bar frame with a natural cotton or linen cover; use white for a light canvas-work ground, dark for dark, so that any shadow created by the inner edges of the bars does not show through. It may also be necessary to lay a piece of cotton batting or interlining on top of the cover if there are loose ends of metallic at the back of the work as this soft interlining will absorb the knots and lumps rather than let them push the surface of the needlework up on the right side.

Leaving the binding in place, fold the excess canvas over the edges of the frame and lace it tightly with strong fine, string. First lace from top to bottom, sewing into the cloth binding or just inside it. Fold in the corners and hold with a few stitches if needed. Complete the lacing, running the string from side to side (see Figure 87).

Now the piece can be handed

Fig. 87

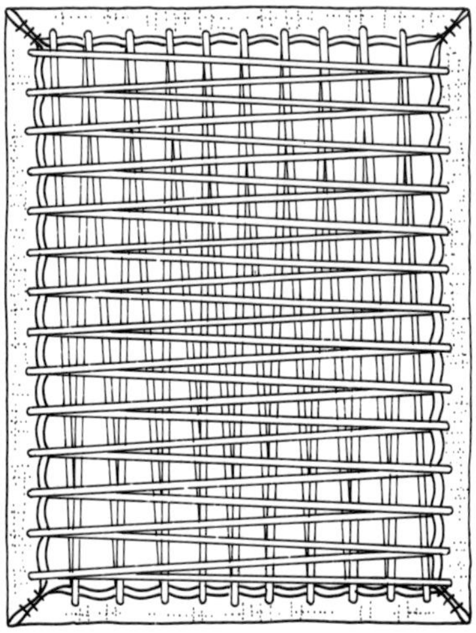

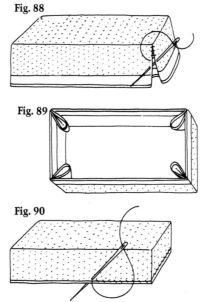

over to the framer and the decorative frame chosen.

Covering the work with glass is a personal choice. However, never, never use non-reflective glass. I prefer needlework left uncovered but you have to decide if leaving it open is practical for where the finished piece is planned. If you do decide to have glass have it specially mounted so that it is not touching the work. If a mount is not appropriate have the framer insert a narrow fillet of wood, mitered at the corners between the stretcher bars and the frame itself.

◇

THREE-DIMENSIONAL PIECES

Although items such as door stops, kneelers and the Country Cottage are all different sizes they are all similar to make-up.

Organize your interior first before stitching. A door stop can have a brick inside and these vary in size quite considerably. Church suppliers make standard high-density foam interiors and special sizes would be extremely expensive or even not available. The Country Cottage can have a

brick with a triangular shape of wood attached or be made as one block of wood. However, it would still be easier to have this ready for checking purposes during the stitching rather than have to make alterations to the completed piece! As always work on a square piece of canvas.

DOOR STOP AND KNEELER: When the needlework is complete fold in all the four unworked corners and stitch them together close up to the needlework, working from the right side and using Binding stitch. A strong matching thread or yarn can be used (see Figure 88). Trim away

Fig. 88

Fig. 89

Fig. 90

the folds that have formed inside to about 1 cm (½ in) and finger press them apart (see Figure 89). Hem them to the back of the needlework. Ease on to the interior. Trim the excess canvas along the base to approximately 1 cm (½ in). Lace with fine string back and forth across the base, as with the picture (see Figure 87). Slip stitch a panel of thick felt (cut to the exact size) to the base (see Figure 90).

COUNTRY COTTAGE: When all three pieces of canvas are worked, trim them to 2 cm (¾ in) along the bases. Iron on fusable fabric to the gable-shaped end pieces and trim to match the canvas points. Stitch one end to the main house, starting at the top of the gable point and matching it to the center of the thatched area of roof on the main piece. Stitch down one side, return to the top and stitch down the other side. Repeat at the end end, always stitching down first one side and then the other. Slip over the wood shape. Lace the spare canvas across the base with fine string and slip stitch thick felt (cut to the exact size) to the base.

◇

RUGS AND CARPETS

Needlepoint rugs are both beautiful and practical. However, they do take time to stitch and so careful planning, even before starting work, is important so that the best possible result can be achieved.

Many rugs are made too small for where they have been planned, so two things are important: first, take a piece of fabric and fold it to the proposed rug size, lay it in the proposed position and see how it looks. If it is in front of a fireplace, does it balance the dimensions? Do the surrounding chairs rest or not rest on it as you would like to see them do? Leave it for a day or two and view from all angles. Second, do you want to make the rug in one or more pieces and is a convenient width of canvas available in the right mesh?

Rugs worked as a series of squares, often 45 cm (18 in) square and then joined together, have long been popular as the working piece is not too large to transport and work on. However, it is extremely difficult to join the completed squares so that the seams do not catch the eye (like narrow-width carpet, it is on the seams that these rugs will first show signs of wear).

Therefore, if after careful consideration this is the format you wish to work, be sure that each panel is surrounded by some decorative pattern or contrast line of stitching to take the eye away from the final seams; it is imperative that all squares are worked in the same direction as canvas mesh across the width does not necessarily match canvas mesh along the length and equally important that all the pieces are taken from the same roll of canvas.

When all the pieces are worked join the panels, following the instructions on page 125. Cut the binding off the ready-seamed edges, hem and miter these edges. Proceed as for the large 'Pigs in Clover' rug (see page 65), laying the felt on to the back of the work and catch the stitching in place. Apply pre-shrunk backing linen and slip stitch in place.

If, however, you can obtain a wide enough canvas that will enable you to make the rug in one piece it really will make a more satisfactory job.

A compromise I frequently suggest, especially when a wide enough canvas is not available, is to work the main area of the rug in one piece and then work four borders to attach on the four sides. The change in pattern between the central area and the border pattern minimizes the joins so that they are virtually impossible to see.

Fringes on either two ends or on all four sides give many rugs a final touch.

◇

WALLHANGINGS

When the needlepoint is complete decide whether you want to make a feature of the mounting.

DECORATIVE FINISH: a decorative wood or brass pole can be run through a series of loops (made from needlepoint, cord or co-ordinating fabric) and either hung from two wall brackets or a strong cord and central hook (see Figure 91). Look at drape poles and brackets in your drapes shop for ideas as the shop will cut these poles any length to order.

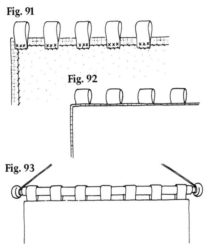

Fig. 91

Fig. 92

Fig. 93

When finishing this type of panel, work the canvas piece (and ribbon-type pieces for loops if wanted), block the main piece, hem all the edges and miter the corners. Line the canvas or fabric loops and stitch together on each side but not at the ends. Attach these loops, doubled over, securely to the back of the canvas, making stitches in to the hemmed edges of canvas, not just into the stitchery. Place them fairly close as, depending on the overall weight of the finished piece, it will tend to sag between the loops. Also allow a loop close to either end so that the corners do

not flap forward (see Figure 92).

To attach the lining slip stitch it in place along the top and down both sides (see Figure 93). Hem the bottom edge of the lining but leave it free from the canvas (as you would when making heavy drapes).

With a large wallhanging it will be necessary to stay stitch the pre-shrunk lining into place at intervals to give even support to the canvas work. To do this, place the hemmed work face down on a clean surface. Measure and mark a central line from top to bottom with a row of dressmaker's pins (see Figure 94). Measure and cut the lining (wash and dry it if not already pre-shrunk) about 5 cm (2 in) bigger on all sides than the hemmed needlework. Lay it over the work with all sides overlapping equally on each side. Fold it back on itself so that the fold is in line with the line of pins. Stitch the lining to the back of the stitchery along this line with a locking stitch (see Figure 95). Start 8 cm (3 in) up from the bottom of the canvas and finish short of the top. Remove the pins.

Fig. 94

Fig. 95

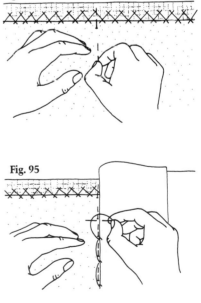

Unfold the lining 15 cm (6 in) and stitch this new straight fold as before. Continue to unfold, in 15 cm (6 in) sections until about 15 cm (6 in) from the side. Return to the center and unfold the lining, working in the other direction. Turn the excess lining in and slip stitch in place on the sides and top of the completed work. Hem the bottom edge of the lining but leave it hanging free from the canvas work.

A large panel will hang better if a series of drapes weights are sewn along the bottom edge of the canvas to hold it down.

INVISIBLE MOUNTING: a slim batten of strong wood or metal can be slipped in to a narrow casing made along the top of the panel in the lining fabric. Simply hand sew an extra line of close stitching through the lining and back of the stitchery about 4–5 cm (1½–2 in) down from the top edge of the piece. The batten can extend at either end and have a decorative cord looped round it for hanging or, if preferred, a cord, finished with tassels at each end could be sewn on for hanging purposes.

Fig. 96

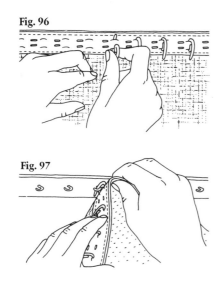

Fig. 97

The wallhanging can also be hung very simply with drape rings from a row of hooks screwed into the wall. Fix a row of small hooks either into a batten on the wall or in to the wall itself (see Figure 96). Either sew on a drape tape (Rufflette) to the top edge back of the canvas work (do not pleat up as for drapes) and slip drape hooks through the special slots (see Figure 97); or sew the drape hooks at regular intervals along the canvas to match up with the hooks in the wall. The heavier the work is the closer the hooks will have to be.

AFTERCARE

Needlepoint was meant to be enjoyed and used and therefore, even if it is protected from undue friction, unnecessary cleaning or bright sunlight, it is still subject to attack from the environment. Daylight fades dyes and weakens fibers, temperature and humidity make the threads move up and down as they take up and give out moisture and fine dirt and chemicals in the air conspire to destroy the textile.

However, there are steps we can take to make finished items wear better and look good for a longer period of time. This section, therefore, aims to guide the reader on protective keeping and safe cleaning; and on pitfalls to avoid that will help all needle-workers. This is not a manual of professional restoration.

If you would like to explore the field of textile conservation the Textile Conservation Centre at Hampton Court Palace, near London, England, runs both short and long courses for professionals. You can also contact the National Trusts in Great Britain or Aus-tralia or the National Trust for Historic Preservation in the United States for details of organized groups of voluntary workers in your area.

FIBERS

The following list of fibers are the ones most commonly found in needlepoint. By knowing the properties of the different fibers the most satisfactory ones can be chosen for a project from the outset. For example, for an upholstered piece wool will give the longest wear. Then, when the piece is in use, it can be cared for in the best possible way.

WOOL: designed as an outer covering for animals, wool will absorb moisture readily. In fact, it becomes hard, dry and brittle if it is in too dry an atmosphere. It tends to decompose in strong sunlight and it is subject to attack by moths. It will mat and shrink if washed in hot soapy water.

SILK: this cannot be washed and must be dry cleaned. Its natural gum-like sericin is taken out during manufacture and then it is artificially weighted in many instances. Sunlight and hot dry conditions make it become dry and brittle.

LINEN: this washes well and is a strong fiber.

COTTON: this has great resistance to heat and does not mind humidity. It stores well and sunlight only causes gradual weakening of the fibers.

MAN-MADE FIBERS: there are two main types, those such as rayon made from natural origins and synthetics such as nylon.

When using man-made fiber on canvas keep a note of the care instructions given on the label accompanying the skein/spool and follow them carefully.

◇

CLEANING

Rugs, upholstered pieces, wall-hangings and pillows should all be vacuum-cleaned regularly with a hand-held nozzle attachment on the vacuum cleaner through muslin. If furniture polish is used near needlework great care should be taken not to get any on the embroidery as the polish will stain the work and attract and hold dust. There are dry cleaners that specialize in delicate fabrics and needlepoint. Find them in your area either through recommendation by your needlepoint shop or other needleworkers who have had first-hand experience with the company and their standard of workmanship.

Washing, even by hand, is seldom appropriate for needlepoint, especially with old pieces. Take them to a specialist and get an appraisal as to their date, importance and possible value before thinking of washing. Washing is a non-reversible step; if colors run nothing can be done to correct it.

However, if you do eventually decide to wash a piece follow this procedure for the greatest chance of success.

Always check the colors are fast by dabbing a scrap of dampened white cotton on to the back or edge of the work and see that no color bleeds on to the cotton.

Make a cardboard template of the needlepoint shape against which you can check the piece after the washing.

Use a bowl, sink or even the bath so that the piece can lie completely flat. Use warm, softened water and only a mild soap-based washing agent well mixed to form suds.

Lower the piece face down into the water and with a sponge pat the work up and down in the water. Do not rub or scrub the stitchery and change the soapy water if the piece is very dirty.

Rinse the work repeatedly in warm, softened water until there are no more suds. Finally, give the work one last rinse in distilled water or in water that has been boiled and then allowed to cool.

Remove the needlepoint and lay it face up on a blocking board. Blot up the excess moisture with a white towel or paper towels.

Check with the template you made for size, pin out and allow to dry naturally for a day or two.

◇

STORAGE

The best method of storage has been proved by the excellent condition of textiles discovered in ancient tombs in Egypt and South America: cool, dry and dark with constant temperature and humidity, unpolluted air and no handling! Excessive dryness, heat and damp can rot fibers, cause mould and grow and attracts moths and bugs.

Stored textiles should be layered between acid-free tissue paper and folded as little as possible. Long narrow pieces can be rolled loosely round lavatory-paper, paper towels or silver-foil cylinders. First wrap the cardboard cylinder with the acid-free tissue and then place sheets of it in between each wrap. Always wrap with the right-side of the needlework out.

◇

DISPLAY

Sunlight and ultraviolet radiation emitted by fluorescent tube lighting are the greatest enemies of all textiles. Filters for absorbing ultra-violet rays can be obtained as a sheet to apply to windows but blinds, systematically used on bright days, are probably most satisfactory for the home. Ordinary light bulbs are safer than fluorescent tubes.

Dust and dirt, especially dirt with gritty particles that work their way into and cut the fibers are bad. Atmospheric pollution, especially in industrial areas, is also bad. Until recent years many homes had dust covers for rooms when not in use or when the family was away.

Having followed these guidelines, enjoy having your needlework pieces around you, making the house look beautiful.

CHAPTER NINE

A-Z OF
*H*INTS AND
*T*IPS

This section is primarily intended for dipping into. I hope that you will find here some tips that you have not thought about before.

The section is arranged alphabetically; an * indicates that further reference can be found under another entry. I like to share my tips and I frequently invite the students in my classes to relate their own favorite tip; drawing on the outside professions of the students, both male and female, it is fascinating to find out what unlikely implements can turn out to be useful to a stitcher. I sincerely hope that anyone who reads a tip in this section that they think they told me in the first instance will feel pleased at its inclusion.

◇

ACID MANTLE: cream that nullifies the acid in perspiration on the hands and does not harm the fibers. Tubes are available from pharmacies.

◇

ALTERNATE STITCHES, PATTERNS OR COLORS: when trying an alternate idea for an area do not unpick the first one until after stitching the second; then the two can be compared – sometimes you may return to the first choice anyway. If the second pattern is stitched in the margin of the canvas, there is an added benefit – when the piece is complete, trim the margin and make small samples with any trial stitches. Mount it in your Reference collection*.

◇

APPLIQUE: mounting one mesh of canvas that is already worked on top of another mesh of canvas; the one to be applied is generally finer than the ground one. There are two methods of appliqué on canvas; in the first method, work the finer piece and then unravel the surrounding canvas, leaving threads of canvas that can be plunged down through the ground canvas and secured at the back; in the second method, used for very fine canvas (24-mesh or finer), turn the upper canvas with a seam allowance and blind stitch into place as you would normally appliqué fabrics. The joining edge in either method can be corded, couched or chain stitched to obtain a neat effect.

◇

AWAY KNOT: a knot used when there is no prior stitching and you have no knowledge of your securing location. Place it 10 cm (4 in) away from the starting point in any direction. Later on, cut the knot and using a sharp needle weave the thread into the back of the stitches.

◇

BARGELLO: the American term for Florentine stitch*.

◇

BARGELLO TUCK: when finishing a thread at the back of the work that only has sparse or long stitches to anchor in, run the thread one way, make a U-turn over one thread (on the back of the work), double back on the original thread, and finish off, leaving no tail.

◇

BLOOD from pricked finger. Spit or white wine, applied immediately, should remove small blood stains.

◇

BOXES: clear transparent plastic boxes such as shoe, sweater or some brands of chocolate boxes with loose lids (so there is no moisture condensation as you would have in a plastic bag), make excellent storage bins for materials.

◇

CENTERING A DESIGN: simply fold the canvas as you would a piece of paper and make a small mark on the two bisecting channels.

◇

CHAIN STITCH and its variations are some of the very few stitches that will form a curve on canvas. They can be used to smooth out any curved edge, either around a piece of appliqué* or where decorative stitchery meets Basketweave tent and the compensation stitches* look untidy.

◇

CHATELAINES: a useful modern equivalent to the antique ones which hung from a lady's waist is a length of firm, wide ribbon, 1 m (1¼ yd) long with scissors, needle-case, emery pad and other items attached at either end to balance each other. This is hung around the stitcher's neck and ensures that her needlework tools are always to hand. A fabric tape measure can also be sewn along the length of the ribbon.

◇

CHEMICALS: the fewer substances used either on the canvas or on the finished work the safer.

◇

CLASS PROJECTS: if you do not intend to finish a piece, cut out the worked areas into neat reference pieces, bind and mount in your Reference collection* to demonstrate the various techniques you have learned – throw the rest away!

◇

'CLEAN' AND 'DIRTY' HOLES: always try and bring the needle up in an empty ('clean') hole and down through the canvas in an occupied ('dirty') hole – this will take any wisps of yarn through to the back of the work.

◇

COMPENSATION STITCHES: This is a term applied to any part of a stitch that needs to be worked either to get a straight edge to the geometric area or to fill in a curve on a pictorial piece. Always try and establish a new stitch across an area so that compensation stitches are not immediately necessary. You may also find it a help to take a piece of paper and cover the stitch diagram being followed so that the edge of paper corresponds with the line on the canvas and hides any part of the stitch not to be worked.

◇

COMPOSITE STITCHES: when two different stitches are worked in an area, either over or beside one another or interlacing. Work with one, two or more needles as the color and ply dictates.

◇

CONGRESS CLOTH can be permanently water-marked if care is not taken when blocking. This is particularly noticeable if areas are left unworked. Always use some sort of frame

when working the piece. When blocking the finished piece spray the back of the work with water, using a hand-spray and damp the fibers from the back only, not the canvas.

◇

DANDRUFF LOOK: when too few ply have been used for satisfactory coverage of the canvas. Always watch when starting an area that no flecks of canvas are showing through your stitching. If in doubt, try an extra ply. See dark backgrounds*.

◇

DARK BACKGROUNDS: consider using ecru or tan canvas or 'paint' the deep-colored areas with a mid-gray marker pen before stitching.

◇

DARK YARNS: These plies may be slightly thinner than light-colored ones from the same manufacturer and so your stitching may need an extra ply for satisfactory coverage of the canvas.

◇

'DIRTY' HOLES: see 'clean' holes*.

◇

DISTILLED WATER: use for blocking and steam ironing if you have many chemicals in your water supply or old rusty pipes in the house.

◇

DITCH: an alternative expression for the channel between 2 canvas threads.

◇

DMC FLOSS: to start a new skein push the two wrapper labels

into a central position; the color reference wrapper has a pair of hands drawn on the back and will show which end to pull the 'head' of the thread from. This top end is looped into the skein so a sharp tap on the back of the hand will make it fall out ready to be cut.

◇

DOCTORS AND DENTISTS: make friends with them. Suture scissors (light plastic ones with a hook on one tip), sterile dressing removers and dental excavators all make excellent tools for ripping*. Dental-floss threaders make fine needle threaders*. Intravenous bottle cap liners make pulling needles through thick stitching much easier.

◇

DRY CLEANING: this is absolutely necessary for Au Ver à Soie silk.

◇

EMERY POWDER: this is good for sharpening and cleaning needles. Attractive small velvet strawberries and other fruit shapes filled with emery powder can be purchased and are pretty to hang on a chatelaine* or neck ribbon. If you wish to make a similar one for yourself, the powder can be purchased from the pharmacy and used alone or mixed with fine sand from a freshwater beach. A very dense lining fabric such as a press-on fuseable fabric or pima cotton must be used as a lining, to avoid the powder leaking under the velvet or satin that is used to represent the shape. If you have an acid skin, the acid will quickly take the nickel plating off the needle. Running your needles through the emery regularly will help repolish them.

◇

ESTIMATING THE YARN NEEDED: work one square inch in the right number of ply with the stitch you plan to use and measure the length of the yarn before and afterwards. When you have the amount for this small area you will be able to estimate the amount you will need for the whole area.

◇

EXTENSION CORDS FOR LIGHTS: these are worth packing on a trip when you hope to stitch. Frequently, the hotel room is not set up as you would like and being able to stitch where you prefer will make it more comfortable.

◇

EYELET STITCH or any stitch that converges to a central hole must always be stitched from the outside in – up in a 'clean' hole* and down in a 'dirty' one. Any thread will lay better if two trips are taken round an eyelet, missing alternate holes on the first circuit and filling them in on the second. Always make all rotations going in the same direction within the same area (clockwise or counter-clockwise), to achieve uniformity.

◇

FLOSS: the American term for stranded cotton*.

◇

FRAY CHECK: a commercially produced liquid that stops fibers unraveling during stitching. It is especially useful for metallics and loose-twisted rayons. Put a small amount on two fingers and 'pinch' both ends of the thread. Allow to dry for a few seconds and then stitch as normal. It dries undetected. It is available from good fabric shops.

◇

FRESH CUT ENDS OF FIBERS should go in the eye of the needle; they are easier to thread.

◇

GARAGES: stitch a series of dense stitches such as Rhodes or Cushion around the blank canvas area of your design (three or four stitches at regular intervals down the canvas on each side). Use these stitches for 'parking' needles that are threaded and in use or resting but needed later on.

◇

GLUE: use fabric glue that dries clear and flexible – never rubber cement or other glues that may invite bugs to your work after it is finished.

◇

HOLIDAYS: check on National Trust listings and research museums in your area. On a dull day a visit to a beautiful collection, even if it is not a needlework one, can frequently give you design ideas.

◇

HUE: the technical name for a family of color, for example green, red or a color that is absolutely pure.

◇

HUNGARIAN POINT STITCH: this is a variation of Florentine.

◇

HUSBANDS: if you do not moan about their hobbies, hopefully they will not moan about yours!

◇

INDECISION: usually a deadly sin but when called 'planning' is excellent. Canvas work can take a long time and it is worth spending time and effort at the early stages to get the effect you wish. See Reference collection*.

◇

INTENSITY OF COLOR: a color scheme can have two or more hues in it but unless one hue has more intensity to it and 'sings' there will be no contrast or excitement in the design. The best way to judge this is to imagine taking a black and white photograph of the finished piece; would the shade of blue chosen appear the same as the adjacent shade of coral? If so, they both have similar intensities and will make for an unexciting end result.

◇

ISLANDS: single stitches surrounded by another color – these give a tweedy effect rather than true shading unless the values are so close together that they are, separately, almost indistinguishable.

◇

JEWELRY PLIERS: these are small curved pliers which are useful to grab the needle with when weaving a long distance under many threads.

◇

JEWELRY ROLLS: a soft roll of canvas work that is finished inside with different size pockets and ring holders to take jewelry when traveling. The bag shown in the Inspirational Stitchery section on page 93 has also been finished in this way.

◇

JOURNEYS: have a small piece of needlepoint in your bag to help the tedium at stations and airports. See also extension cords*.

LAMPS: pack an extra bulb for your high-intensity lamp when traveling as these special bulbs and fittings are sometimes difficult to find.

◇

LAYING TOOLS are useful for getting really smooth stitches, especially for silk and floss. My favorite is a curved Swedish rug needle but thick needles, collar-stays or stiletto punches can also be used.

◇

LEFT-OVER FIBERS: make sure they have their reference number still on them if you are keeping them or throw them away.

◇

LENGTH OF THREAD: never be tempted to use a longer thread than recommended, it does not save time in the long run. It will wear thin before finished and give an uneven appearance to the completed project.

◇

LIGHT AND DARK THREADS: work the light color first, then the dark one, otherwise the light wool will pick up the fuzz from the dark one as it is stitched. If, despite your care, a little fuzz does appear on the front of the work, it can be picked off with small tweezers. Always pay attention to the direction of a waste knot with dark thread so that dark stitches cover their own tail. Do not run dark threads behind light stitches as they will show through the canvas.

◇

LIGHT BULBS: pack a 60-watt or stronger bulb when traveling as hotels have a tendency to put 40-watt ones in bedroom fittings.

◇

LIGHT-COLORED WOOLS: these are frequently fluffier and softer than dark shades. Sometimes they will need 1-ply less for the same stitch than a dark one would.

◇

MEASURING YARN: with a project of any size always test stitch an area to assess the overall quantity needed.

◇

METALLICS: use a needle threader when working with metallics – the head of the thread will be less damaged and, therefore, less likely to unravel. Thread the needle with only a short tail (about 5 cm/ 2 in) as it will tend to fray at the eye of the needle and be unusable.

◇

MISSED STITCHES: when a piece is completed, hold it up to the light to check for any stitches that may have been missed; if any need to be filled in, use only half the number of ply originally used for that area, weave in from one direction, make the stitch twice in the same hole and and weave out to the other direction. This will avoid unnecessary bulk at the back of the work.

◇

NAIL VARNISH: a small touch of clear nail varnish behind the work will tame any metallic threads that are popping out.

◇

NAP: this is the right and wrong direction of the yarn. As explained on page 11 certain fibers have a more distinct rough and smooth direction than others. Check when using a fiber for the first time. The work will look much better with the nap running the right way. An alternative way to running Paterna Persian lightly against your upper lip to find the nap is to loop a piece of the 3-ply wool in one hand so that the two ends project evenly about 2 cm (½ in) between the thumb and forefinger. Rub these two ends vigorously round and round over the back of the other hand. After a few moments examine the two ends; one will still be smooth and should be threaded and the other will be frayed, ragged and bent.

◇

NEEDLES: a threaded needle is less likely to get lost than an unthreaded one. Use garages* for parking needles on a piece in progress. Use a larger needle for Pulled-thread work to assist in canvas displacement. When faced with a bunch of needles and you don't know their size, drop one through your canvas – if it drops through or just stops before the eye – you have the right size for that canvas.

NEEDLE STORAGE: when making a needle booklet or needle-roll be sure to use a 100 per cent natural fabric for sticking the needles into. A synthetic one will attract moisture and so rust your needles.

◇

NEEDLE THREADERS: two types are common; one is a metal disc with two holes at either end, one large and one small and is extremely useful; the other is a metal or plastic disc with a fine metal loop but it is not strong enough for canvas work except for threading a single ply into a beading needle. Failing one to hand, a small piece of thin paper folded along the length with the yarn inside (without the tip showing) can be guided through most needle eyes.

◇

NUBS ON PLASTIC CANVAS: always use the commercially trimmed edge of the plastic canvas sheet when possible. On all other edges trim the nubs (the sharp pointed ends of the canvas) off before stitching the pieces together. If you do not these sharp ends will poke through the stitching and ruin the end result.

◇

ORGANIZATION: the few minutes spent before starting work to get threads properly cut and mounted makes for more relaxed stitching.

◇

ORTS: a smart term for the small pieces of thread that are trimmed from the canvas, the waste knot and tail that has to be trimmed after running through the back of stitches to finish off a thread. They can be used for stuffing small pincushions.

◇

ORT-POTS can be made from either any plastic carton that has a lid or a plastic or paper bag. Simply cut a small round hole in the lid of the pot to pop the ort through or, attach a plastic or paper bag to the edge of your table with some masking tape so that the lip remains open to take the bits and pieces. Either is simple to empty.

◇

PARKING LOTS: these are a series of mixed plies mounted on a card. See page 22 for full details about mounting these on a project card before working a shading piece. It really makes changing shades faster and easier, even in poor light.

◇

PEARL COTTON: do not work with this thread when your hands are hot as the sheen on it will disappear.

◇

PENCIL: the graphite will come off on your thread, so, if you have used a pencil to mark your canvas take some paper towels and give the whole canvas a good rub. Alternatively, spray it with a crystal clear fixative spray.

◇

PENS: Nepo and Pilot SC-UF pens are the two brands of waterproof markers I have personally used. However, always check any pen to find out whether it is waterproof on the very piece of canvas you plan to use. Draw on, allow to dry, wet and rub with white paper towels and if any color comes off do not use. Never use ball-point pens for marking the design. See also water-soluble pens*.

◇

PILLOW CASES: these are excellent for storing items or for transporting large pieces on stretcher-bar frames.

◇

PLAGIARISM: nothing can be gained from copying someone else's design and trying to pass it off for your own. It is much smarter to ask the original designer's permission and then to stitch with a clear conscience. Similarly, is it not more impressive to say, 'I learned this technique from a wonderful teacher in . . . and I was inspired to make this adaptation'?

◇

PLASTIC BAGS: avoid storing threads in sealed or zip-locked bags in a warm climate. Moisture will condense inside and the hairs of wool will stand up and later matt down to make a terrible tangle. Wool is affected most but other fibers can be spoilt too.

◇

POCKET LENSES FOR MAGNIFICATION: with or without a light, these are a wonderful gadget to have in your bag to examine exhibits in museums and needlework shows as well, of course, as the road map or telephone directory. Stationers also have plastic cards of magnification in various sizes, for example 5 × 7 cm (2 × 3 in) or 21 × 27 cm (8½ × 10½ in).

PULLED-THREAD WORK: use a larger needle, an awl or stiletto punch to make the holes larger before stitching into them. When possible halve the ply needed and make each stitch twice (immediately one after the other). This will give two pulls at the same pair of threads. Counting threads accurately is essential as, if errors are made, they have to be ripped* and the canvas threads re-aligned to their original position. If arrows or numbers are shown on a Pulled-thread diagram follow them closely. Some people like to damp the canvas slightly with a small sponge before working an area to make the displacing of threads easier.

QUEEN OR ROCOCO STITCH: my least favorite stitch. However, as it was so frequently used for small items like purse fronts in the eighteenth century I have graphed it in the Stitch Glossary and suggest you try it.

QUICK POINT: a term applied to needlework done on canvas larger than 10 mesh with multiple-ply or rug wool.

REFERENCE COLLECTION: this is immensely useful when looking for a stitch for a particular area. Use a ring-binder with clear plastic pockets to mount the pieces of canvas in. See alternate stitches*, class projects* (and indecision*) for a painless way to keep the collection up-to-date.

RESTORATION should be done by professionals only. Some museums offer an appraisal and/or valuation or may be able to recommend or put you in touch with qualified restorers. As the work is liable to be expensive and lengthy get a written estimate from more than one source, asking them to state both the cost and the probable time needed. See also sentimental pieces.

RIPPING can be called retro or reverse stitching if it makes you feel better. However, if something is not right, try an alternative sooner rather than later. Never rip in anger: canvas threads get cut and repairing them takes even longer.

RUNNING OUT OF THREAD: if you think you might be short, stop stitching and take any unstitched wool to the shop. It is easier to match unstitched wool. When you resume stitching, combine the new and the remaining old wool, plying together until all the old is used up and only new wool is left (see page 14). The transition of two dye lots can be smoothed together in this way.

SELVEDGES frequently have red thread running along the woven edge. Remember 'Selvedge at Side' and you will not turn your work incorrectly.

SENTIMENTAL PIECES: unfinished pieces worked in the past should be mounted as they are, unless there is extremely little in an obscure area to finish or a color that does not need to be matched with existing stitching. See restoration*.

SHADE: any hue mixed with black.

SHOE BAGS: the old-fashioned bags with a drawstring at the top are good for storing things and can be hung in a cupboard so that the air can circulate.

SHOT BAGS: these are small, cotton bags filled with lead shot and are useful for resting on the rear portion of a stretcher-bar frame when sitting at a table to stitch. Architectural suppliers have ready-made ones, used as weights to hold down drawings.

STAINS: If coffee or tea are spilled, let cold water from the tap run through the area. Do not put the whole piece in water and do not rub it. Rest it on a towel and blot up as much moisture as possible with another one. Leave flat to dry. If a ball-point pen has been used the only solution is to rip the discolored stitches.

STRAIGHT STITCHES almost always need one or two more plies than diagonal ones to give good canvas coverage.

STRANDED COTTON: the British term for floss*.

THREADING THE NEEDLE: for wool, hold the eye of the needle between the thumb and forefinger of the right hand, bend the correct number of plies over the needle, squeeze them tight and slip off the point of the needle with the left hand. Turn the needle and push the tight loop through the eye. For metallics, use a needle threader* to avoid damaging the tip of the thread. For other threads, push the fresh cut end* through the needle eye. See also needle threaders* and metallics*.

◇

TYING EQUIPMENT ON TO THE FRAME: laying tools*, needle threaders* and other small items get lost less easily if they are tied on to the edge of the stretcher bars with a bright colored thread.

◇

TINT: a hue or color with white added.

◇

TONE: a color mixed with its relative value, for example a gray that will absorb or reflect light to the same extent.

◇

TWISTED THREADS: if the yarn twists during stitching, simply allow the needle to dangle and the thread unwind itself. If you find your threads twisting more than those of your fellow stitchers and it bothers you, try wearing two rubber finger covers, on the righthand thumb and forefinger. This will quickly stop you rolling the needle as you stitch.

◇

UNFINISHED PROJECTS: always called 'works of art – in progress' – that way you feel better!

UNPICKING: the English term for ripping*.

◇

VALUE OF A COLOR: the amount of lightness or darkness in a color.

◇

VELCRO: good as a belt closure if a suitable buckle cannot be found. A Velcro dot stapled to the canvas frame holds floss threads while you strip or divide each strand before stitching.

◇

VERSATILITY: always try out stitches in different color combinations, in varying scales on the opposite diagonal.

◇

WASTE KNOTS: always position the knot in the direction of your immediate stitching so that the tail behind the work can be covered as quickly as possible. When the waste knot is reached and before that hole is used for stitching, pull it firmly up and snip below the knot so that nothing is visible on the right side of the work.

◇

WASTE TAILS: if it is more convenient than weaving through the back of existing stitches, the almost finished thread can be brought through to the right side of the work some distance ahead and again in the immediate direction of stitching. The tail can be trimmed when reached as a waste knot*.

◇

WASTE KNOTS AND TAILS WITH BASKETWEAVE TENT: this is

the one exception to the rules above. When working down a diagonal row, finish the thread by bringing it through the canvas vertically below, the new waste knot should be horizontally to the side. When working up a diagonal row, finish the thread by taking the tail horizontally to the side and bring the new thread in vertically from below.

◇

WATER-SOLUBLE PENS: there are some pens on the market that claim to wash out after the work is complete. My advice would be to avoid these pens for various reasons. The carefully drawn-on pattern can disappear if the weather is either humid or damp, a hot iron can make the design permanent, the dye can be picked up by white wool and congress cloth* watermarks so it cannot be wetted and silk has to be drycleaned*.

◇

WIRE HANGERS: looping leftover yarn on wire hangers is an excellent way of keeping it neat, and easy to refer to when planning other projects. Depending on the quantity you have, there could be a hanger for each color. Hang them in a cupboard but do not cover them with plastic.

◇

YARN: any fiber that is spun into strands. It can be wool, silk, cotton, synthetic or a blend.

◇

ZIG-ZAG LINES: zig-zag or curved lines worked in Continental tent stitch must be watched carefully so the Continental stitch does not become Half-cross stitch.

CHAPTER TEN
STITCH GLOSSARY

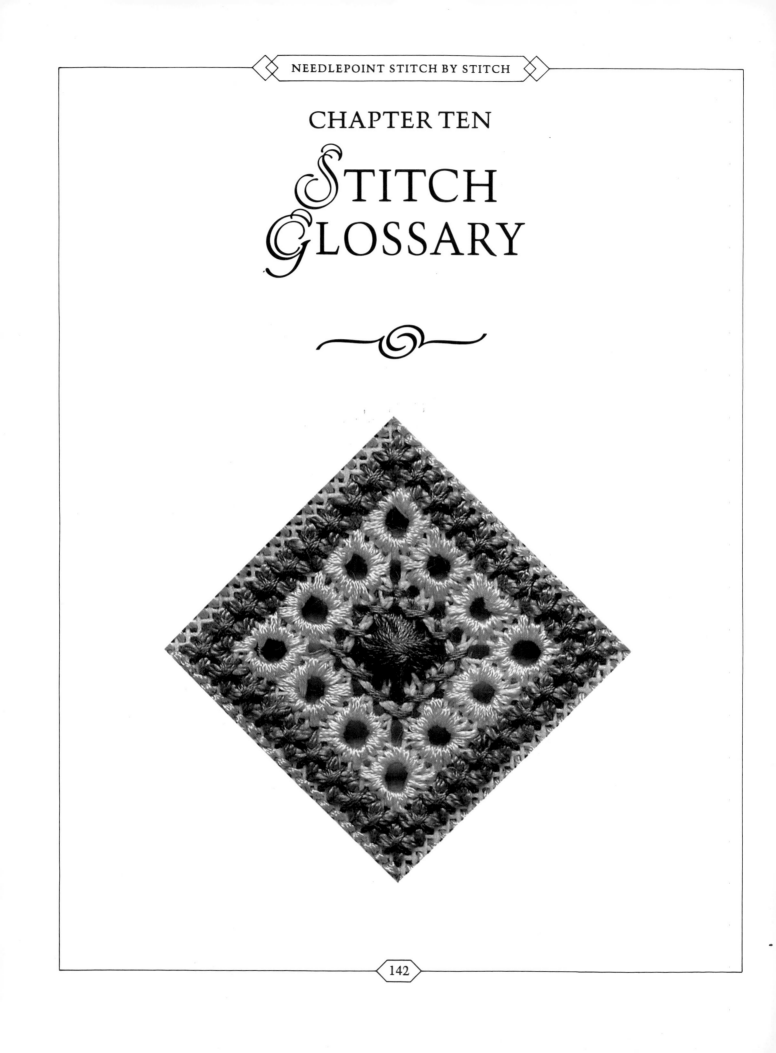

BINDING STITCH

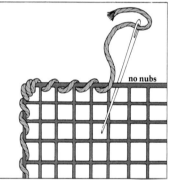

This stitch covers the edge of the canvas and is also used in joining two pieces of canvas. It may be necessary to go through the holes several times on the corners to get a good coverage.

If worked on plastic canvas (see Simple Tent stitch page 21) it is important to remove any 'nubs' from the edge of the plastic pieces before working the stitch.

Simply stitch the wool over and over the edge of the canvas, covering one of the outside horizontal threads.

BRICK STITCH

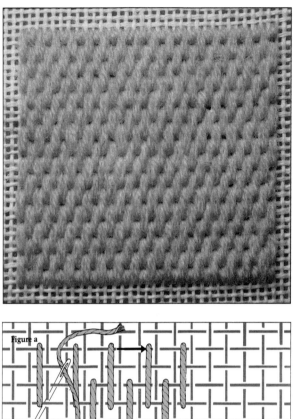

This stitch consists of vertical stitches over 4 threads of canvas with 2 threads of canvas between each stitch. Work on horizontal rows backwards and forwards across the canvas. The stitches of the second and subsequent rows fit half-way into the gaps left by the previous row.

In order to get a straight edge at the top or bottom of an area, compensation stitches are necessary. It is generally easier to work these when the pattern is well established and the bare threads can be seen.

Figure b shows compensation stitches. These should be worked in the same color.

BRICK STITCH, DOUBLE

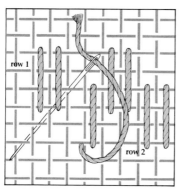

This is very similar to Brick stitch but two vertical stitches over 4 threads are worked side by side. Leave 3 threads of canvas before stitching the next pair. Work in horizontal rows and fit the stitches of the second row into the gaps left by the previous row.

When complete, pairs of compensation stitches will be needed along the top and bottom edges of an area in order to obtain a straight line.

BULLION KNOTS

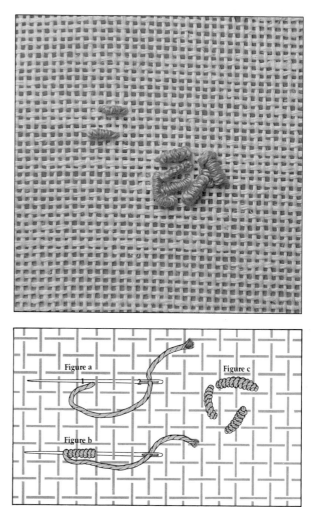

These are also known as Caterpillar stitches which is very descriptive. This is a traditional embroidery stitch but worked on top of other needlepoint on canvas to give accents.

Bring the needle up at 1. Take a 'sewing', not a 'stab' stitch, and go down at 2 (2 or 3 threads away in any direction). Bring the tip of the needle up again at 1 and wind the thread around the tip until the coil is the same length as the distance between 1 and 2. Pull the needle gently through the canvas, holding the coil down on the surface with the left-hand thumb down the length of the thread until the coil lays smoothly on the canvas. Stitch down through the canvas at 2. Some practise will achieve more even results. To make a flowerhead such as a rose, work three knots close together, overpacking each time which will make them curl as in Figure c.

BYZANTINE VARIATION WITH BOXES

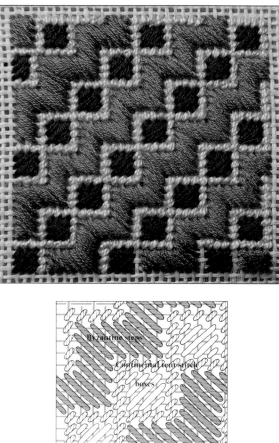

CHAIN STITCH AND DETACHED CHAIN STITCH

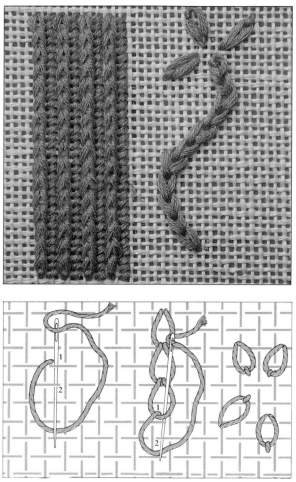

Work one diagonal interlocking outline in Continental tent stitch to form a series of boxes across the canvas from the upper right to the lower left.

Work the Byzantine stitch in steps of five stitches across and five stitches down (the pivot or corner stitch is counted twice) on either side of the Tent stitch.

Work another diagonal interlocking outline in Continental tent both above and below before working the Byzantine stitch steps again. The boxes over 1, 2, 3, 2 and 1 threads of canvas fit in when the other stitches are complete.

The angle of the boxes matches the angle of the Continental tent stitches and are on the opposite diagonal to the Byzantine steps.

In the Simple Stitchery project on page 82 the canvas needs to be turned one quarter before working the upper-left and lower-right corners.

This is one of the few stitches that can be used on canvas to work a curve. It can be worked as a solid filling, but it is more satisfactory to work it with a row of Continental tent stitch in between each row to set off the texture. When working one or more rows they should all start at the same end. Never start a row without sufficient yarn to finish.

Bring the needle and all the thread up at 1. Form a loop and hold it. Re-insert the needle again at 1 and pass it under 2 threads of canvas and bring it up at 2. Holding the looped thread below the point of the needle, draw the needle gently through to form the first loop. Always put the needle back in the hole it has just come out of inside the last loop. To finish a row, take a final catching stitch outside the final loop.

Detached chain stitch: Work a single Chain stitch and anchor it down with a small stitch.

COBBLER FILLING

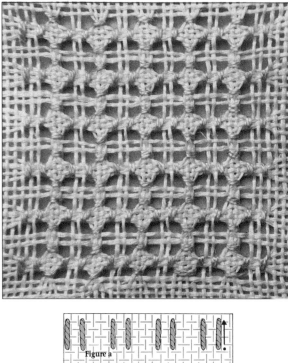

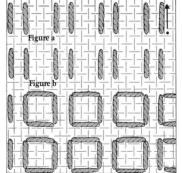

COUCHING

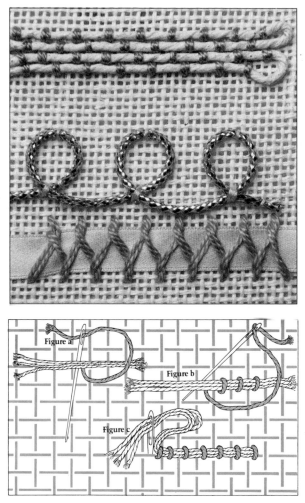

This is a Pulled-thread stitch and is similar to the Framed Cross (see page 157). Work all the upright stitches first, starting at the spot (see Figure a). Each pair has 2 threads of canvas between them and then 4 threads between the pairs.

When the area is complete turn the canvas and work the next pairs in a similar pattern at right angles (see Figure b).

This is used to attach a thread or ribbon that is too thick or fragile to stitch up and down through the canvas. Lay a good length of the thread to be couched along the surface of the canvas. With a single ply of the stitching thread in the needle, come up on one side of the wide thread and go back down through the canvas on the other side. Do not pull too tight (see Figures a and b). When complete the wide threads are 'plunged' to the back and finished off. Place a large-eyed needle halfway through the canvas in the same hole as the last couching stitch, thread the couched thread through the eye and gently pull it to the back of the canvas to finish off (see Figure c). If the thread is too thick for any needle, make a strong lasso with another thread, come up through the canvas in the last hole, go over the couched thread and back through the same hole. Pull gently.

CROSS STITCH

CROSS STITCH, BROAD

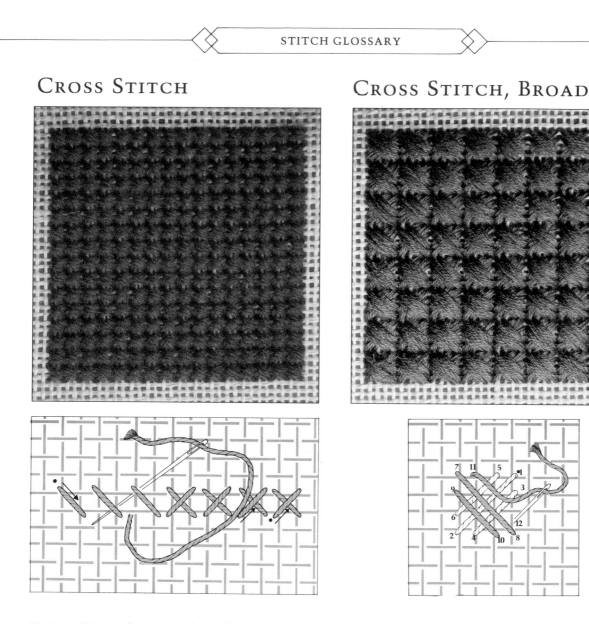

Basic or Diagonal cross stitch can be worked quite satisfactorily in two different ways. The first method is to work a row of half crosses, all slanting on the same angle, right across the area and then to return, completing the second and top stitch on the bisecting diagonal. On the return journey go back over one cross and forward under two. This is the way I find most convenient for all canvas work. The alternative method is to complete each cross in turn before moving on to the next one. I find this the best method for working samplers where a great deal of the ground fabric is left uncovered.

Always work any area of Cross stitch in the same order to make the top stitch always lie on the same diagonal. This gives a neat appearance to the work.

Work a diagonal stitch over 4 threads from the upper right to the lower left, then work a stitch over 3 threads on both sides. Next, work a diagonal over 4 threads from the upper left to the lower right and a stitch over 3 threads on both sides. The numbers in the diagram show the correct order.

Work all the stitches in the same order so that the slope of the top stitches is uniform.

CROSS, BROAD WORKED IN GROUPS OF FOUR

CROSS STITCH AND SMYRNA CROSS

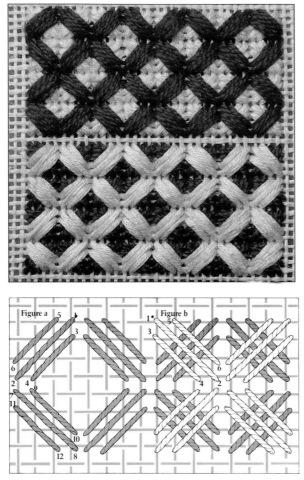

Work this stitch in groups of four. Work the first three stitches only in each group (1–6) and angle each group alternatively so that they form a series of diamond shapes (see Figure a).

When complete, work the upper stitches over each group on the other diagonal to the base stitches (see Figure b). The photograph shows how effective this stitch can be; the upper area has a dark thread on top of a pale one and the lower area shows the reverse.

Work a Small-scale Smyrna stitch over 2 threads (this stitch has already been used on the Simple Cross stitch pillow on page 57 but over 4 threads). The Small-scale version is a Diagonal cross over 2 threads of canvas with a vertical cross on top (the horizontal stitch is last). Then, with a contrasting color and appropriate ply count, work a Diagonal cross over 2 threads of canvas between the Small-scale Smyrna stitches. The second row fits a Smyrna under a Diagonal cross and a Diagonal cross under a Smyrna.

The photograph shows (above) Smyrna and Diagonal cross over 2 threads; (center) Smyrna and Crossed corners over 4 threads; (below) Smyrna and Rhodes worked alternatively over 4 threads.

CROSS STITCH, LARGE AND STRAIGHT

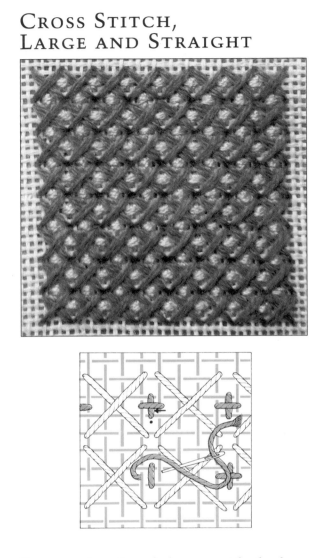

CROSS STITCH, LONG-LEGGED

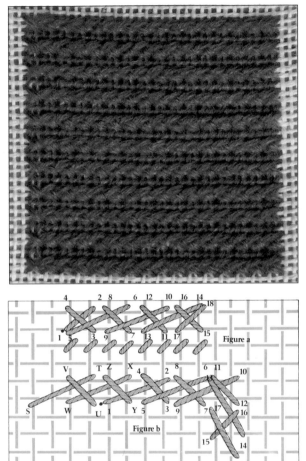

First complete the whole area with the large Diagonal crosses, working over 4 threads of canvas. Always cross in the same order. Then work the small Upright crosses over 2 threads of canvas with the horizontal stitch on top. Work each complete cross in turn.

Only work small crosses in the full spaces between the Diagonal crosses, do not work half crosses around the edge of an area. The Diagonal and Upright crosses can be worked in contrasting colors if preferred, as in the photograph.

When worked in horizontal rows (see Figure a), the row always starts and finishes with a Basic cross stitch (1–4). The Long-legged stitch itself starts at 5. Work a long leg to 6, come up at 7 and stitch back to 8. Come up at 9 and take a long stitch out to 10. Come up at 11, stitch back to 12 and down to 13. Start a new Long-legged cross stitch here. Continue along to the end of the row and finish off with a Basic cross stitch (15–18). There will be a series of short, upright stitches behind the work. Underneath the row of Long-legged cross stitch a row of Continental tent stitch worked from right to left makes the return journey.

Figure b shows the stitch worked as a border. Start with a long leg and follow the numbers to get you round the corner. When the circuit is complete, follow the letters in the diagram to work the final stitch over the long leg that you started with.

CROSS STITCH, SMALL-SCALE

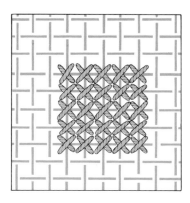

CROSS STITCH, STAGGERED

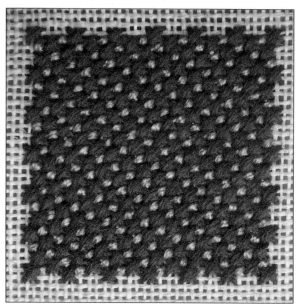

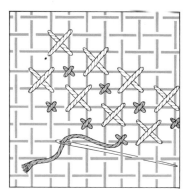

This stitch is similar to the Basic cross stitch (see page 147) but is worked diagonally over only 1 thread of canvas. Start at the left-hand side of an area and work this stitch in the same way.

This stitch works well on coarse-mesh canvas or as an alternative to Tent Stitch for sampler work as it gives a more dense effect. Shown here in the photograph is a small area in a single color; a series of concentric squares in alternate colors (this is best worked from the centre out); two small border designs and a pair of initials.

Work the first diagonal row of Cross stitches over 2 threads of canvas across a wide area, starting at the spot to allow the shallow step pattern of only 1 thread drop between Cross stitches to emerge.

Then, using a contrasting color if required, work the Small-scale cross stitches over 1 thread before working a second row of the larger Diagonal cross stiches. Compensate where necessary.

The photograph shows the pattern worked with the Basic cross stitch over 2 threads and the Small-scale cross stitch over 1 thread, worked in contrasting colors.

CROSS STITCH, TALL

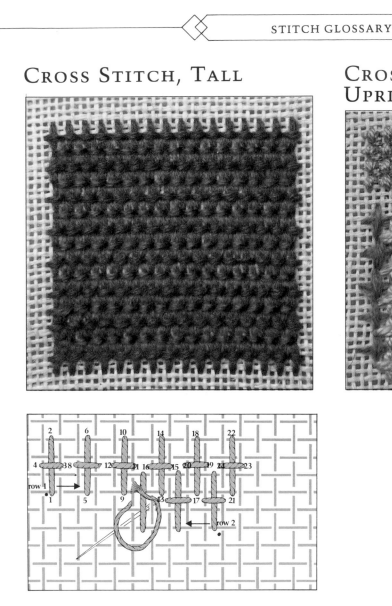

CROSS STITCH, UPRIGHT GONE WRONG

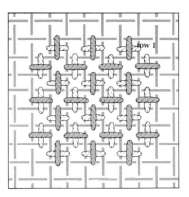

Work a vertical stitch over 4 threads and then cross it with a bar over 2 threads; follow the arrows in the diagram to get the best effect.

The second row (in a contrasting color if required) fits up into the spaces left between the first row of stitches. The top of the upright stitch shares with the two bars from the previous row and the new bar shares with the bottom of the two previous long stitches.

The photograph here shows alternate rows of color with the bar stitch worked in the same shade as the upright stitch.

Instead of always keeping the horizontal stitch on top break the rule with this stitch. Alternate the rows with, first, a row of the vertical stitch being worked on top, and then a row of the horizontal stitch on top.

Continue to work all the odd-numbered rows (from where you first started) with vertical stitches on top and all the even-numbered rows with horizontal stitches on top.

The photograph shows (above) the stitch worked over 2 threads and (below) over 4 threads.

CROSS STITCH, UPRIGHT & DIAGONAL INTERLOCKED

VERTICAL CROSS STITCH

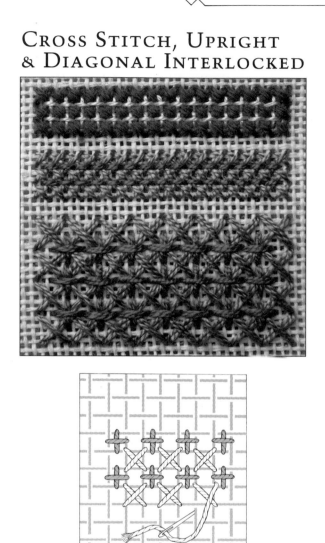

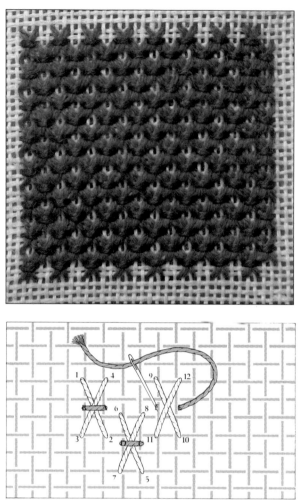

First work a horizontal row of upright crosses over 2 threads and then fit in a row of Basic crosses. Continue to work the rows of crosses alternately in the pattern area.

The photograph here shows (above) the Basic cross worked in a thick thread and a fine thread for the upright cross worked afterwards between the Basic crosses. This would allow a thread such as a metallic one to lie on top attractively. (Center) rows of the two types of cross, worked alternately, both in a similar weight thread. (Below) the pattern rescaled over 4 threads and the rows worked alternately as before.

This is worked from left to right. Work a tall Cross stitch over 4 threads of canvas high and 2 threads wide. Work the tie-stitch in the same color or in a contrasting color, as in the photograph, using a second needle. Work this tie-stitch before dropping down and over 2 threads to start the next Vertical cross stitch. The third Vertical cross stitch starts up 2 threads.

CROSSED CORNERS STITCH

CROSSED CORNERS, UPRIGHT

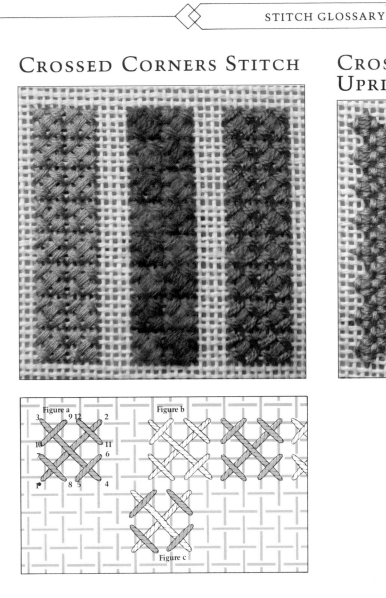

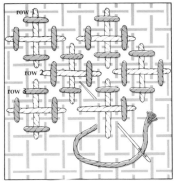

First work the large cross over 4 threads of canvas and then tip each corner in turn.

This stitch looks effective worked in different color combinations; either worked completely in one color (see Figure a and the left-hand area in the photograph); worked alternately in two colors to give a checkerboard effect (see Figure b and the middle area in the photograph); or with the large base cross worked in one color and the tips worked in a contrasting color (see Figure c and the right-hand area in the photograph).

This is closely related to the traditional Crossed corners but turned on its side!

Work a horizontal row of large upright crosses over 4 threads of canvas (the horizontal stitch is always last); when the row is complete, work the tipping stitch over each arm of the cross, using a contrasting color. The order of these tipping stitches does not matter.

The second row of upright crosses fits up into the first row as the diagram shows.

CUSHION STITCH

CUSHION STITCH, VARIATION

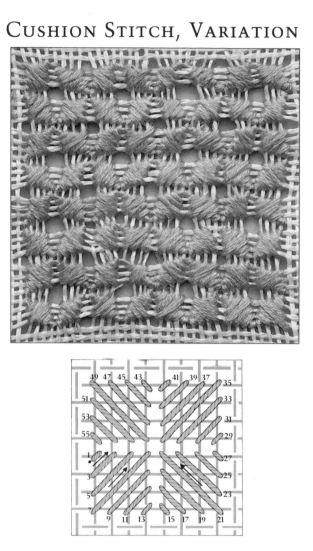

This is a group of seven stitches worked over 4, 3, 2 and 1 threads to form a small box. Four similar groups are worked on alternate diagonals to form a larger box over 8 threads.

This is a traditional canvas-work stitch and not pulled. It can also be rescaled for other projects.

Frequently, the pattern is worked in two contrasting colors and two boxes of one color are worked on the same diagonal before stitching the other two boxes in a contrasting color on the other diagonal as in the photograph.

The previous stitch can also be worked as a Pulled-thread variation. Follow the numbers given in the diagram, starting at the spot. Come up on the odd numbers and follow the arrows. When all four boxes are complete use the back of the stitches to get to the starting-point of the next box without trailing behind any holes.

EGGS IN A BASKET

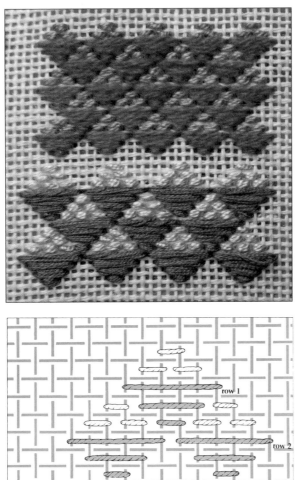

EYELET, DIAMOND

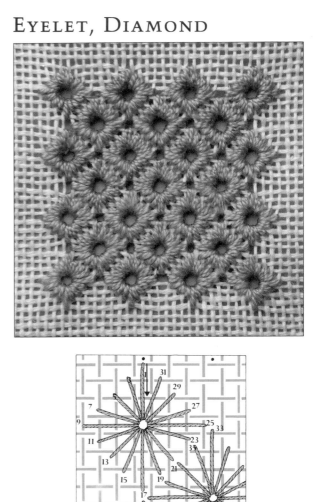

The 'basket' is formed by three horizontal stitches over 6, 4 and 2 threads of canvas. There are three 'eggs' in each basket, each over 2 threads of canvas.

This stitch looks good in two contrasting colors as in the photograph and is best worked unit by unit, with two needles, horizontally across the canvas. The second and subsequent rows fit in to the gaps formed by the previous row.

This stitch can be rescaled to give a larger basket (8, 6, 4 and 2 threads) with six eggs in it as shown in the lower area of the photograph.

This is a Pulled-thread stitch. Bring your needle up at the spot and work counter-clockwise, always going down in the central hole.

If a single horizontal row is required, start each eyelet at the top and work counter-clockwise, leaving 8 threads between the starting-points of the stitches. A spot marks the starting-point of the second eyelet.

If a solid area is to be worked in Diamond eyelet stitch it in diagonal lines from the upper left to the lower right, turn the canvas and work back up again on the diagonal.

If a single diagonal row is needed, as in the frame in the Simple Pulled thread project on page 101, start off at the upper left and work to the lower right. Turn the canvas one quarter at each point and continue to follow the numbers in the diagram.

EYELET, SQUARE

Figure a | Figure b

FLORENTINE STITCH

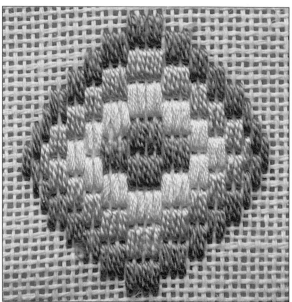

This is also known as Bargello and Irish stitch. It is generally an upright stitch over 4 or 6 threads with a jump up or down between stitches. Many variations can be worked by altering the length of stitch, the number of stitches worked in a group and the size of the jump between groups. The Florentine patterns used in the projects in this book are diagrammed within the Florentine chapter between pages 32 and 53.

This is a Pulled-thread stitch. It is worked over 8 threads of canvas in the Simple Pulled-thread project on page 100 (see Figure a and the upper area in the photograph); there are 32 stitches worked down into the central hole. Following the numbers, start at the spot, make the first circuit, missing alternate holes and complete the circle on a second trip to get the neatest result.

In the Advanced Pulled-thread project on page 104 this stitch is worked over 6 threads (see Figure b and the lower area in the photograph). There are 24 stitches down into the central hole. Follow the numbers for the correct order.

This stitch can easily be rescaled over 10 or 12 threads for other projects.

FOUR-SIDED EDGE STITCH

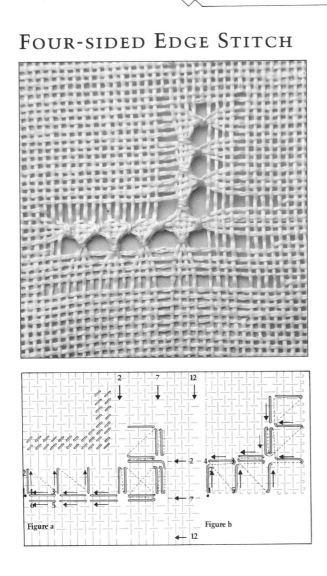

FRAMED CROSS STITCH

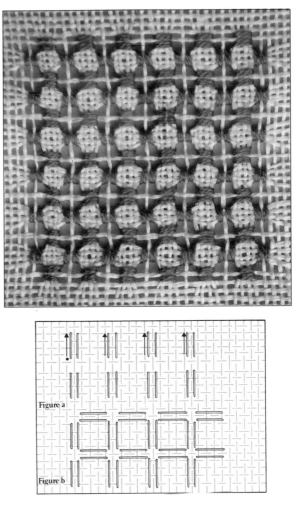

Leaving the canvas on the frame, remove the threads of unworked canvas along each side of the completed design according to the instructions. To remove a thread snip it centrally along one side with pointed scissors and then, with the point of a needle, pick it completely out. Working from left to right follow Figure a. The vertical stitches are worked once and the horizontal stitches twice. Work extra overcasts at corners. After completing the journey round the whole design remove the canvas from the frame. Turn back any spare canvas, and finger press along the base of the stitches, aligning the threads in both layers. Now make a second journey, following Figure b and working all the stitches twice. The stitches are diagrammed once only; simply treat each one as a double wrap. The photograph shows all the canvas threads removed on a corner and the first journey of stitches completed.

This is a Pulled-thread stitch. Follow Figure a and work all the upright stitches first, starting at the spot; each pair is over 4 threads and has 1 thread between them and then 4 threads of canvas before the next pair.

When the area is complete, turn the canvas and work the next pairs in a similar pattern at right angles (see Figure b).

FRENCH KNOTS/ FRENCH KNOTS ON STALKS

GOBELIN STITCH, STRAIGHT

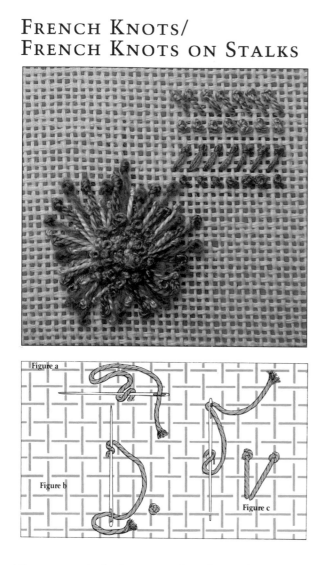

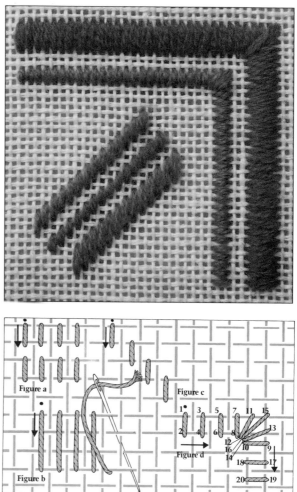

These are stitched on top of traditional canvas-work stitches. Bring the needle and all the thread up through one hole. Hold the needle at '9 o'clock' close to the canvas and wrap the thread around it once (see Figure a). Turn the needle to '12 o'clock' and take it back through the canvas one hole above and to the right of the hole it came up in (see Figure b). Never wrap more than once. If you want a larger knot, use a thicker thread.

French knots on stalks: These are used for larger flowerheads. Come up at 1, wrap and turn the needle as for a French knot. Re-enter the canvas 3 or 4 threads away to form a knot on the end of a stitch. They can be used singly or overlapping closely. They can radiate out in a circle or be used round a group of ordinary French knots. The photograph shows both French knots and French knots on stalks and you can see how effective they are when grouped together.

This is an upright stitch worked in horizontal rows, backwards and forwards across the canvas. Work a stitch in to every hole (see Figures a and b).

It can be worked over any number of canvas threads but over 2 and over 4 threads are the most usual and are the ones charted and photographed here.

The stitch can also be worked on a diagonal (see Figure c and the photograph), each stitch stepping down 1 thread from the previous one. If worked as a single row, as an outline for a square, follow the numbers in Figure d in order to get a neat corner.

GOBELIN STITCH, SLOPING

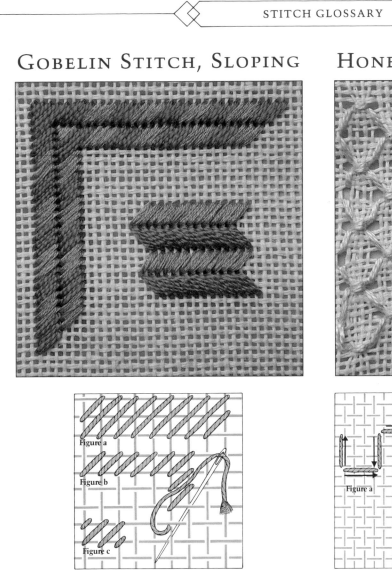

HONEYCOMB STITCH

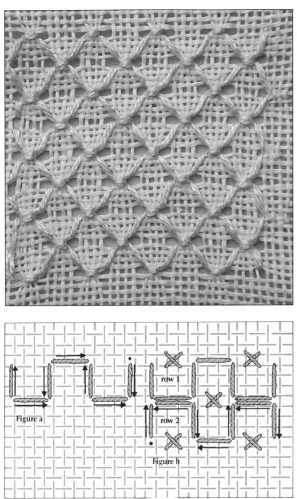

Work this stitch in horizontal rows over 2, 3 or 4 diagonal intersections of the canvas. When working a single row as a border stitch maintain the same stitch slant down both sides as established along the top (see Figure b).

Combinations of differing lengths of Sloping Gobelin can combine to form both horizontal and vertical block shapes. The bricks, window panes and garden posts in the Country Cottage on page 83 are worked this way. In Figure c a horizontal block has been formed from one stitch and over 1 thread, two stitches over 2 threads and then one over 1 thread.

This is a Pulled-thread stitch. Start at the top right of the area at the spot and work from right to left, following the arrows carefully – a back stitch is taken over all the horizontal threads (see Figure a).

When working the second row from left to right, start at the spot and note that there is a second wrap on the lower horizontal bar of the first row (see Figure b).

If when starting a new row you should want to come up in a hole you have just gone down in, simply catch the thread in the back of surrounding stitches to anchor before coming up the necessary hole.

A small Basic Cross stitch over 2 threads can be worked as diagrammed. Work these on a diagonal line so as not to trail any thread behind the pulled areas.

HUNGARIAN STITCH

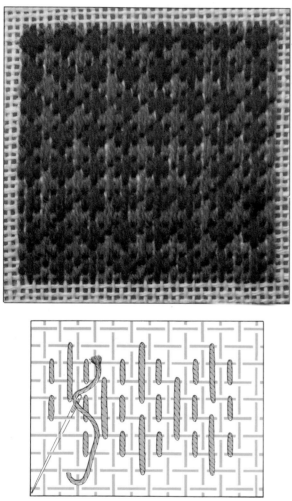

LEVIATHAN STITCH

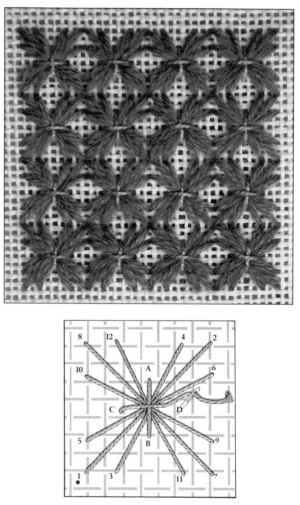

This stitch is worked in horizontal rows in groups of three stitches, over 2, 4 and 2 threads of canvas, with a gap of 2 threads in between each group.

Follow the diagram when starting the second row. The stitch over 4 threads fits into the gap between the groups in the previous row. This stitch may be worked in one or two colors. Work compensation stitches at the top and bottom edges of an area in order to achieve a neat edge.

Alternate rows can be worked in contrasting colors as shown in the photograph.

This stitch is worked over 8 threads. Starting at 1, bring the needle up on the odd numbers and down on the even. When the large diagonal cross is completed, work the upright cross, following the letters. This upright cross can be worked in a contrasting color as shown in the photograph, using a second needle.

MOSAIC WITH TENT STITCH

MOSAIC VARIATION

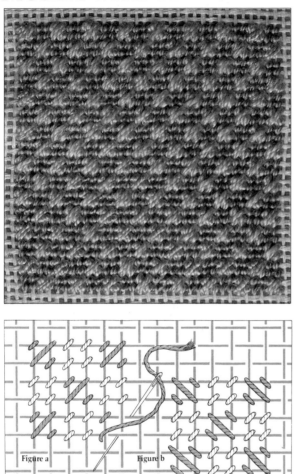

Figure a   Figure b

row 1

row 2

Three diagonal stitches over 1, 2 and 1 threads are worked to form a small square box (the Mosaic square). Four Tent stitches are then worked beside them to form another small square (the Tent square). The squares of Mosaic and Tent stitches alternate across the canvas. When working the second and subsequent rows a square of Tent stitch fits under the Mosaic and vice versa.

This stitch can also be worked in diagonal rows. First stitch a diagonal row of Mosaic squares, and then a diagonal row of Tent squares. Generally, both the Tent and Mosaic stitches slope on the same diagonal, from the lower left to the upper right. If required, the Mosaic can slope on the other diagonal (see Figure b). The Tent stitch never slopes the other way.

When working in two contrasting colors use two needles for ease.

Four diagonal stitches, each over 2 threads of canvas, are worked to form a small diamond. When the whole area is worked with these diamonds, small Upright cross stitches over 1 thread of canvas are fitted in between the diamonds. The horizontal stitch of the Upright cross is always worked last.

PARISIAN STITCH

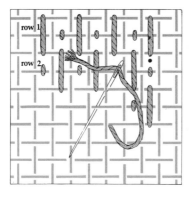

QUEEN OR ROCOCO STITCH

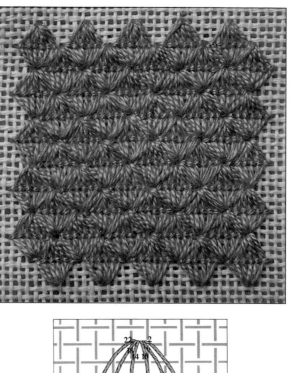

This stitch is worked in horizontal rows over 1, 3, 1, 3 and 1 threads of canvas, starting at the spot. When working the second row the stitch over 1 thread fits below the stitch over 3 threads in the previous row and the stitch over 3 threads under the stitch over 1 thread.

This stitch needs to be worked on a frame and pulled quite firmly. Following the numbers on the diagram carefully, come up for the tie-stitch before the long upright stitch is fully pulled down on to the canvas.

Work each stitch from left to right and each row diagonally from the upper left to the lower right. At the end of the row, turn the canvas upside down and work back down diagonally again. I have charted and stitched it here with six upright stitches over 6 threads of canvas. I used pearl cotton – a tight, twisted thread that is not too thick works best. It can be rescaled easily with four stitches over 4 threads of canvas.

RAISED NEEDLEWEAVING

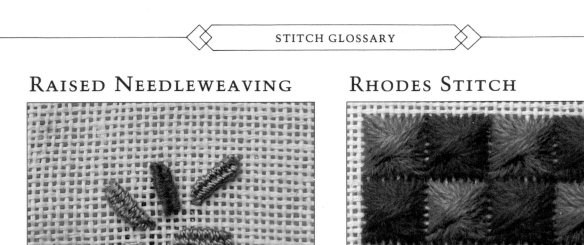

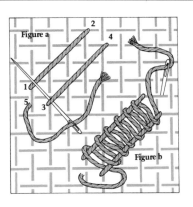

RHODES STITCH

This is used for leaves on existing canvas work. When used on canvas this stitch is more attractive worked on an angle with the two long stitches worked in next door holes. Lay two stitches the same length diagonally over a few threads (usually 3 or 4). Bring the needle up again close to or at the starting-point, taking a long stitch behind the work to hold the tension (see Figure a).

Start to weave without going down through the canvas. First go over the left-hand thread and under the right; then go over the right-hand thread and under the left. Pack the existing stitches close together every time the needle passes between the two threads. It is easier to turn the canvas so that the stitches grow away from you. When the bars are closely packed take the needle down through the canvas, making a point between the first two long stitches (see Figure b).

This is a dramatic stitch that can be rescaled easily over 4, 6, 8, 10 or 12 threads, depending on the size required.

Here, the stitch has been diagrammed over both 4 and 8 threads. (In this book I have called the version over 4 threads Small-scale Rhodes stitch.) The photograph shows Rhodes stitch over 8 threads, each alternate stitch worked in a contrasting color.

Bring the needle up at the odd numbers and down at the even numbers. It is important to start each Rhodes with a stitch at the same angle and to travel round the square in the same direction (as in the diagram). This means that the last stitch in each Rhodes will lie at the same angle.

RIBBED SPIDER

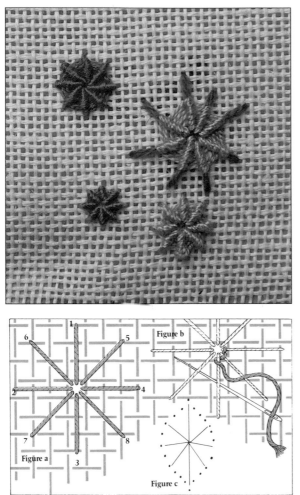

ST GEORGE AND ST ANDREW

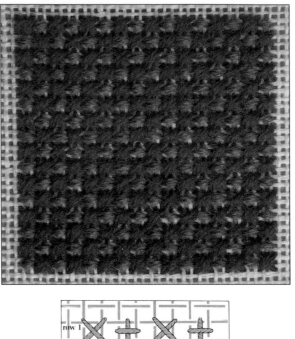

This is usually worked over an area that is already stitched with Basketweave tent stitch but it can be worked on blank canvas too. Set up the ribs first, four straight stitches are stitched at right angles, all over 4 threads of canvas and sharing a central hole. Then, work four diagonal stitches over 3 threads of canvas, sharing the same hole as the first four stitches (see Figure a).

When these are complete bring the yarn (either matching or contrasting) to the right side of the work between two ribs and weave under two ribs and back over one, under two and back over one (see Figure b). Pull firmly so that the early stitches are tight around the center and continue weaving until all the ribs are closely packed. Take the yarn to the back of the canvas and finish off.

As used in the Advanced Florentine project, the ribs are adapted to fit the space (see Figure c).

This is a Basic cross stitch over 2 threads followed by an Upright cross stitch over 2 threads. These crosses are worked alternately (in contrasting colors if required as in the photograph) across the canvas.

In the second row the Upright cross fits under the Basic cross and vice versa.

For large areas the pattern can be worked on the diagonal: work all the Basic crosses in one line before working the next diagonal line with Upright crosses, in a contrasting color if preferred.

SATIN STITCH VARIATION WORKED HORIZONTALLY

SATIN STITCH VARIATION WORKED VERTICALLY

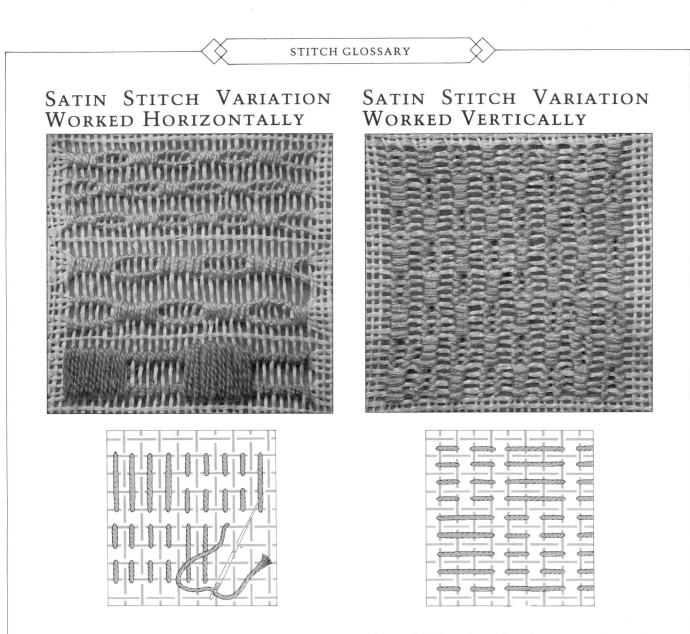

This Pulled-thread stitch is worked across the area in groups of four stitches over 4 threads of canvas and then two groups of four stitches over 2 threads of canvas alternately. In the second and subsequent rows the short stitches fit under the longer ones and vice versa.

This stitch can easily be rescaled, either by covering more threads with each stitch (for example, 3 and 6 as shown in the middle area of the photograph) or by working longer groups of each stitch (for example, 8 and 8 as shown in the bottom area of the photograph).

This Pulled-thread stitch is the same as the stitch above but is worked vertically instead of down an area. It can also be rescaled over different numbers of threads.

SPACED SATIN

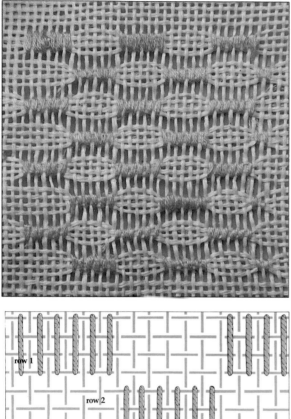

SMYRNA STITCH

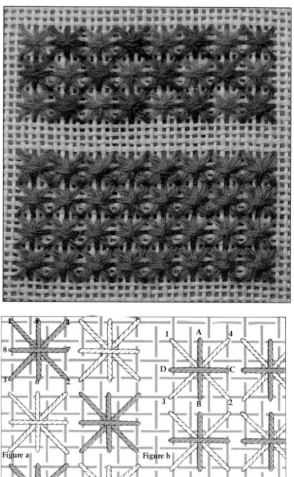

This Pulled-thread stitch is worked in horizontal rows in groups of six stitches over 4 threads of canvas. There are 7 threads of canvas between each group.

When working the second row the group of six stitches fits below an unstitched area immediately above.

This stitch pattern can easily be rescaled if required; for example, five stitches with 6 threads between the groups.

First work the base cross over 4 threads, then the vertical and finally the horizontal stitch.

The diagrams and photograph show how two colors can be used to give different effects. Either use the colors alternately for each complete stitch to give a checkerboard look (see Figure a and the upper area in the photograph); or stitch the base cross in one color and then the upright one in a contrasting color (see Figure b and the lower area in the photograph).

SMYRNA STITCH, REVERSED

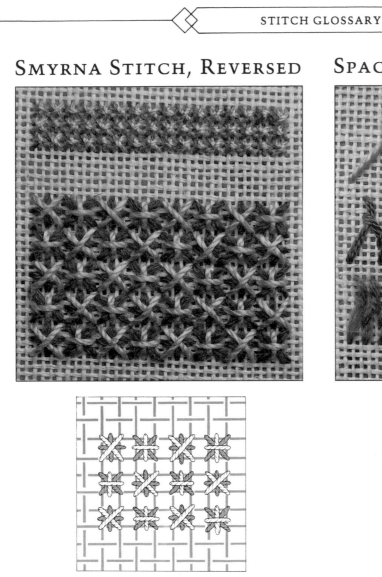

SPACED CRETAN STITCH

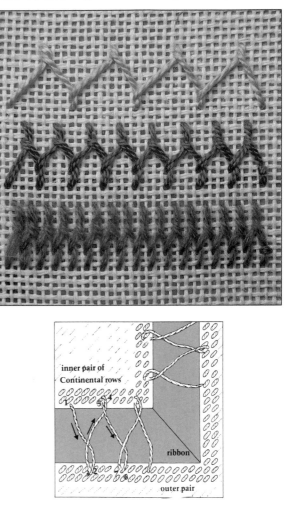

Work horizontal rows of first an Upright cross over 2 threads and then a Basic cross stitch over 2 threads. Continue working these stitches alternately until the row is complete.

Then, with a contrasting color if required, work a Basic cross stitch on top of the Upright and an Upright on top of the Basic cross. Be sure to always have the same diagonal stitch and the same horizontal stitch worked last.

When working the second row the stitch with the Basic cross uppermost fits under one with the Upright cross on top and vice versa.

The photograph shows (above) the pattern over 2 threads; (below) the pattern rescaled over 4 threads.

This stitch is worked from left to right. Turn the canvas if necessary.

Come up at 1, go down at 2 and come up at 3 (immediately inside 2). Make sure that the yarn is under the point of the needle before pulling it through. Go down at 4 and come up at 5 (immediately inside 4). The closer 1 and 4 are the thicker the braid will be. The Advanced Pulled-Thread project on page 106 uses the spaced Cretan stitch as charted here. The photograph above shows various widths of stitch.

When working a border it is more convenient to finish off each side as you come to a corner and start the next side afresh.

SPLIT STITCH

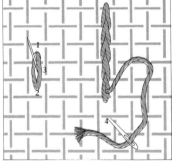

This is another stitch that can be used to form curves on canvas. (The other is Chain stitch.) Bring the needle up at 1, go down at 2, usually 2 canvas threads away. Take the thread down through the canvas so that the stitch rests neatly on the right side. Bring the needle up at 3, the mid-point between 1 and 2, and pierce the thread in the middle. Take the needle down at 4 (2 threads from 3 but only 1 from 2) and come up at 3.

To form a smooth line it is important always to come up in a hole that has previously been used for going down. On straight lines the size of the stitch may be increased, but on tight curves the stitch must be kept short.

TENT STITCH, BASKET-WEAVE OR DIAGONAL

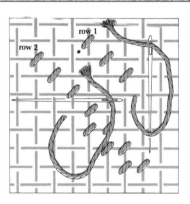

This method of Tent stitch gives a neat basket-weave appearance on the back of the canvas and prevents distortion and pulling. It is worked diagonally over 1 thread from the top right-hand corner of the work, starting at the spot. There is no need to turn the work. The needle passes horizontally under 2 vertical threads and vertically under 2 horizontal threads (see row 2).

This is the only version of Tent stitch that can be recommended for anything but a single row.

TENT STITCH, CONTINENTAL

This stitch should only be used when working one row. It covers 1 diagonal thread from the lower left to the upper right, starting at the spot. The needle passes under 2 vertical threads, making a long stitch on the back of the work and therefore, is hardwearing.

When working a single row of Continental from the lower right to the upper left it helps to run a long thread under the stitches afterwards as shown in the photograph.

When working a single row around a completed design from right to left, it is possible to come up in an empty hole and achieve a long stitch behind the work. However, when working from left to right, in order to get the necessary long stitch behind the work, you have to come up in a 'dirty' hole, which is not desirable.

It is very easy, therefore, to fall into the trap of working one side in Continental tent stitch and the next one in Half cross stitch with minimum wool behind the work. Even the front of the work looks uneven but examination of the back shows how patchy the wear would be on a piece worked in this fashion.

Half cross stitch looks similar from the front but inspection of the back shows how little padding the completed piece would have and therefore, how unsatisfactory the wear would be.

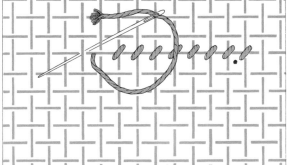

TENT STITCH, SKIP

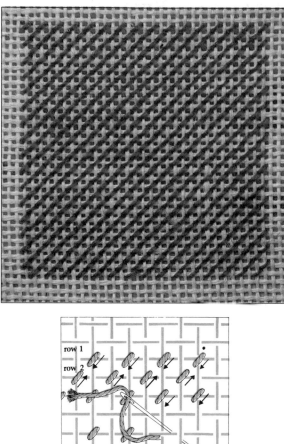

TRELLIS

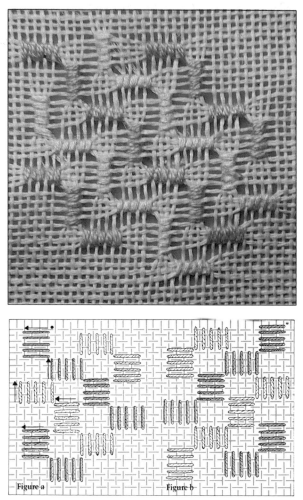

Before working any area with this stitch be sure that there are no trailing threads as a light, lacy look is necessary to the beauty of this stitch. Follow the diagram carefully, starting at the spot. There is very little thread behind the work and the second and subsequent rows form a diagonal line on the canvas.

Before starting a line of Skip tent stitch, always check that you have sufficient thread to finish it and anchor off in surrounding solid stitchery as any finishing or starting thread will show through.

This Pulled-thread stitch is worked in groups of five over 4 threads. When working a single area follow Figure a, starting in the upper left-hand corner at the spot and working a diagonal row towards the lower right-hand corner. Work subsequent rows up and down the canvas, always on the diagonal.

If, as in the Advanced Pulled-thread project on page 106, there are four areas for the pattern to radiate out from the center, follow Figure a for the lower right-hand quarter and turn the book and follow Figure a again for the upper left-hand area. Follow Figure b for the lower left-hand area and turn the book again for the upper right-hand area.

TRELLIS BARS WITH CROSS STITCH VARIATION

TRELLIS BARS WITH DIAMOND EYELETS

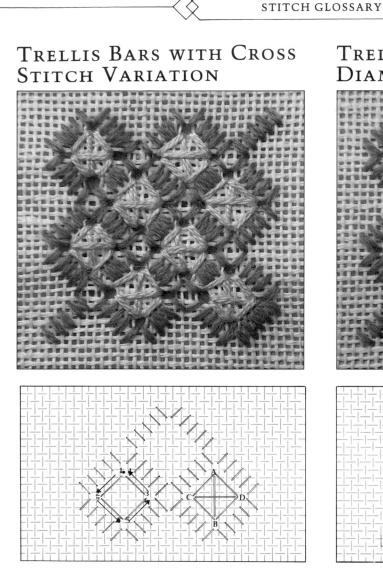

This is a Pulled-thread stitch. Set up the Trellis bars first without pulling the canvas. These are groups of five stitches over 2 diagonal canvas threads.

When the area is filled work the Cross-stitch variation. The left-hand stitch in the diagram shows the four diagonal stitches which are worked first. Follow the numbers carefully. The right-hand stitch shows the upright cross which is worked immediately afterwards, with the horizontal stitch on the top.

This is a Pulled-thread stitch. Work the Trellis bars first. These are groups of five stitches over 2 diagonal canvas threads, without pulling.

When the area is filled with Trellis bars work a Diamond eyelet in each gap, i.e. eight stitches going down into the central hole. Use the Trellis bars to anchor the thread.

2, 4, 6, 4, 2 WITH BACKSTITCH

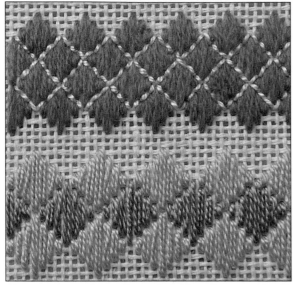

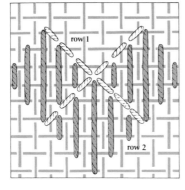

This stitch consists of large, diamond shapes formed with vertical stitches over 2, 4, 6, 4 and 2 threads of canvas. The diamonds are worked in horizontal rows, leaving 2 threads of canvas between each group. On the second and subsequent rows the diamonds fit up in to the gap left by the first row, the stitch over 2 sharing with the previous one over 4, the one over 4 sharing with the previous one over 2, and the stitch over 6 fitting in to the gap.

When the whole area is complete a Backstitch can be worked between the diamond shapes, generally in a thinner thread than that used for the vertical stitches as shown in the upper area of the photograph.

This stitch can successfully be rescaled over 2, 4, 6, 8, 6, 4 and 2 threads as shown in the lower area of the photograph; and over 3, 5, 7, 5 and 3 threads.

TWO-SIDED ITALIAN STITCH

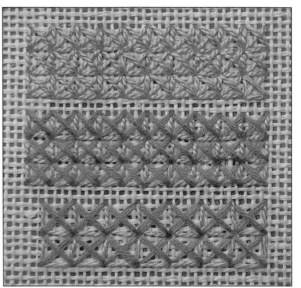

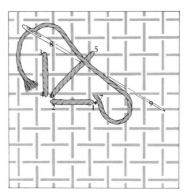

This is a traditional stitch used in eighteenth-century samplers as a more dense covering than Basic cross stitch. Work three stitches over 3 threads in turn down into one corner hole. Come up again at 7 and cross over to 8. Start the next complete stitch 3 threads to the right at 9. Work in horizontal rows back and forth across the canvas. The stitch can be rescaled over 4 threads.

The photograph shows (above) the stitch worked over 3 threads; (center) worked over 3 threads and using a contrasting color for part of the stitch; and (below) worked over 4 threads, again using a contrasting color for part of the stitch.

WEBB VARIATION

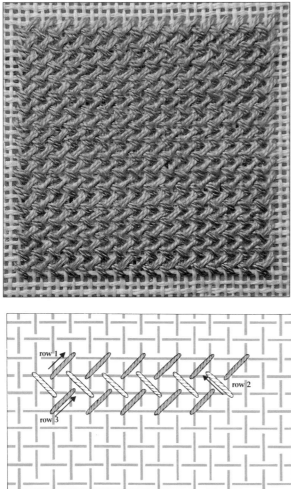

WICKER CROSS STITCH

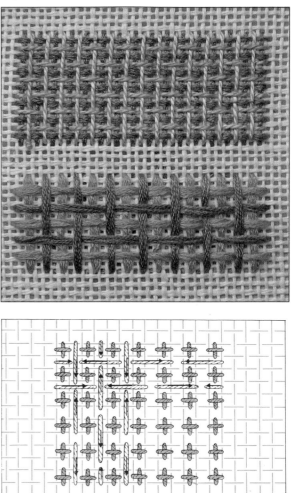

Work the first row from left to right over 2 threads diagonally with a straight stitch behind the work.

Work the second row from right to left with stitches on the other slant and tucking up in to the previous row of stitches. Continue to work back and forth across the rows with alternating slants.

If the area is to be worked with two colors, as in the Advanced Cross stitch project on page 64, always start one color from the left side and the second color from the right. Fasten off at the end of each row or, if the distance back to the correct starting-point is very short, use the back of the stitched area to get you back neatly.

Work the whole area with Upright cross stitch over 2 threads first. This can be worked backwards and forwards across the canvas.

When complete work the long vertical stitches; all these stitches are over 4 threads except where necessary at the edges of the area. Follow the arrows on the diagram as it is necessary to do backstitches. Work up and down the area.

Finally, work the long horizontal stitches, again back and forth across the area. The piece will wear better if you stitch these as the vertical ones rather than weaving under the previous stitches but not through the canvas.

The photograph shows (above) the stitch scaled over 2 threads; (below) scaled over 4 threads.

USEFUL ADDRESSES

These suppliers are good sources of yarns used in this book. In case of difficulty write to the suppliers concerned below who will send you details of your local stockist. Always enclose a stamped addressed envelope.

CITY STITCHER,
46E Chicago Avenue,
Chicago 60611,
Illinois
(*Paterna, Medici and Balger*)
CUSTOM NEEDLECRAFT FINISHING,
113 East Las Tunas Drive,
San Gabriel, CA 91776
(*Custom finishing for pillows, framing, rugs and many other items, list available.*)
DEDE NEEDLEWORKS,
4754 California Street,
San Francisco, CA 94118
(*Unusual fibers including Twilley, bags as shown on page 47, hand-painted canvas; regular newsletter*)
MEISEL FISCHER,
7934W. 3rd Street, LA, CA 90048
(*Custom finishing for bags, rugs, pillows, etc.*)

NATALIE,
144 N. Larchmont Blv.,
LA, CA 90004
(*Appleton's Crewel, Paterna, Medici, DMC and Balger*)
NEEDLEWORK FANTASIES,
6248 North Federal Hwy,
Ft Lauderdale, FL 33307
(*Paterna, Medici, DMC and Balger.*)

GUILDS AND ASSOCIATIONS DEDICATED TO FINE NEEDLEWORK AND EDUCATION
AMERICAN NEEDLEPOINT GUILD,
Pat Blailock (President),
The American Needlepoint Guild,
20 West Oaks Drive,
Houston, TX 77056
EMBROIDERERS GUILD OF AMERICA,
Membership:
200 Fourth Avenue,
Louisville,
Kentucky 40202

PUBLIC COLLECTIONS
COOPER HEWITT MUSEUM,
SMITHSONIAN INSTITUTION'S NATIONAL MUSEUM OF DESIGN,
Smithsonian Institution,
2 East 91st Street,
New York, NY 10028
(*Permanent collection and loan exhibitions.*)
DAUGHTERS OF THE AMERICAN REVOLUTION MUSEUM,
1776 D Street, N. W.,
Washington, D.C. 20006
(*Needlework and sampler collection, Period rooms.*)
HENRY FRANCIS DU PONT WINTERTHUR MUSEUM,
Wilmington, Delaware 19735
(*Furniture and special needlework tours.*)
HENRY FORD MUSEUM & GREENFIELD VILLAGE,
Oakwood Boulevard,
Dearborn,
Michigan, 48121
(*300 years of Americana.*)
PHILADELPHIA MUSEUM OF ART,
Parkway at 26th Street,
Philadelphia, Pa 19130
(*Whitman sampler collection.*)

ORDERING KITS

The following projects in the book can be ordered. No instructions are included as each project is fully explained in the book. All canvas (except the plastic) comes ready taped. Three needles are included for the Pulled-Thread projects and two for all the others.

Simple Tent stitch, Apple box (*page 21*)
(includes plastic canvas, wools and needles)
Simple Florentine stitch, cushion (*page 33*)
(includes 14 mesh de luxe canvas, wools and needles)
Simple Cross stitch, cushion (*page 55*)
(includes 14 mesh de luxe canvas, wools and needles)
Simple Stitchery, cushion (*page 77*)
(includes 14 mesh de luxe canvas, wools and needles)
Advanced Stitchery, Country Cottage (*page 83*)
(includes 18 mesh de luxe canvas, threads, beads and needles)
Simple Pulled Thread, cushion (*page 99*)
(includes 13 mesh linen canvas, threads and needles)
Advanced Pulled Thread, cushion front (*page 102*)
(includes 17 mesh linen canvas, threads, ribbons and needles)

Please write for full details to **Pearson Design, 25 Kildare Terrace, London W2 5JT, England.**

FURTHER READING

Stitchery
Ambuter, Carolyn. *Open Canvas*. Workman Publications, New York, 1982.
Eaton, Jan. *The Complete Stitch Encyclopedia*. Barron, New York, 1986.
Enthoven, Jacqueline. *The Stitches of Creative Embroidery*. Van Nostrand Reinhold, New York.
Ireys, Katharine. *The Encyclopedia of Canvas Embroidery Stitch Patterns*. T. Y. Crowell, New York, 1977.
Lantz. *A Pageant of Pattern for Needlepoint Canvas*. Andre Deutsch Ltd, London.
McNeill, Moyra. *Pulled Thread*. Unwin & Hyman Ltd, London, 1986.
Wilson, Erica. *Erica Wilson's Embroidery Book*. Scribner, New York, 1979.
Color
Itten, Johannes. *Elements of Color*. Van Nostrand Reinhold, New York, 1970.
Lambert, P. et al. *Color and Fiber*. Schiffer, West Chester, Pennsylvania.
Finishing and Aftercare
Finch & Putnam. *Caring for Textiles*. Watson Guptill Publications, New York.
Ireys, Katharine. *Finishing & Mounting your Needlepoint Pieces*. T. Y. Crowell, New York, 1973.
History
Bridgeman, Harriet & Drury, Elisabeth. *Needlework*. Paddington Press, London, 1978.
Clabburn, Pamela. *The Needleworker's Dictionary*. Macmillan Ltd, London, 1976.
Swan, Susan B. *Plain & Fancy: American Women & Their Needlework, 1700–1850*. Henry Holt & Co, New York, 1977.

INDEX

Illustrations are indicated with page numbers in *italics*, if separated from the text to which they apply.